# (Re)constructing Armenia in Lebanon and Syria

# STUDIES IN FORCED MIGRATION
General Editors: Roger Zetter and Jo Boyden

# (Re)constructing Armenia in Lebanon and Syria

ETHNO-CULTURAL DIVERSITY AND THE STATE
IN THE AFTERMATH OF A REFUGEE CRISIS

*Nicola Migliorino*

*Berghahn Books*
New York • Oxford

First published in 2008 by

*Berghahn Books*
www.berghahnbooks.com

© 2008 Nicola Migliorino

**Library of Congress Cataloging-in-Publication Data**

Migliorino, Nicola.
  (Re)constructing Armenia in Lebanon and Syria : ethno-cultural diversity and
the state in the aftermath of a refugee crisis / Nicola Migliorino.
    p. cm.
  Includes bibliographical references and index.
  ISBN 978-1-84545-352-7 (hardback : alk. paper)
  1. Armenians--Lebanon--History--20th century. 2. Armenians--Syria--History--
20th century. 3. Armenians--Lebanon--Social conditions--20th century.
4. Armenians--Syria--Social conditions--20th century. 5. Armenians--Lebanon--
Political activity. 6. Armenians--Syria--Political activity. 7. Armenians--Lebanon--
Economic conditions--20th century. 8. Armenians--Syria--Economic conditions--
20th century.  I. Title. II. Title: Reconstructing Armenia in Lebanon and Syria. III.
Title: Ethno-cultural diversity and the state in the aftermath of a refugee crisis.

  DS80.55.A75M54 2008
  305.891'99205691--dc22

                    2008015223

**British Library Cataloguing in Publication Data**

A catalogue record for this book is available
from the British Library

Printed in the United States on acid-free paper

ISBN 978-1-84545-352-2 hardback

# Contents

# List of Tables

*To Gianni, Gianna, Ludovica and Anna*

# Note on Transliteration

For Arabic, I have adopted a simplified version of the transliteration guidelines used in the *International Journal of Middle Eastern Studies*. In particular, all diacritical marks (dots and macrons) have been omitted. Exceptions are made, for personal names or names of places with accepted English spellings (for example Nasser instead of Nasir). Some inconsistencies are inevitable.

For Armenian, I have adopted a transliteration system used for Western Armenian in R.G. Hovannisian (ed.). 1997. *The Armenian People from Ancient to Modern Times*, Basingstoke and London: MacMillan. I have – for example – used the spelling *Dashnak* instead of *Tashnag*. As in the case of Arabic, some exceptions have been made for names of persons and places when a widely accepted spelling is available. Some inconsistencies are, here too, inevitable.

# Acknowledgements

This book owes much to the assistance of a great number of people and institutions. To all of them, I am deeply grateful. I wish, first of all, to thank all the persons in Lebanon and Syria who have contributed to my work by sharing with me their knowledge, their memories and their views, by lending me their time, patience and trust, or by simply supporting me with their friendship. Throughout the time I spent in Lebanon and Syria researching this book, I felt that my interest in the Armenian community was almost invariably welcome. For me, an outsider of both the *Bilad As-Sham* and of the Armenian world, that feeling was a tremendous encouragement, and helped me to carry this project through.

In Lebanon, I am particularly indebted to Mireille Abi Moussa, Father George Assadourian, Dr. Christine Babikian-Assaf, Armen Balian, Raffi Berberian, Manoushag Boyadjian, Krikor Chahinian, Hagop Doniguian, Berge Fazlian, Tamar Guédikian, Nieves Gurbindo, Rev. Paul Haidostian, Marie-Helène Kassardjian and family, Dr. Paolo Kazazian, Sevag Keshishian, Hasmig Khanikian, Talar Khatchigian and family, Sarkis Najarian, Dr. Levon Nordiguian, Hagop Pakradouni, Rev. Robert Sarkissian. In Syria, I owe special gratitude to Marieke Bosman, Antonella and Ciro Fiorillo, Varti Keshishian, Vahé Hovaghimian, Mihran Minassian, Jirair Reissian, Simone Ricca and Nada Al-Hassan, Hamo Sarkissian and family, Dr. Vahé Seferian. I am also deeply grateful to the staff of the Italian Hospital of Damascus; my thoughts go, in particular, to Suor Maria, Suor Marisa and to the late Suor Fiorin.

Over the last few years I have benefited enormously from the academic environment of the Institute of Arab and Islamic Studies at the University of Exeter. Faculty, staff and students have contributed greatly to the improvement of my work and helped me to make my stay in Exeter a pleasant and life-enriching experience. I am indebted, in particular, to Professor Tim Niblock, whose experience, knowledge and vision have provided me with crucial inspiration. My colleagues Dr. Anita Mir, Dr. Julia Droeber, Dr. Shahira Sami, and Dr. John Measor have also contributed greatly to the ideas contained in this work.

My research in Exeter and my fieldwork in Lebanon and Syria would not have been possible without the generous financial support that I have received from the Anthony Parsons Memorial Fund and from two travel scholarships: the Furthering Understanding Award made available by

H.R.H. Prince Walid bin Talal bin Abdulaziz Al-Saud, and a travel grant from the Council for British Research in the Levant. To these institutions, and to the persons involved, I address my sincere thanks.

In Beirut, Haigazian University and its precious library have been a crucial source of information and ideas during several periods of fieldwork. I owe deep thanks to all the staff and faculty who have provided support. I also owe thanks to the School of Humanities and Social Sciences at Al Akhawayn University in Ifrane, Morocco, for granting me the time necessary to complete this project.

I am deeply grateful to my publisher, Marion Berghahn, and all the staff at Berghahn Books for the trust they placed in me and in this project, and for their patience and hard work in helping me to complete it.

Three colleagues deserve a special place in these acknowledgements: Dr. Ara Sanjian, now at the University of Michigan in Dearborn, Dr. Vahé Tachjian of the Bibliothèque Nubar in Paris, and Dr. Mohammed Al Masri of the Center for Strategic Studies, University of Jordan. In different ways and at different moments, their friendship and advice has contributed crucially to this work. The mistakes that remain, regrettably, are entirely my own making, and I take full responsibility for them.

Finally, I wish to thank my wife, Anna, my parents, Gianni and Gianna, and my sister, Ludovica, for their love and continuous encouragement and support. It is to them that this work is dedicated.

**Nicola Migliorino**
**Lympstone (UK), and Ifrane (Morocco), July 2007**

# Introduction

This book is about the experience of the Armenian people as a culturally diverse community settled in Lebanon and Syria. The ideas behind it have taken shape over a long period of time, as I repeatedly came across Armenians and Armenian culture during travels and a number of stays in Lebanon and Syria. Of those repeated encounters I recall two initial observations. The first was that the Armenians appeared to me to be remarkably 'different' people compared to the majority: Christians of a discrete faith and non-Arab in a prevailingly Arab and Islamic world, they could speak their non-Semitic language, write using their own alphabet, and run a number of communal institutions, including schools, political parties, cultural clubs, welfare and recreational organisations, and so on. The second was that they did not appear as a fully excluded or marginalized community. Although a significant part of the life of many Armenians in Lebanon and Syria seemed to revolve around communal institutions, spaces and affairs, Armenians did not look isolated from the rest of the society and from its wider set of institutions. Armenians were present in many sectors of the society, economy and – at least in Lebanon – even government: I came across businessmen, professionals, members of parliament, ministers, the head of a national administration of statistics, and members of the national Lebanese and Syrian cultural scene.

There was, also, a third observation: the Armenian community was much more visible in Lebanon than in Syria, despite the fact that Armenians represented a similar sized minority in each. The number and variety of Armenian establishments in Lebanon was indeed impressive, and included a university, several daily and monthly publications, musical production, two national football teams, just to mention a few. Spaces and occasions in which Armenian life would become visible were numerous in Syria too, but the profile of the Armenian presence was remarkably lower.

I have always enjoyed my encounters with Armenian culture in the Arab East and have constantly held that the presence of such a diverse community added interest and value to the experience of living in Lebanon and Syria and, in general, to the two countries as human communities. At the same time, I have for long been aware that culturally diverse communities throughout the world are often facing a dramatic choice between assimilation into dominant cultures or sheer exclusion.

That is, the price that culturally diverse communities pay in order to live in a society, enjoy social and economic success (or sometimes in order to simply survive) is often that of having to give up their own culture – their language, traditions, religious practices, etc. – or else, being excluded and rejected. Does the case of the Armenians in Lebanon and Syria tell us a different story, of how a community of 'different' people can successfully 'find its place' in the contemporary Middle East without being either assimilated or excluded? A positive *modus vivendi*? And, if this is the case, how could Armenian cultural diversity manage to survive and develop in the context of contemporary Lebanon and Syria? Also, can we now assume that Armenian cultural resilience in these two countries is sustainable and that the presence of Armenian cultural diversity will continue to be a feature of Lebanese and Syrian societies?

This book attempts to answer these questions by studying the exceptional cultural diversity of the Armenians of Lebanon and Syria from three main perspectives. The first, inevitably, focuses on the circumstances in which the bulk of the contemporary community was formed during the twentieth century. Certainly, the presence of Armenians in Lebanon and Syria is considerably older: the Armenians, whose ancient homeland is in large part located within the borders of contemporary Turkey, were for centuries a component of the human geography of Aleppo and of many other centres of the Arab East, where they were often engaged in trade and crafts. However, there is no doubt that most Armenians of Lebanon and Syria can trace back their family history to the mass population displacements that began during the Genocide of 1915–16. By the end of the First World War, and during the turbulent years that followed it, large numbers of survivors found themselves resettled as refugees in the new countries formed in the post-Ottoman regional order. Lebanon and Syria took arguably the largest part: by the mid-1920s Beirut, Aleppo and its environs, the valley of the Euphrates, the Jazeera, but also Hama, Homs, Damascus, and even the far Dera'a, all hosted an Armenian refugee population. From this first perspective this book tells a refugee story, one of the many from a region where the Palestinian case remains by far the most well-known and the most studied in the scholarly literature. Indeed, the Armenian case could be seen to add an extra dimension to refugee studies in the region.

But this book also explores how the Armenian refugee community has struggled to find, beyond the initial phase of emergency, its 'permanent' space as a distinct cultural community in the Arab East. From a second perspective, therefore, this work observes the path of the Armenian community in search of a model of cultural integration within Lebanon and Syria. This perspective calls for an enquiry into a range of different dimensions and different meanings of the presence of the Armenians in the Levant. On the one side, it involves looking at what Khachig Tölölyan has recently described as a historical transition, within Armenian communities worldwide, from the reproduction and cultivation of a post-Genocide, post-eviction Armenian 'nationalism in exile' to a condition of 'diasporic transnationalism'.[1] In other words, it entails a study of the Armenian communities of Lebanon and Syria as diasporas based in the contemporary Middle East. On the other side, it requires an analysis of the relations between two Middle Eastern states and the cultural diversity present within their societies: the study of the type of approach that Lebanon and Syria have adopted towards cultural diversity, of how that approach has evolved over the years as an aspect of the political history of the two countries, and of what impact that approach had on the Armenian communal strategies and on the Lebanese and Syrian social attitudes towards diversity.

Neither dimension has received adequate attention in contemporary literature on the Middle East, which only makes the task of this book harder. The question of ethno-cultural diversity in the region has been traditionally analysed with the tools of ethno-politics and ethnic conflict theory, and mostly from the perspective of the state, the political system, or the regime: minority groups, ethnic or sub-ethnic communities, and primordial solidarities tend to be studied either as *threats* to the territorial integrity of states and to the stability or legitimacy regimes, or as *opportunities*, as tools that can be used to mobilize and control key sectors of the population, to win and maintain power. The traditional ethno-political approach, however useful, disregards important dimensions of the presence of culturally diverse communities in Lebanon, Syria and in the wider region. On the one hand, it tends to say little on those 'discreet minorities' which are not engaged in the 'struggle for power' and are, thus, neither a threat, nor a primary strategic resource for regimes. On the other, it tends to neglect the meaning of minority cultures when considered *per se*, as alternative ways of 'being Lebanese' or 'being Syrian' and living in these countries. It fails to capture the variety and richness of forms in which diverse ethno-cultural groups run their life and pursue their alternative cultural strategies and projects. In doing so, it also misses the fine details of how diverse groups organize their relations with the state, the society at large, and the world of their transnational connections.

This of course is not to say that the ethno-political approach has lost its usefulness, or that it is not relevant to the experience of the Armenians of Lebanon and Syria. In fact, that approach constitutes the third perspective which this book intends to adopt. Hopefully this third perspective will also contribute to a deeper understanding of Lebanon and Syria by shedding light on a minority which has so far received little scholarly attention.

2. See, for instance, H.H. Karekin II, Catholicos of Cilicia. 1989. *The Cross Made of the Cedars of Lebanon*, Antelias: Catholicosate of the Great House of Cilicia; also see the sermon given in Antelias, Lebanon, by H.H. Aram I, at his consecration and enthronement as the new Catholicos of Cilicia on July 1st, 1995, English translation reported in H.H. Aram I, Catholicos of Cilicia. 1997. *The Challenge* · *to be a Church in a Changing World*, New York: The Armenian Prelacy, 11–15.

3. N.B. Schahgaldian. 1979. 'The Political Integration of an Immigrant Community into a Composite Society: the Armenians in Lebanon, 1920–1974', Ph.D. thesis, New York: Columbia University. No published English language comprehensive study of the Armenians of Lebanon and Syria exists. A few books which cover or include coverage of the Armenian experience in the Middle East are available in Arabic and in Armenian: see for example H. 'Azazian. 1993. *Nubdha Tarikhiya Mujaza 'an al-Jaliyat al-Armaniya fi al-Bilad al-Arabiya*, Latakia: publisher unknown; M. Rif'at al-Imam. 1995. *Al-Arman fi Misr: al-Qarn al-Tasi' 'Ashar*, Cairo: Nubar Printing House; M. Rif'at al-Imam. 1999. *Tarikh al-Jaliya al-Armaniya fi Misr*, Cairo: al-Hay'ah al-Misriyah al-'Ammah lil-Kitab; M. al-Mudawwar. 1990. *Al-Arman abr al-Tarikh*, 2nd ed., Damascus; A.F. Raslan. 1997. *Arminiya: al-Ummah wa al-Dawlah*, Cairo. A. Alpoyachian. 1941–1961. *Patmut'iun Hay Gaghtakanut'ian: Hayeru Tsruume Ashkharhi Zanazan Masere* [History of Armenian Emigrations: the Dispersal of Armenians in Different Parts of the World ], 3 Vols., Cairo: Nor Astgh; Academy of Sciences of the Armenian SSR. 1967–1984. *Hay Joghovrdi Patmut'iun* [History of the Armenian People], 8 Vols., Yerevan; A.G. Abrahamian. 1964–1967. *Hamarot Urvagits Hay Gaght'avayreri Patmut'ian* [Concise Outline of the History of the Armenian Expatriate Communities], 2 Vols., Yerevan: Hayastan.

# 1

# The Origins of the Armenian Presence in Lebanon and Syria: A Brief Historical Account

## Introduction

Why are there Armenian communities in Lebanon and Syria? Under what circumstances have they been formed? Any attempt to answer these questions should start from the fact that the Armenian people originated and developed in a geographical region overlapping the periphery of the contemporary political Middle East.[1] Large parts of what is commonly described as historical Armenia fall within the borders of contemporary Turkey and Iran. The history of the Armenian people is thus deeply intertwined with some of the most significant facts of the history of the region: these facts have at times taken the Armenians away from their homeland and have scattered them in a number of countries in the Middle East and beyond.

## The Armenian Homeland

Who are the Armenians, and where are they originally from? A long-established geographical and historical tradition identifies the Armenian homeland in the mountainous plateau located between eastern Anatolia and the southern side of the Caucasus. The presence in those uplands of a people called Armenian is documented in writing since the sixth century BC, although the origin of the Armenian people is in all probability significantly more ancient. Since then, some form of Armenian presence in the lands included between the upper part of the valleys of the Tigris and Euphrates to the south and west, around Lake Van, and along the upper valley of the river Arax to the east, has been almost continuously recorded.[2] Known to Herodotus and then to Xenophon, who described them in the *Anabasis*, the Armenians developed a language of their own, which is classified as an 'independent, one-language family within the Indo-European group'.[3]

From the administrative point of view, historical Armenia constituted at times through history an area where independent political units were established. However, with the exception of the *âge d'or* under King Tigran the Great (95 to 55 BC),[4] Armenia never rose to the status of regional power. Its destiny was that of a politically and militarily weak area bordering much stronger states. On account of its strategic position, Armenia was at times invaded and became part of large empires: that was the case, for example, under the Persian Achaemenids (550 to 331 BC), following the Arab conquest (from 645 AD) and under the Ottomans (from the second half of the sixteenth century). At other times Armenia was a buffer region or a disputed area dividing stronger and hostile regional players (the Romans and the Parthians, the Romans and the Sassanids, the Ottomans and the Persian Safavids, the Ottoman and Russian Empires). In addition to that, Armenia suffered from different waves of invasion from peoples moving from Central Asia. Between the eleventh and the fourteenth century Turkic and Mongolian tribes repeatedly swept across historic Armenia.

The early adoption of Christianity by the Armenians is a fact that deserves attention due to the importance that it had in the history of the Armenian people, in the process of formation of an Armenian ethnic identity and for the role that it still plays in defining the boundaries of that identity. Through the centuries, the culture of Armenian Christianity has become closely interwoven with Armenian history, myths, language, folklore, arts, to the point that, until today, it is hard to imagine non-Christian Armenians, except at the very margins of the community. According to a long-established tradition, Christianity has been present in Armenia since the second half of the first century, thanks to the preaching of two Apostles of Jesus Christ, Saint Thaddeus and Saint Bartholomew.[5] It was at the beginning of the fourth century, between 301 and 314 AD, that the Armenian King Tiridates III (298–330) was converted by Saint Gregory the Illuminator and decided to adopt Christianity as the religion of the state. Saint Gregory is also considered the founder of the original church of all the Armenians, the Armenian Apostolic Church, or Armenian Gregorian Church. The common expression Armenian Orthodox Church also identifies the Armenian Apostolic Church. In fact, from a theological point of view, the church is one of the Oriental Orthodox churches: it is one of those churches – together with the Coptic, the Ethiopic, the Syrian Orthodox and the Malankara Syrian Orthodox – which did not accept the dogmatic positions of the Council of Chalcedon of 451 on the nature of

Christ. The Council had censured monophysitism and affirmed the double nature – human and divine – of Christ.[6] The Apostolic Church is also often referred to as the Armenian National Church, a denomination that underlines the close, historical link between this church and the Armenian people. As it will appear later in this work, the term *national* is effective in reminding us of the primary political role that the Armenian Apostolic Church played throughout the centuries as a representative of the Armenian people.

## Armenian Migration to and within the Middle East: The Pre-Ottoman Era

It is hardly surprising that a people living in a troubled region like Armenia has gone through recurrent waves of migration. In fact, migration and displacements seem to be a distinctive feature of Armenian history from old to modern times. Historical migration of Armenians from their homeland could be related to a variety of sometimes concurrent causes.

One of these is the recurrent plague of invasion and war suffered by historical Armenia. Wars could have the immediate effect of displacing the population but could also cause economic hardship by ravaging the land. People would have to leave because villages, fields, irrigation systems, flocks, stocks etc. had been destroyed. Armenian agriculture had traditionally had its strength in the fertile, volcanic land but it required substantial artificial irrigation. The damages caused to villages and irrigation systems by wars and invasions resulted at times in severe agricultural crisis and famine, inducing local communities to emigrate. Although war-ignited agricultural crises were probably recurrent throughout Armenian history, these became particularly severe during the era of the Turco-Mongol raids and invasions between the eleventh and the fourteenth century. The first invasions of Turkmen and Seljuks from Central Asia, which began in the 1040s, and a second wave – this time Turco-Mongol – in the thirteenth century, are considered to be at the origin of the first *en masse* migration of Armenians to the west and southwest: to Cappadocia and, further on, to Cilicia and Cyprus.[7] A further substantial emigration from the Armenian homeland occurred in the late fourteenth century as a consequence of the campaigns of Tamerlane, perhaps the most brutal of all.[8]

Armenians were sometimes forcibly displaced and re-located due to their potential as settlers. Resettlements could serve the double purpose of developing the local economy and providing resources and logistic bases to protect the land from foreign attacks. This type of migration has probably contributed to the establishment of some of the Armenian communities in Iran. Under Seljuk domination, a sizeable community of Armenians was relocated to Isfahan. Resettlement had also been a common practice in the Byzantine Empire. In particular, during the late tenth century the Empire pursued the policy of removing Armenian nobility from Armenia by assigning them new titles and lands in Cappadocia and northern Mesopotamia.[9]

A certain reputation of the Armenians as soldiers distinguished for courage, loyalty and discipline can also help in accounting for some Armenian migrations. Armenian soldiers and generals served Byzantium at different points in time and in different parts of the Empire, sometimes with the task of garrisoning and defending peripheral areas. As far as the Middle East is concerned, the Armenian presence in Cilicia was strongly reinforced from the eleventh century by the imperial policy of assigning lands to Armenian officers. In the later period of crisis in the Byzantine Empire, these Armenian chieftains assumed a position of leadership in the region: the most notable case was that of the Armenian Prince Ruben, who, in 1080, formed a barony independent from Byzantium and laid the bases for the foundation of the Armenian Kingdom of Cilicia (1199–1375).[10]

Traders, professionals and functionaries represent a further, rather separate class of Armenian migrants. Since ancient times Armenian merchants were operating on the main trade routes connecting Persia and the Far East to the Black Sea and the Mediterranean. At times taking advantage of the special treatment they received as an elite minority and thanks to their communal connections, Armenians gradually established themselves as successful commercial intermediaries in virtually all the major cities of Anatolia and the Levant.[11] Since the Byzantine conquest of Armenia, history records that the Armenian elite also provided functionaries for the governmental institutions dominating the area. In the course of Byzantine history a number of Emperors were Armenians or of Armenian origin, a fact which probably determined the injection of Armenian cadres in the state administration.[12]

Some early Armenian migrations to and within the Middle East can be understood in the context of the Armenian Christian faith. This accounts in particular for the case of the Armenian presence in Jerusalem whose focal centre, since perhaps the seventh century, is the Cathedral and Monastery of Saint James, a traditional place of Armenian learning and pilgrimage.[13] Armenian presence is also documented in the Monastery of Saint Catherine in the Sinai during the late Middle Ages.

## The Armenians and the Ottoman Empire

It is hard to re-construct a detailed demo-geographic picture of the Armenians at the end of the Turkic and Mongol invasions, as extensive

and reliable information concerning population and migrations is missing. It seems, however, safe to assume that the three-century-long epoch of invasions and raids which terminated in the early fifteenth century severely affected the Armenian homeland and determined a significant change in the human geography of the Armenian people. Although information can be hardly unequivocally confirmed, it is indeed possible that, by the time the last Timurid campaign ended in 1403–4, Armenians were no longer a majority in many parts of the lands of historical Armenia.[14] From the point of view of the demographic composition of the Armenian homeland and Anatolia, the Turkic-Mongol invasions seem to have dramatically accelerated the centuries-long process by which the Armenian presence spread from the homeland to central and west Anatolia, the northern part of the fertile crescent, and – to the north – the Caucasus.

Contacts between the Armenians and the Ottomans date back to the very first decades after the foundation of the Ottoman Empire. Starting in the early fourteenth century from an area around Bursa, and overcoming the setbacks of the Timurid raids, the Ottomans conquered Anatolia in the span of two hundred years. As the Ottomans expanded, Armenians would gradually become subjects of the Empire. Again, precise population data is missing. However, it is known that at the time of the Ottoman conquest Armenian communities were living in Bursa, Kütahya, Constantinople, Ankara, Karaman, Trebizond and that some of these cities had an Armenian bishop.[15] There is little doubt that the Armenian population in these cities was fairly small. In Constantinople, where a census of shops was conducted by the authorities in 1478, a quarter of a century after the conquest of the city, estimates indicate that the Armenians were possibly 5,000 or 6,000 out of a total population of 100,000 to 120,000.[16]

There has been speculation about an alleged forced migration of Armenians from the newly conquered lands to the cities of western Anatolia, and in particular to Istanbul. Some historical accounts report that, after the fall of Constantinople in 1453, Sultan Mehmet II forcibly resettled Armenians to the city, in order to replace the many Greeks who had fled.[17] Recent historical works, however, tend to play down the importance of these resettlements since no proof seems to be available that these involved a large number of households.[18]

On the contrary, a new substantial wave of Armenian migration was certainly triggered in the sixteenth and seventeenth century in the framework of the confrontation between the Ottoman Empire, the Mameluks and the Safavids, when Cilicia, the Levant and most of historical Armenia were conquered. The Ottoman expansion at the expense of the Safavids, which only terminated in 1639 with the Treaty of Zuhab, was particularly hard for the Armenian homeland, cut across by the war front. Ottoman offensives and Safavid responses repeatedly ravaged the land. Anarchy, famine and destruction forced many to leave towards the cities of Cappadocia and western Anatolia, or southwards, probably towards Aleppo and Beirut. Through an analysis of fiscal registers of the sixteenth century, Kouymjian has been able to provide data that can help in understanding the extent of the migration phenomenon. The registers of Erzerum, in Armenia proper, report that the city was empty and destroyed in 1523, in the midst of the first phase of the Ottoman-Safavid conflict. Kayseri, on the north east margin of Cilicia, recorded in the same period a dramatic increase of Armenian population: between 1523 and 1583 the Armenian population increased by more than 500 per cent.[19] Among all destinations of migratory movements, Istanbul became arguably the most important. At the beginning of the 1600s a Polish-Armenian cleric estimated the Armenian immigrant population at 40,000.[20] By the mid seventeenth century the overall figure of the Armenian population of Istanbul rose possibly to 58,000, of which 50,000 were immigrants.[21] The Treaty of Zuhab marked symbolically a turning point in Armenian history: from the end of the Ottoman-Safavid wars until the First World War, the destiny of the largest part of the Armenian population was tied to that of the Ottoman Empire. Eastern Armenia, where a much smaller number of Armenians lived, was to remain fully under Persian control until the expansion of the Russian Empire began in the eighteenth century.

As far as Lebanon and Syria are concerned, the migrations of the sixteenth and seventeenth centuries came to integrate the previously established Armenian communities dating from the fourteenth century or before.[22] In Aleppo the influx of new settlers reinforced the position of the Armenians as important traders and contributed to opening the 'golden age of Armenian Aleppine commerce, with the natives of Julfa occupying a position of pre-eminence'.[23] Aleppo, undoubtedly the most important Armenian settlement in the region, was also a major centre of Armenian arts and crafts – textile weaving, tanning, gold smithing and tailoring being the activities for which the community was best known. Other sizeable Armenian communities were present in Antioch and Latakia, while in the smaller centres of northern Syria Armenians lived as peasants.

## *Laying out the Ottoman-Armenian Relations: The* Millet *System*

How were Armenians accommodated within the Ottoman state as they became new subjects? The general approach of the Ottomans *vis-à-vis* these new non-Muslim, non-Turkish subjects was informed by a mixed spirit of tolerance and interest. The Ottomans manoeuvred with a certain degree of flexibility to bring new human and economic resources into the state, allowing the Armenians – as well as other non-Muslim communities – to find a mutually beneficial place within the Empire. Recent historical literature on the Ottomans suggests that the success of the Empire over six hundred years of history was due to that fact that it 'incorporated the energies of the vastly varied peoples it encountered'.[24] Countering a certain tradition of 'stereotypes and preconceptions', Quataert also argues that 'inter-group relations during most of the Ottoman history were rather good relative to the standards of the age' and that minorities enjoyed 'fuller rights and more legal protection in the Ottoman lands than, for example, did minorities in the realm of the French king or of the Habsburg emperor'.[25]

The Ottoman approach was of course inspired by Islamic doctrine concerning non Muslim peoples. Since its appearance, Islam introduced a clear distinction between the community of Islam, considered as both a religious and a political community, and other communities. According to the classical Islamic model of relations with non Muslims, unbelievers and pagans were not in principle tolerated and, as the Islamic community expanded, forcibly converted, if not killed; believers in monotheistic revelations, like Jews and Christians, enjoyed however the privileged status of *dhimmi*, 'protected' peoples, although they were never considered on an equal basis to the Muslims as far as the political sphere was concerned.[26] The actual modes of co-existence between Muslim, Christians and Jews in the Middle East, and the precise definition of the religious and socio-political limitations imposed on the *dhimmi* through written or unwritten norms, were subject to changes over time. Sometimes these changes could be dramatic, but the classical *ahl al-dhimma* model of relations was substantially maintained as a reference. In particular, two cardinal principles of the *dhimma* concept were relevant to the Ottoman conquerors: first, as Christians and, thus, 'people of the book', the Armenians deserved the protection of the state. Second, Armenians could not be considered as being of equal status with Muslim citizens: they would be bearers of a diminished, second-class citizenship, a fact that excluded them from the formal leadership of the state and the society.

In the context of the Ottoman institutional system and practice, the adoption and assimilation of the *ahl al-dhimma* principle is traditionally described by the term and concept of *millet*. It is generally agreed that the establishment of the so-called *millet* system was the result of a complex process of evolution which, starting from the earliest times of the Empire, was only completed in the nineteenth century.[27] What is important here is that the Ottomans, without significant breaks in relation to Islamic tradition,[28] engaged from the start in the establishment of a system by which the state recognized some religiously defined communities as subjects of rights and duties. Disregarding ethno-linguistic or territorial differences, the Ottoman Empire would define *millet*, or 'nations' and distinguish its subjects on the basis of religious faith. The approved leadership of the recognized non-Muslim communities, which included since early Ottoman history the Orthodox Greeks, the Jews and the Armenians, entered some form of agreement with the Muslim ruler, playing an important mediating role between non-Muslim citizens and the state. On the one hand, the community submitted to the Muslim rulers and accepted paying a poll tax (*jiziya*); on the other, the state – at least in principle – guaranteed protection and granted a fairly substantial autonomy in a significant number of community-sensitive areas.[29]

When the *millet* system reached its 'classical' form, the head of each community – the patriarchs for the Christians, and the members of the rabbinic hierarchy for the Jews – had jurisdiction over the entire population of the respective *millet*. The role that the *millet* leadership and its local representatives played in the Ottoman system was relevant in many areas of the everyday life of the non-Muslim citizen: with some important limitations,[30] most matters regarding religious doctrine and practice, personal status, 'but also a large part of civil and penal law',[31] education and – in general – any culture-specific institution, were left to the autonomous management of the community. The head of the *millet* was also invested with the task of collecting part of the taxes due by the non-Muslim subject to the state, *ipso facto* playing the function of an administrative officer of the state.[32]

## The Evolution of the Armenian Millet

The *millet* formula sketched above provides the main framework for a description of the institutional regulation of the relations between the Armenians and the Ottoman state until the second half of the nineteenth century. As mentioned earlier, however, the Ottoman formula in dealing with inter-community relations went through a complex process of evolution and definition. In the case of the Armenians it is possible to identify at least two important trends in the course of this process: the first concerns the progressive extension of the jurisdiction of the Armenian clergy of Constantinople to cover, eventually, most of the Armenian community of the Empire. The second concerns the definition of the leadership of the Armenian community: it is a path by which the *millet* leadership, although remaining formally assigned to the Church, was gradually taken over by Armenian laity. These two trends and, more generally, the whole case of the Armenian *millet* until the mid nineteenth century, clearly show that, within the limits imposed by the *ahl al-dhimma* principle, the Ottoman approach in dealing with religious diversity was fairly successful in adapting dynamically to local differences and historical change and in reflecting both the general developments of the Empire and the socio-economic evolution of the Armenian community.

I shall first look at the question of the jurisdiction of the Armenian *millet*. Some sources traditionally date the symbolic origin of the

Armenian *millet* to 1461, shortly after the conquest of Constantinople, when the Armenian primate of Bursa, Bishop Hovakim was invited by the new rulers to move to the new capital and was 'conferred upon [...] the title of "patrik", thus placing him on the same footing as the patriarch of the Greek community'.[33] In general, contemporary scholarly tradition in fact rejects the idea of the establishment, on that date, of an Armenian *millet* (in the sense described above) and stresses that the formation of the *millet* has to be regarded as a gradual process. 'Bishop Hovakim was merely the prelate of the capital and held no jurisdiction over the Armenians in the rest of the empire' while the title of patriarch 'was not officially used to designate the head of the Armenians in Constantinople until the reign of Süleyman Kanuni (1520–66)'.[34] The jurisdiction of the head of the Armenian church over the rest of the population was then extended gradually, through a process which, according to Berbérian, was only completed in the sixteenth and seventeenth century and, for Barsoumian, in the middle of the eighteenth.[35] Barsoumian also adds that, even when the process of extension of the jurisdiction was completed, some areas of the Empire remained excluded: these areas included 'the catholicosate of Sis (whose territory comprised essentially Cilicia), the catholicosate of Aghtamar (whose area of influence was limited to a number of towns and villages in the south of Lake Van), and the patriarchate of Jerusalem (which exercised authority over communities in Palestine, southern Syria, Lebanon, Cyprus and Egypt)'.[36] These facts confirm that, within the boundaries of the Islamic tradition of the *ahl al-dhimma*, the application of the formula regulating inter-confessional relations took different forms at different times and places throughout the 600 years of Ottoman history. As the Ottoman conquest progressed, new communities of Armenians would be incorporated acknowledging, when necessary, local specificities, as in the case of the Catholicosates and of the patriarchy of Jerusalem. It is beyond any doubt, however, that the general trend throughout the history of the Armenian *millet* was that of a progressive extension of the prestige and importance of the centre (the patriarchy in Istanbul) over the periphery.

The second important aspect of the evolution of the Armenian *millet* regards the definition and control of the *millet*'s leadership. At the time when the relations between the Armenians and the Ottomans were first laid out, and probably until the seventeenth century, the Armenian Church held a fairly clear position of leadership within the community. This may be related in part to the fact that, under the *ahl al-dhimma* principle, the Muslim conquerors needed to link the 'diversity' they were bringing into the state with a religious identity, and, thus, they were inclined to consider the Armenian clergy as their counterpart. But, more importantly, the Church was probably the only organized centre of power that could represent the Armenians. The importance and power of the traditional Armenian nobility, the *nakharars*, had been weakened and declining for centuries; 'whatever role [it] may have had in the second half of the fifteenth century [...], by the sixteenth century there [sic; read "their"] presence [was] not strongly felt in Armenian national life. The Church [seemed] to keep the nation together'.[37]

Until the end of the seventeenth century or the beginning of the eighteenth, Armenian society seems not to have been very differentiated. The vast majority of Armenians were peasants and lived in villages; the only other group that could be easily recognized, apart from the clergy, was the 'active and wealthy middleclass' of Armenian merchants (*khodjas*, or *xojas*).[38] Not entirely urbanized, the *khodjas* played an important role in capital accumulation and in developing communications between Armenian communities, but they were unorganized and, thus, did not comprise a leadership.[39]

Conditions changed in the eighteenth century when the importance of the Armenian communities in the cities of western Anatolia, and particularly in Istanbul, increased. Most urban Armenians successfully engaged in trade and handicrafts, playing a significant role in some sectors of the Ottoman economy. But, more important, the eighteenth century saw the appearance of a rich and influential Armenian upper class. Members of this elite, who were later to be known by the name of *Amiras*, roughly belonged to two groups: the first was composed of the so-called *sarrafs*, former money-changers who had become bankers; the second included a large number of civil servants who had reached important positions within the Ottoman administration. Both groups had effectively seized the opportunities that the Ottoman system granted to members of non-Muslim minorities.[40] The rise of the power and prestige of the *sarrafs* was, for example, related to the key role they played as guarantors and moneylenders in the functioning of the tax-farm system (*iltizam*).[41] Within the Armenian *millet* structure, it was inevitable that the *Amiras* expanded their influence at the expense of the traditional monopoly of power by the clergy. The appearance of the *Amiras*, with their important connections within the Ottoman administration and with the financial weight which they could use to back the patriarchate up in moments of need, resulted in a significant evolution of the *millet*: the function of representation and mediation between the Armenian community and the Ottoman state was now shared with the laity.

A further important step in the evolution of the structure of the *millet* was taken when representatives of the world of the Armenian traders and manufacturers started to make an impact on the political scene of the community. This function of representation was taken up by the Armenian guilds or *esnafs*. Guilds organising and regulating professions, handicraft and, in general, all various economic activities had already existed for a long time, but it was only after the second half of the seventeenth century that community-specific (i.e. Armenian, Muslim, etc.) guilds were formed.[42] The first official participation of the *esnafs* in important moments in the life of the *millet* date back to the eighteenth century,[43] but it was only in the nineteenth century that the guilds effectively started to challenge the power of the *Amiras* and progressively gain more control in the running of the patriarchate.

### *Armenian Catholics, Armenian Protestants and the Armenian* Millet

A third, important example of the adaptability of the Ottoman system to the changing realities of its Armenian community can be observed in the process that led to the establishment of two Armenian Churches which broke away from the Armenian Apostolic Church: the Armenian Catholic Church and the Armenian Evangelical Church.

Even after the Council of Chalcedon, which set the Armenian Apostolic Church on a different path from the Church in Rome, contacts were never completely severed between Armenia and the Holy See. Throughout the centuries a number of Armenian clerics maintained relations with the Vatican; either acting individually or representing small communities, these clerics kept Catholic Christianity alive among the Armenians. For its part, the Papacy never renounced to try bringing the Armenian National Church under its control and, from the seventeenth century it intensified its missionary activities in the Ottoman Empire. The reaction of the Apostolic Church was strong and suppressive. The Church saw its authority challenged and Armenian Catholics suffered persecution: under patriarch Avedik 'papal Armenians were not only denied the ordinances of baptism, matrimony, and burial, but also punitive measures, in the form of fines, exile, and imprisonment, were inflicted upon them'.[44] Many Armenian Catholics took refuge in the Lebanese mountains, an area which had for long been a sanctuary for minorities. It was in 1742 that, largely thanks to the intercession of the Maronite Church, Pope Benedict XIV recognised the head of the Armenian Catholic community in Lebanon as Patriarch, a fact that can be considered as the founding moment of the modern Armenian Catholic Church. The See of the Patriarchate was fixed in the region of Kesrouane, in the mountains north of Beirut. In that area, the Armenian Catholics founded the monastery of Bzoummar, which became the focal point of their faith and the starting point for proselytizing and for supporting Catholic Christianity in Armenia and Anatolia.[45]

From the point of view of the Ottoman authorities, the position of the Catholic Armenians, insubordinates (if not secessionists) of the Armenian *millet*, was – strictly speaking – illegal. The law required every non-Muslim citizen of the Empire to obey to the rules and authorities of the *millet* to which he or she formally belonged. However, certainly under pressure from foreign powers, the Ottoman government increasingly took a pragmatic approach and, in the early nineteenth century, encouraged a diplomatic process of reconciliation within the *millet*.[46] Finally, in 1831, the Sublime Porte established a Catholic *millet*, emancipating the Armenian Catholics from the authority of the Apostolic Church.[47]

A similar succession of events marked the establishment of the first Armenian Evangelical Churches.[48] The spread of Protestant Christianity among the Armenians was sparked by the activity of American and, to a minor extent, British missionary activities. The first Protestant mission dedicated to proselytizing among the Armenian community was established in Istanbul in 1831; the opening of a high school in Pera (1834) and the establishment of the first Armenian Evangelical church (1846) followed. It would be wrong and simplistic, however, describing Armenian Protestant Christianity as a mere consequence of missionary apostolate. In fact, foreign missionary activity was surely coupled with a spontaneous quest for spiritual renewal and religious reform which had pervaded some sectors of Armenian Ottoman society for long time.

As in the case of the Catholics, the activities of the early Protestant missionaries, which largely focused on education, were strongly opposed by the Apostolic Church: in 1839 Patriarch 'Step'an issued a patriarchal letter forbidding any Armenian to participate in the Protestant activities', and participants and 'all those who concealed facts about the Protestants were severely punished'.[49] It was not until 1850, when a decree of the Sultan established the so-called Protestant *millet*, that Armenian Protestants – along with other, non-Armenian Protestants of various denominations – could proselytize more freely in the Empire.[50]

## The Unmaking of the Millet System and the Crisis of Ottoman–Armenian Relations

The Armenians developed through the centuries a reputation as the 'loyal *millet*' of the Ottoman Empire, the *millet* that the Sultan could trust.[51] In the last part of the nineteenth century and, further on, until the tragic epilogue triggered by the First World War and the collapse of the Empire, the situation changed dramatically and everything in Ottoman-Armenian relations went terribly wrong. Attempts to interpret and understand this change are complex.

It is initially important to say that the facts that eventually led to the quasi disappearance of the Armenians from Anatolia must be analysed in the wider context of the crisis of the Ottoman approach to diversity epitomized by the *millet* formula. The deterioration in inter-communal relations did not involve the Armenian community alone; it was part of a much wider phenomenon that revolved around the crisis of the notions of citizenship and subject-state relationships. But why was the *millet* formula in crisis, if it had been 'working well' for centuries?

Some authors have in fact argued that the Ottoman system went into crisis precisely because it was *not* 'working well'. Putting the stress on the limitations inherent in the principle of *ahl al-dhimma*, these authors more or less explicitly argue that the *millet* system was responsible for an accumulation of tension and reasons for conflict until the conflict itself eventually broke out. For Barsoumian 'The millet system was an offensive scheme, which functioned well so long as the non-Muslims accepted their status of inferiority and subservience. Once they refused to accept the restrictions and bonds imposed on them, then the whole system gradually collapsed'.[52] For Dadrian, '*[l]es musulmans [...] étaient destinés à rester la nation des maîtres et seigneurs. Les non-musulmans étaient relégués au rang d'infidèles admis, tolérés et soumis. Ces catégories jumelles permettaient de maintenir les divisions entre les deux communautés religieuses et étaient ainsi source d'un conflit permanent au sein du corps social*'.[53]

The status of inferiority and submission concerned both the symbolic-psychological sphere (as in the case of the dressing laws) and the material one, most notably in the case of tax disparities.[54] It is argued that the Armenian population in the provincial areas of the Empire, in eastern Anatolia and Armenia proper, was particularly discriminated against and received less protection from abuses of various kind. Barsoumian argues that the 'Armenian rural population, as well as those [Armenians] in towns who were involved in agriculture, were exploited in various ways: onerous taxation, corvée, misuse of their lands by others, illegal appropriation of their products, expropriation, forced loans, and cheap labor'. In addition to the Ottoman taxes, 'the Armenian peasant also paid several taxes to the Turkish or Kurdish *agha* (feudal lord), who "owned" or "protected" the village or the district'.[55]

A slightly different position is taken by those authors who, while rejecting the idea that the Ottoman model was inherently conflict-generating, recognise that the *millet* system did not encourage unity and patriotism either, a fact that increasingly became a potential weakness for the state.[56] In other words, the Ottoman approach, as inspired by Islamic law and tradition, was responsible for maintaining and encouraging a system of parallel allegiances: to the state but also, most importantly, to the respective (religiously defined) community. The case of the guilds, mentioned earlier, is useful for making the point here: mixed guilds did not disappear when separate, community-specific guilds were established, but within these, mobilization sometimes took place along communal lines.[57] The alternative allegiance system was always present and could be activated under certain circumstances.

Changing perspective, some of the literature has convincingly underlined a number of historical successes, comparatively speaking, of the Ottoman approach to diversity. The first of these is merely demographic: recent research argues that, during the centuries of the

Ottoman Empire the non-Muslim population of Anatolia and the Arab East not only increased, but it did so at a faster rate than the Muslim population. Courbage and Fargues describe the Ottoman era as an epoch of recovery for Christianity, after the quasi annihilation caused by the Turk-Mongol invasions. In Anatolia 'four centuries under the rule of Islam had enabled Christianity to regenerate itself from the inside. From the 8 per cent recorded in the censuses of 1520 and 1570, by 1881 the Christian population of Anatolia had reached 16 per cent'.[58] In the Fertile Crescent 'Under the Ottomans [...] the trend of the previous millennium was reversed enabling Christian communities to make an extraordinary recovery';[59] according to Courbage and Fargues the Christian population in this area increased from a mere 7 per cent at the time of the Ottoman conquest in the sixteenth century to 20–30 per cent at the end of the Empire. The reasons for this demographic increase should be understood in connection with the status of *dhimmi* of the Christians: exempted from military service, Christians did not risk their lives in war and were not taken away from their households, facts that resulted in higher marriage and birth rates.[60] In conclusion, the retrospective demographic picture seems to suggest that the coexistence of the Muslims and non-Muslims under the Ottomans was successful in so far as it did not eradicate religious diversity from Anatolia, but rather the opposite.

The preservation of the non-Muslim communities under the group rights-oriented arrangement offered by the *millet* model had a further crucial implication: it allowed the preservation of communal religious beliefs and of the communal culture at large. It seems undisputed that religion and culture were the areas where the autonomy of the non-Muslim community was exercised at its best. Armenians were allowed to preserve their language and educational system and maintained autonomous control over all issues regarding their faith and the organization of the Church, probably to a larger extent than was admissible under Byzantine domination.[61]

A look at inter-communal relations at the non-institutional level also seems to confirm that the Ottoman system worked comparatively well in making coexistence of different communities workable. As far as residential patterns or economic relations are concerned, for example, Quataert rejects the view that 'each community lived in isolation one from the other'[62] and dismisses as 'gross and untenable generalizations' theories of the 'ethnic division of labour' in the Empire.[63]

It may be observed that it is not academically sound to try and strike a balance of centuries of Ottoman experience in applying the traditional Islamic approach in dealing with inter-communal relationships: too many variables should be taken into account in assessing the Empire's treatment of diversity over such a long period of time. However, if something can be said, it is that it seems that the argument of the disparity of treatment alone explains only in part the crisis of inter-communal relations in the last phase of the Ottoman Empire. Disparity had been present for centuries. What made it unworkable in the last part of the nineteenth century?

A closer look at the context in which the crisis of the *millet* system took place seems to suggest that the demise of the traditional approach to diversity was not the effect of a 'rebellion' of the submitted peoples as much as the result of a process of modernization in large part initiated and supported by the Ottoman state itself. The crisis of the *millet* system and, as we mentioned earlier, of the traditional state-subject relation in the Ottoman context, should be seen in the light of a combination of internal and external challenges that the Empire was facing in the course of the nineteenth century. In particular, military defeats and territorial losses in the Balkans and elsewhere represented the symptom of a wider problem: the Empire was not able to keep pace with the industrializing European powers. The Ottomans had previously been able to adapt to military technology improvements: when muskets had become a standard in seventeenth century armies, Ottoman industrial capabilities had been able to follow. But 'as technology advanced and factories were needed to make masses of new weapons, the Ottomans fell behind'.[64] It was not a strictly military problem: 'countries that wished to compete militarily with the Europeans were forced to emulate that way of life'.[65] The perception of this weakness by the Sublime Porte prompted the activation of a process of reform that could not be limited to the army alone but had to be directed, more widely, towards the modernisation of the state and society.

A major feature of the Ottoman 'Westernizing' reforms, perhaps initiated under Selim III (1789–1807) and culminating with the so-called *Tanzimat* and the Constitution of 1876, is that they were in general aimed at increasing the centralization of power. The needs of a rationalized bureaucracy, fiscal system and military service, for example, called for the abolition of those institutions that were damaging the efficiency and coherence of state action and for the introduction of new instruments of state administration and control. All male citizens, including Christians and Jews, were to be made available for the military needs of the state; the inefficient tax-farming system had to be abolished and tax-collection was to be centralized; new governmental schools would have to prepare a generation of citizens who could support the project of modernization; a new system of government, including Western-style ministries, was to be introduced.[66]

From the perspective of minority groups, the reforms announced an epochal reversal of the traditional approach in state-diversity relations: the Rose Garden decree of 1839 (*Hatt-i Sherif of Gülhane*) and the *Hatt-i Hümayun* of 1856 promised equality of treatment and justice for all Ottoman subjects, regardless of their religious affiliation. It has been argued that, to a significant extent, the old disparities did not disappear and that there was a gap between the principles announced and their actual application;[67] what is important, however, is that, at least at a formal level, the state was moving from a group rights-oriented approach to diversity to a new approach by which the Sultan would regard every subject as an individual subject, rather than as a member of a tolerated *nation*. Whether the measures of reform were introduced genuinely and consciously for the purpose of developing a new model of citizenship or rather – more practically – for curtailing the power and jurisdiction of the *millet* institutions may be an object of controversy; but this does not reduce the magnitude of the change in approach.

It is important to stress that the Sultan did not formally abolish the *millets* as institutions: on the contrary, the edicts of reform included formulas that confirmed the concessions and guarantees originally granted to the recognized religious groups.[68] However, important functions of the *millet* were gradually transferred to the state, weakening the *millet* leadership as a centre of power autonomous from the Sultan. This was most evident in the case of the administration of justice: communal courts were not abolished but their importance and jurisdiction was gradually lost to the advantage of newly established mixed and secular courts.[69]

For the Armenians, as for other minority groups, the change introduced by the Ottoman reforms was potentially a double-edged weapon. On the one hand, it could bring an end to the traditional system of discrimination, particularly in fiscal issues and in the administration of justice; Armenians in the Eastern *vilayets* had probably much to gain from the reaffirmation of Ottoman central authority against the abuses of the local Kurdish *aghas*. On the other hand, rather paradoxically, the reforms represented a danger for the autonomy and privileges that the minorities had been granted by the traditional system.

It is not surprising, therefore, that the process of reform of state-minority relations encountered some degree of opposition, not only within the Muslim majority, who saw its political, social and economic leadership threatened,[70] but among the *millet* peoples themselves. The case of the clothing law of 1829 is emblematic. The law was intended to bring an end to a long epoch in which differences in clothing were markers of affiliation to different communities or professions. By requiring all male citizens to adopt a single type of headgear, the *fez*, the law sought 'to create an undifferentiated Ottoman subjecthood without distinction'.[71] Quataert has shown that the new headgear was often rejected by 'Muslims and non-Muslims alike', who perceived the new state rules as an attempt to undermine a system of intermediary social institutions which had enjoyed privileges and autonomies.[72]

At least one example of cold welcome for the reforms was specific to the Armenian community. The introduction of measures to suppress the tax-farming system seriously undermined the core business of the Armenian aristocracy, the *Amiras*, marking the beginning of their decline in the leadership of the *millet*. In the internal political balance of the *millet* the destabilization caused by the weakening of the *Amiras* was followed by a process of realignment that led to the widening of the political participation of the community to the affairs of the patriarchate, most notably granting a stronger representation to the Armenian guilds.

The process of 'democratisation' in the management of the affairs of the Armenian *millet* provides a further opportunity to assess the aims and scope of the Ottoman reforms. The reordering of power relations within the patriarchate took place within a framework provided by the *Hatt-i Hümayun* in 1856: in that document the Sultan had asked the community to 'examine into its actual immunities and privileges, and to discuss and submit to [the] Sublime Porte the reforms required by the progress of civilisation and of the age'.[73] The response of the community was contained in the drafting of a constitution that restructured and regulated the administration of the *millet*, reflecting the new internal balance of power. The fact that the Sultan still recognized the juridical personality of the *millet* at the time when he approved the draft of the constitution in 1860 should not be overestimated. The case may be useful as an indication of the gradualism of the reform process, but in fact many of the traditional powers of the patriarch had already been limited.[74]

The argument that the demise of the *millet* system was initiated by the Ottoman state in response to the need of modernizing the state and society helps in understanding more about the reasons of the crisis of inter-communal relations. In conclusion, two remarks seem particularly crucial. The first is that the reforms generated some degree of resistance: in the Muslim community, which was losing its position of social dominance, but also, as we have seen, within the minorities that should have – at least theoretically – benefited from the change. Inter-communal tension and conflict may indeed have been increased by the process of reform. The second is that, even if we play down the argument concerning resistance to the reforms by the different communities, we might have to accept that the demise of a system of inter-communal relations that had been in place for centuries may have understandably destabilized the society as a whole creating a sense of insecurity and mistrust. Is this enough to account for the sharp conflict that exploded between the end of the 1870s and the First World War?

Further elements for an understanding of the crisis of inter-communal relations in the Ottoman Empire may be found by looking at the international context and, in particular, at the role that some foreign states played in the so-called 'Eastern question'. The influence of the West and of Russia on the internal affairs of the Empire during the nineteenth century was significant and took a variety of forms.

One level of discussion is surely that of the influence of Western values and culture. It is always difficult to account for the history of the migration of ideas, but there is little doubt that, increasingly in the second half of the nineteenth century, European culture played a role in the education of new generations of Ottoman elites. For what is more relevant here, the ideals of many Ottoman supporters of the reform of the state along constitutional and democratic lines as well as the ideals of the first nationalists (in the Balkans but also in Anatolia and other parts of the Empire) were necessarily to be put in relation with European models and precedents. The influence of Western cultures on the Ottoman Empire had of course a long history, particularly considering the background of the commercial relations in the Mediterranean and of various systems of privileges granted to foreigners. However, the phenomenon took a different shape and scope in the nineteenth century when some of the elite Ottoman youth received a European-style education by either travelling abroad or by attending new Western schools that were opened in the Empire. It is not argued here that these schools necessarily prepared generations of radical reformers and nationalists, but it seems accepted that the diffusion of Western education made new ideas available and contributed to the challenging of traditions. Of particular importance is the fact that, in the cultural environment that resulted from this cultural contamination, a number of separate nationalist movements emerged: an Ottoman nationalism but also ethnic-based movements, including a Turkish nationalism and, among others, an Armenian nationalism.

As far as minority groups are concerned, Western education played a prominent role and may have contributed to widening the cleavages between different communities. The case of the Armenians is no exception: the impact of foreign missionary education and of Western education in general was important in redefining the community's identity. Already in the first part of the nineteenth century a small elite of Ottoman Armenians, sons of rich *Amiras* but also students from poor families supported by philanthropists, took the opportunity of receiving higher education in Italy and France. The experience of life and study abroad acted as a catalyst in the process of formation of a renewed Armenian consciousness, even if only at the elite level. In Paris, in 1849 a group of those who became later known as the 'young Armenians' founded the Ararat Society, an association of Ottoman Armenian students aimed at the promotion of what started being defined as the Armenian 'nation'. This Armenian liberal youth brought back to the Empire complaints about the 'miserable condition' suffered by the Armenian nation and the need for improved Armenian education.[75]

In the economic sphere, the impact of the West on inter-communal relations was also relevant. By looking at the recruiting practices of Western firms operating in the Empire, Quataert has observed that these discriminated in favour of Ottoman Christians, relegating Muslims to the 'lowest-ranking, lowest paid jobs'. The system linked back to the Western-style education that Christians were more likely to receive: 'foreign capital interacted with the local (Ottoman) society to produce a workforce in which the coreligionists of the foreign investors were privileged'.[76] Quataert regards this example as a 'metaphor for the impact of west European penetration on Ottoman society as a whole', and concludes that 'the increasing economic, political, social, and cultural power of the West had set in motion a transformation that was overturning the existing order in the Ottoman Empire'. These and similar observations suggest that the attitude of Western businesses played against inter-communal co-operation and contributed to the isolation of the Ottoman Christians; the special relations that these were offered by the West placed them in a bad light to both Muslim traditionalists and emerging Turkish nationalists.

Finally, it is well known that the influence – or interference – of foreign states in the affairs of the Ottoman Empire was by no means limited to the non-governmental and unofficial, non-material level. On the contrary, on several occasions it involved foreign offices and armies of the European powers. It is also known that the treatment of minorities became in the course of the nineteenth century one of the important files in their relations with the Sublime Porte. It is probably unfair to deny that this reflected to some extent a true concern for the conditions of fellow Christians under Ottoman authority. Public opinion in Europe and North America was uncomfortable with the idea of Christians being ruled by Muslims.[77] But philanthropic and humanitarian inclinations should not obscure the fact that the underlying reasons for the intervention of the European powers in the affairs of the Empire were actually more prosaic.

European states had considerable economic interests in virtually all sectors of the Ottoman economy. In particular, since the aftermath of the Crimean War of 1853–1856, the Ottoman state relied increasingly on Western investors in order to finance the expansion of its military and bureaucracy. By the 1870s, international debt was out of control and Western diplomacy started acting forcefully in protection of respective national interests.[78] Russia, for its part, had clear strategic interests at stake. For a long time the Empire of the Czars had sought territorial expansion towards the Black Sea, the Straits and the Mediterranean, all at the expense of the Ottomans. Given this international framework, it is understandable that the protection of minorities was most importantly a powerful Trojan Horse that European powers could use to interfere in the internal affairs of the Ottoman Empire; minorities were to a large extent cynically used as pawns in the protection of the powers' strategic and economic interests, exposing them to the risk of local revenges. In the case of Russia, the inclusion of discussions on the issue of Christian minorities became a pattern in its foreign relations with the Ottomans from the time of Catherine II (1762–96). Peace treaties signed at the end of recurrent military confrontations between the Empires usually included clauses whereby the Ottomans gave Russia some forms of right of protection of Christian minorities.[79] Similar arrangements were obtained by other Western powers, in part to counter the expansion of Russia towards the Mediterranean. It is no mystery that the two most famous documents introducing the *Tanzimat*, the mentioned *Hatt-i Sherif of Gülhane* and the *Hatt-i Hümayun*, were written taking into account a number of pressures from European governments, particularly those that concerned minorities. In some cases, as in Lebanon in 1860 but also during the complex phase of Ottoman retreat from the Balkans, the Europeans did not hesitate to use their armies in order to back up their protected minorities and their interests.

## The Era of Massacres: The End of the Empire and the Armenian Genocide

The years between the 1890s and the First World War mark a tragic, crucial phase in the history of the Armenian people. In these twenty-five years or so the position of the Armenians in the Ottoman Empire, at the time the largest Armenian concentration in the world, progressively deteriorated: as a result, the size of the community was dramatically reduced and its geographical distribution in the Middle East and in the world radically transformed. In the period mentioned most Ottoman Armenians were either killed or driven out of Anatolia and Turkish Armenia. By the end of the First World War survivors found themselves starting a new life as refugees outside Turkey. Only a relatively small number remained in their homeland, within the new Turkish state.

The existing literature on the last phase of Ottoman history and, specifically, on the tragic events that affected the Armenians, is extremely vast and it is the object of sharp controversies to the present day. Controversy is fuelled by the strong significance attached by Armenians and Turks alike to the issue of the public general recognition of the Genocide of the Armenians. The Turkish authorities have so far denied such recognition. Scholarly research, not only Armenian and Turkish, has sometimes suffered from lack of impartiality or simply from lack of some important pieces of reliable, unbiased information. Although not central to the present work, the question of understanding the nature of the events that led to the quasi disappearance of the Armenians from Turkey is important in providing a background for the following chapters. This is for two main reasons: first, because the very dynamic of these events crucially explains the dramatic migration and inflow of Armenian migrant refugees to Syria, Lebanon and other parts of the Middle East.

Secondly, because the particular destiny of the Ottoman Armenians – being victims of a genocide, and of its denial – has deeply marked the collective identity of the Armenian diaspora communities, including those studied in this research.

The beginnings of the most tragic period for the Ottoman Armenians must be traced back to the aftermath of the Russo-Turkish war of 1877–78. One of the war fronts cut across Armenia and, during operations, Russian forces occupied significant parts of Ottoman Armenia. The severe political and economic crisis that followed the Ottoman defeat contributed to redefining the political position and demands of the community in the Empire. Since the outbreak of the war, the Armenian leadership, at the official, *millet* level, had given important signs of its loyalty to the Sublime Porte.[80] After the war, however, the need of supporting the Armenians of the eastern provinces, particularly hit by the effects of the conflict and once again ill-protected by the central government,[81] encouraged the Armenian leadership to take an important initiative: official Armenian delegations contacted Russian and other European powers' representatives to obtain international protection and guarantees for the Ottoman Armenians. The similar cases of Bosnia, Herzegovina and Bulgaria provided a model for the Armenian request of obtaining a form of autonomous administration in the eastern *vilayets*. The Armenian official initiatives were an important sign of the political self-consciousness that the community had developed *vis-à-vis* the state to which it belonged.

The failure of the Armenian diplomatic efforts and the prospects of the Ottoman restoration, under the autocratic rule of the new Sultan, Abdülhamit II, are key elements in understanding the formation, from the mid-1880s, of the first important Armenian nationalist and subversive organisations: the Armenakan Party, the Hunchakian Revolutionary Party and the Armenian Revolutionary Federation (*Dashnaksoutioun*).[82] These groups shared the dream of an autonomous or independent Armenia, but were in fact different in backgrounds and strategies.

The first of these, the Armenakan Party, was founded in Van in 1885. Inspired by an educator of upper-class Istanbuli background, Megerditch Portugalian, the party operated on a small scale, mostly in eastern Turkey. Its members engaged in arms smuggling from Persia, military training, diffusion of revolutionary propaganda and attacks against Turkish police or Kurdish local chieftains. The Hunchakian Revolutionary Party (hence simply the Hunchak)[83] had more developed ideological foundations and a more ambitious, trans-national vision. The party was founded in Geneva in 1887 by seven Russian Armenian students strongly influenced by Marxism and by the Russian revolutionary movement of the time. Ideologically, the Hunchaks associated the Armenian national question with the fight for social justice: the revolutionary struggle for the independence of the Armenian people was to be conducted with the key involvement of peasants and workers and was meant to establish a new model of society where social privilege and exploitation would be banned. Armenian nationalism combined with a socialist program were also the basic principles of the Armenian Revolutionary Federation (hence simply the Dashnak). Founded in 1890 in Tiflis, the party was the result of an effort to join together the forces of a number of Armenian patriotic groups; it shared with the Hunchak the commitment to revolutionary methods but, at least in the first phase, it supported a program of autonomy and reform for the Armenian *vilayets* rather that aiming at the full independence from the Ottoman empire.

By the early 1890s the Armenian revolutionary organisations started engaging in acts of protest and attacks on Ottoman institutions. Literature has been split on two fronts regarding the extent of these attacks, the context in which they took place and even the targets they were aimed at. Versions favoured by pro-Turkish audiences tend to describe the activities of the Armenian organisations as 'guerrilla warfare' which was responsible, among other things, for slaughtering innocent Muslim villagers to provoke an Ottoman reaction and, eventually, foreign powers' intervention.[84] Versions favoured by Armenian audiences tend to describe the early activities of the revolutionary groups as acts of resistance and self-defence or as merely symbolic attacks on Ottoman institutions.[85] Only at a later stage would Armenians organize guerrilla bands but, even then, these would target 'officials, informers, and hostile tribal elements'.[86] There is little doubt, however, that the Armenian revolutionary organizations never had the strength and mass support necessary to pose a serious threat to Ottoman sovereignty in the eastern regions of the Empire.[87] The Ottoman response to these first forms of Armenian resistance, by contrast, was often out of proportion and indiscriminate, and made use of the same unruly Kurdish raiders whose actions were at least in part at the origins of the Armenian question in the east.[88]

Ottoman repression was conducted with unprecedented violence in 1895 and 1896. Most centres in the Ottoman east were hit by a wave of anti-Armenian violence. Attacks seemingly followed a standard pattern: a mob, including Ottoman militaries, would attack Armenian businesses and residential areas, killing and plundering.[89] Ottoman authorities would let the attacks last for a few days before intervening. It is hard to assess the impact of the 1895–6 violence on the Ottoman Armenian population. In the aftermath of the events the German pastor Lepsius estimated victims at more than 88,000.[90] Hovannisian estimates at 100,000 the number of Armenian victims in the massacres of the two-year period. A number of Armenians fled the country.

A second wave of massacres took place during the events that led to the fall of Abdülhamit II, in 1908–9. Armenian revolutionaries had co-operated with the Young Turk opposition, in the effort of bringing down the Sultan.

When the Ottoman constitution of 1876 was restored in the summer of 1908 a number of Armenians ran for election and fourteen became members of parliament.[91] Inter-communal relations seemed to improve. However, during the attempted restoration by the Sultan's supporters in the spring of 1909, another outbreak of violence took place in Ottoman Cilicia: Adana and the surrounding villages were the theatre of brutal attacks on Armenians and their properties.[92] Many were killed and others fled.

Violence against Armenians reached a peak in 1915–16 when it assumed the character of a genocide. The final inter-communal crisis that resulted in the tragic events of 1915–16 was triggered by the combination of at least two elements: first, the emergence in the leadership of the state of an autocratic triumvirate (Talât Pasha, Enver Pasha and Cemal Pasha) deeply imbued of Turkish nationalist and Pan-Turkist ideology.[93] Second, the outbreak of the First World War, in which the Ottomans participated on the side of the central empires. Both elements played against a positive resolution of the Armenian question. On one side the Armenians, as well as other non-Turkish communities, became an obstacle to the realization of a strong Turkish nationalist state. On the other, they were once again caught in the middle of another phase of the centuries-long Russo-Turkish conflict. Given the recent precedents in Ottoman-Armenian relations and the community's stronger presence in the eastern theatre of the war, it is not surprising that the government regarded the Armenians as a dangerous fifth column.

As for the Armenians, the community took different approaches to the war. Many enrolled in the Ottoman army obeying what has been described as an 'old fashioned loyalty to Ottomanism'.[94] It is also reported that Armenian clergy encouraged the community's support for the Ottoman war effort. Others, such as the Armenian revolutionary organisations, actively engaged in organizing military actions against the Empire.

The first phases of the war were unfavourable to Turkey, and Russian troops advanced deeply on the eastern front. Evidence indicates that, under the threat of a potential mass defection of the Armenians, a number of high ranking figures in the government decided to prevent it by the most tragic of all means: the physical elimination of the Armenian Ottoman population of Anatolia. Taking advantage of the general weakness of the constitutional institutions in Istanbul, the decision was dissimulated; a secret corps, the *Teflkilat-ı Mahsusa* (Special Organisation), was created with the main task of implementing the plan.[95]

The issue of the Turkish intent to annihilate the Armenians, crucial in determining the case for genocide, is not surprisingly the most contested of the whole Armenian question.[96] What is generally agreed upon – even by official Turkish authorities – is that, starting in the spring of 1915, Armenians serving in the army were disarmed, and the Armenian population of most cities and villages in the Eastern *vilayets* and elsewhere was ordered to leave their homes at short notice, so that they could be transferred away from the war zones. However, the reports of a large number of eyewitnesses unequivocally points to the fact that the alleged 'relocations' turned out to be in most cases mass roundups and deliberate killings of a disarmed population. For many, the events developed in a strikingly similar pattern throughout the country, including areas geographically distant from the war front. The adult men would be jailed for a few days, then forced to march out of the centres and killed. Women, children and the elderly would be then forced to march away from their homes, generally to the south, on the way to Aleppo and Deir Ez-Zor, along the Euphrates valley. The defenceless columns were then often attacked on the way by brigands, irregulars and other forces. Thousands, virtually deprived of any food and water, exposed to harsh climate, died on the marches.[97]

## The Victims of the Genocide and the Refugees

How many Armenians were victims of the Genocide? How many became refugees? Answers to these questions can only be, at best, educated guesses. Given the circumstances in which the events took place in 1915–16, no official record of the dead was kept. A number of estimates has been put forward in the literature; in examining them, the first thing that one notes is, once again, the striking contrast between the various figures presented. To mention only some of the most quoted accounts, figures range from 1,500,000 (put forward by Bernard Lewis in 1968 in a classic work on modern Turkey) to 301,000 (Gürün, writing in 1985). For Toynbee, writing in 1916 from a British point of observation, victims were between 460,000 and 860,000. For Lepsius (immediately after the end of the First World War) around 1,000,000; for McCarthy (writing in 1983) close to 600,000.[98]

Figures are often based on simple subtractions of data on population in Anatolia before and after the First World War. The number of those 'missing' from Anatolia at the end of the war minus the number of refugees should give the number of those who perished in the massacres. The problem is that there is little agreement on all the primary figures involved, beginning with the number of Armenians living in Turkey before the war started. Data range dramatically from less than one million to over two million.[99]

A critical analysis of existing figures on the Genocide victims is out of the scope of this book. For the purpose of this work it is sufficient to note that accounts and figures agree on a general fact: the events that began with the Genocide of 1915–16 resulted in the quasi disappearance of the Armenians from Turkey. With the most notable exception of Istanbul, an important and ancient component of the Ottoman society was reduced, in the demo-geographic picture of the new Turkish state, to a negligible minority. The first Turkish census after the war, conducted in 1927, did not count Armenians as an ethnic group; however, on the basis of the religious classifications that it employed, it is possible to estimate that only 110,000–120,000 were Armenians, out of a total population of about 13.6 million; that is, less of 1 per cent of the total.[100]

As we move the focus from the victims to those who survived as refugees, the importance of figures, as far as this book is concerned, increases. How many Armenian refugees fled from Anatolia and Armenia to neighbouring regions? In particular, what was the demographic impact of this new migration on the pre-existing Armenian communities in the Middle East, in the Levant and beyond?

Unfortunately, once again, the information available is less than satisfactory. To begin with, given the circumstances in which the population displacements took place, information on the mass of refugees who were driven south into Syria is only available in the form of rough estimates rather than being based on counts or registers. Kevorkian suggests that the survivors of the deportations were about 240,000 and that about 70,000 of these hid in and around Aleppo until the Ottoman military's retreat in late 1918.[101] The marches scattered the refugees in the centres along the course of the Euphrates, in the valley of the Khabur, and along the route leading from Aleppo to Hama, Homs, Damascus and beyond.

Secondly, a proper assessment is made difficult by the fact that population movements involving the Ottoman Armenians were not limited to the displacements of 1915–16, but continued throughout the period between the two World Wars and beyond. A first, important movement took place after the British and French armies secured the control of Cilicia in 1918: a number of refugees ranging between 120,000[102] and 150,000[103] travelled 'backwards' to that region. Some of these were returning to their lands and homes in Marash, Zeitoun, Aintab, Hadjin, and so on; others, originally from other parts of the Ottoman Empire, were following them hoping to join a new Armenian homeland or – at least – to move closer to their homes.[104] The movement was reversed at the end of 1921, when France renounced control of Cilicia and signed the Accord of Ankara (20 October 1921) by which Turkey would re-occupy the region. The recent and continuing experience of violence and fear made it impossible for the Armenians to remain and an estimated 80,000 left Cilicia again for Lebanon and Syria.[105] A third wave of Armenian refugees left Turkey between 1929 and 1930 following further vexation and strong pressures to make the Armenian population leave; a fourth, in 1939–40, was a result of the French Mandatory's cession of the Sanjak of Alexandretta to Turkey.

An estimation of the number of refugees by 1925 was attempted by Hovannisian in 1974, in an article which has remained ever since fairly influential. Hovannisian's figures, are reported in the following table.[106]

**Table 1.1. Armenian refugees in the countries of the Middle East, 1925**

| Country | Number of refugees |
| --- | --- |
| Syria | 100,000 |
| Lebanon | 50,000 |
| Palestine & Jordan | 10,000 |
| Egypt | 40,000 |
| Iraq | 25,000 |
| Iran | 50,000 |

With the exception of Walker, who presented remarkably smaller figures, most of the literature has reached conclusions which are generally compatible with Hovannisian's.[107] McCarthy, who critically analysed the possible sources of information on the refugees, mentioning censuses of a number of western countries and League of Nations data, accepted in full Hovanissian's figures and included them in a wider overview of Armenian refugees.[108] Dekmejian estimated at 200,000 the number of refugees who settled in Iraq, Syria, Lebanon, Jordan and Palestine; a figure which seems roughly compatible with Hovannisian's.[109] For Sanjian 'by the mid-1920s, there were about 100,000 Armenian refugees and orphans settled in Syria, over 40,000 in Lebanon, some 10,000 in Iraq, a similar number in Palestine and Transjordan, and another 25,000 in Egypt'.[110]

Bearing in mind the difficulties in assessing the population displacements, it is beyond doubt that, in most areas of the Middle East, the refugees largely outnumbered the previously existing Armenian communities, perhaps with the exception of Egypt. Speaking of Lebanon and Syria, Varjabedian has presented a useful breakdown of the estimated Armenian population in 1922, based on a report prepared by the department of sociology of the American University of Beirut in 1925.[111]

**Table 1.2. Armenian refugees in Lebanon and Syria, 1922**

| Location | Natives | Refugees | Total |
| --- | --- | --- | --- |
| Beirut | 1,500 | 20,000 | 21,500 |
| Suburbs of Beirut | – | 5,000 | 5,000 |
| Tripoli | 50 | 1,900 | 1,950 |
| Sidon | – | 1,500 | 1,500 |
| Zahleh | – | 1,500 | 1,500 |
| Jounieh, Antelias, Jbeil | – | 1,500 | 1,500 |
| Azez | 13,000 | 2,500 | 15,500 |
| Aleppo | 13,000 | 35,000 | 48,000 |
| Djarablous | – | 2,000 | 2,000 |
| Bab | – | 250 | 250 |

| | | | |
|---|---|---|---|
| Mambedge | – | 250 | 250 |
| Raqqa | – | 600 | 600 |
| Deir Ez-Zor | – | 600 | 600 |
| Villages | – | 300 | 300 |
| Damascus | 800 | 14,000 | 14,800 |
| Hama and Homs | – | 2,500 | 2,500 |
| Alexandretta | – | 7,000 | 7,000 |
| Latakia | 370 | 1,950 | 2,320 |
| Sweida | 7,500 | – | 7,500 |
| | | | |
| Near East Relief orphans* | – | 10,000 | 10,000 |
| | | | |
| Total Lebanon | 1,550 | 31,400** | 32,950** |
| Total Syria | 34,670 | 66,950** | 101,620** |
| Total Lebanon and Syria | 36,220 | 98,350** | 134,570** |

* Breakdown Lebanon/Syria not available
** Excluding Near East orphans

The figures presented by Varjabedian raise more than one doubt in the column regarding the non-refugee component of the Armenian population (particularly in the case of Sweida and Alexandretta); however they are compatible with the totals presented by Hovannisian for 1925 and, with some corrections, could be roughly indicative of the demographic impact of the newcomers. The radical demographic transformation of the Lebanese and Syrian Armenian communities is also evident in the figures put forward in 1986 by Topouzian and presented in the two tables below.[112]

**Table 1.3. Armenian refugees in Lebanon, 1923–1924**

| Area | 1923–1924 | | |
|---|---|---|---|
| | Natives | Refugees | Total |
| Beirut and suburbs | 1,500 | 25,000 | 26,500 |
| Tripoli | 50 | 1,900 | 1,950 |
| Saida, Tyre and surroundings | – | 1,500 | 1,500 |
| Zahleh, Rayak, Ba'albak and other Beka'a | – | 2,000 | 2,000 |
| Antelias, Jounieh and surroundings – | 3,000 | 3,000 | |
| Mount Lebanon | 50 | 500 | 550 |
| Orphans | – | 7,141 | 7,141 |
| Total | 1,600 | 41,041 | 42,641 |

**Table 1.4. Armenian refugees in Syria, 1923–24**

| Area | 1923–1924 | | |
| --- | --- | --- | --- |
| | Natives | Refugees | Total |
| Aleppo and surrounding villages | 13,000 | 37,435 | 50,435 |
| Sanjiak of Alexandretta | 11,000 | 6,800 | 17,800 |
| Latakia and surroundings | 1,370 | 2,750 | 4,120 |
| North-eastern Syria | – | 4,750 | 4,750 |
| Damascus | 800 | 14,000 | 14,800 |
| Hama and Homs | – | 2,500 | 2,500 |
| Armenian orphans (Aleppo) | | 1,500 | 1,500 |
| Total | 26,170 | 69,735 | 95,905 |

If we accept these figures as roughly correct, we may conclude that, with the exception of a few areas where the Armenian presence was already a solid reality before 1914 (Aleppo and its surroundings, the Sanjak of Alexandretta and Latakia), most of the Armenian communities of Lebanon and Syria were formed as a direct consequence of the inflow of refugees. How this community of newcomers found its place in the post-Ottoman Levant is the object of the next chapter.

# Notes

1. It goes without saying that the expression *Middle East* is not fully straightforward. In this context I am using the expression in the 'classical' meaning that it has acquired in contemporary English language literature: it identifies a group of political units in the area including the mid and lower Nile valley, the Levant, the Arabian peninsula, Mesopotamia, Anatolia and the Persian plateau.
2. For a geographical description of historical Armenia see R.H. Hewsen. 1997. 'The Geography of Armenia', in R.G. Hovannisian (ed.), *The Armenian People from Ancient to Modern Times*, Vol. 1, Basingstoke and London: Macmillan, 1–17; D.M. Lang. 1970. *Armenia, Cradle of Civilisation*, London: Allen and Unwin, Chapter 1.
3. Lang, *Armenia*, 37.
4. During the reign of Tigran II political Armenia reached its largest extension. 'Greater Armenia' included all the territories between the Azeri Caspian coast in the east, parts of contemporary Georgia on the Black sea to the north, upper Mesopotamia and the Syrian and Cilician coast on the Mediterranean to the west; see Lang, *Armenia*, Chapter 6.

5. On the origins of Armenian Christianity and of the Armenian Apostolic Church see, among a vast literature, Archbishop M. Ormanian. 1955. *The Church of Armenia*, London: A.R. Mowbray and Co; L. Arpee. 1946. *A History of Armenian Christianity*, New York: The Armenian Missionary Association of America; D.H. Boyajian. 1962. *The Pillars of the Armenian Church*, Watertown: publisher unknown; R.P. J. Mécérian S.J. 1965. *Histoire et Institutions de l'Eglise Arménienne*, Beirut: Imprimerie Catholique; A.J. Iskandar. 2000. *La Nouvelle Cilicie: Les Arméniens du Liban*. Antélias: Catholicosat Arménien de Cilicie.

6. On the participation of the Armenian Church in the Council of Chalcedon, see H.H. Karekin II Sarkissian, Catholicos of Cilicia. 1984. *The Council of Chalcedon and the Armenian Church*, Antelias: Catholicosate of Cilicia.

7. See R. Bedrosian. 1997. 'Armenia during the Seljuk and Mongol Period', in Hovannisian, *The Armenian People*, Vol. 1, 241–271; A.K. Sanjian. 1965. *The Armenian Communities in Syria under Ottoman Dominion*, Cambridge, Massachusetts: Harvard University Press, Chapter 1.

8. According to Bedrosian, 'Armenia during the Seljuk and Mongol Period', p. 268, a severe famine occurred as a consequence of the first Timurid campaign in 1386–87: 'Due to the disruptions [Tamerlane] had caused, crops were not planted, and now there was nothing to harvest. Cannibalism was reported in some areas'.

9. Ibid., 243.

10. Sanjian, *The Armenian Communities*, 9–10. On the Armenian kingdom of Cilicia see A. Atamian Bournoutian. 1997. 'Cilician Armenia', in Hovannisian, *The Armenian People*, Vol. 1, 273–290.

11. See Bedrosian. 1997. 'Armenia during the Seljuk and Mongol Period', 261–262.

12. See Sanjian, *The Armenian Communities*, 8. Sanjian mentions Flavius Mauricius Tiberius (582–602), Philippicus and Romanus Lecapenus as emperors of Armenian origin. Other sources include Heraclius I (610–641), Leo V 'the Armenian' (813–820), and Basilius I (867–886).

13. The first Armenian settlements in the Holy Land would date back to the fourth and fifth century; see R.H. Dekmejian. 1997. 'The Armenian diaspora', in Hovannisian, *The Armenian People*, Vol. 2, 427. Also Sanjian, *The Armenian Communities*, 3–4.

14. See Bedrosian, 'Armenia during the Seljuk and Mongol period', 241.

15. D. Kouymjian. 1997. 'Armenia from 1375 to 1604', in Hovannisian, *The Armenian People*, Vol. 2, 10.

16. Ibid.

17. See V. Artinian. 1988. *The Armenian Constitutional System in the Ottoman Empire 1839–1863*, Istanbul: publisher unknown, 4.

18. Kouymjian, 'Armenia from 1375 to 1604', 13.

19. Ibid., 28.

20. Ibid., 26.

21. Artinian, *The Armenian Constitutional System*, 6, referring to the estimates of a French diplomat of the seventeenth century.

22. On this subject, see Sanjian, *The Armenian Communities*, Chapter 3. 'The Armenian communities which existed in northwestern Syria during the hegemony of the Crusaders were considerably augmented by the influx of settlers from Cilicia after its occupation by the Mamelukes, and continued to survive during the entire period of Ottoman dominion', 53.

23. Ibid., 49.

24. D. Quataert. 2000. *The Ottoman Empire 1700–1922*, Cambridge: Cambridge University Press, 2.

25. Ibid., 173.

26. There is extensive literature on the *dhimmi* formula. See, among a vast literature, R.S. Humphreys. 1991. *Islamic History: a Framework for Inquiry*, London and New York: I.B. Tauris, Chapter 11.

27. The term *millet* itself seems to have been used to indicate non-Muslim communities only in the early nineteenth century. See Quataert, *The Ottoman Empire*, 173. A detailed analysis of the concept and practice of *millet* falls outside the scope of the present work. See, among others, B. Braude and B. Lewis (eds.). 1982. *Christians and Jews in the Ottoman Empire*, New York and London: Holmes & Meier; L. Chabry and A. Chabry. 1984. *Politique et Minorités au Proche Orient: les Raisons d'une Explosion*, Paris: Maisonneuve et Larose, Chapter 2; A. Pacini (ed.). 1996. *Comunità Cristiane nell'Islam Arabo*, Torino: Fondazione Agnelli; B. Masters. 2001. *Christians and Jews in the Ottoman Arab World*, Cambridge: Cambridge University Press.

28. See in this sense H. Inalcik. 1998. *Essays in Ottoman History*, Istanbul: Eren, 202, with reference to the fact that 'Mehmet the conqueror did not have to innovate in establishing a system to handle relations with his non-Muslim subjects'; Inalcik mentions examples of pre-Ottoman documents or agreements regulating relations between Muslims and non-Muslims.

29. The submission of non-Muslims was never in doubt until the *Tanzimat* in the nineteenth century. The status of 'second class' citizens was reinforced by a number of prescriptions concerning the behaviour of the *dhimmi* in public. In particular, 'Clothing laws [...] stipulated the dress of both body and head, that persons of different ranks, religions, and occupations should wear', Quataert, *The Ottoman Empire*, 44.

30. Examples of these limitations could include the issues of proselytizing and – in general – public manifestations of faith, conversion, construction or restoration of churches or synagogues and the religion of the offspring.

31. Pacini, *Comunità Cristiane*, 6.

32. See Inalcik, *Essays in Ottoman History*, 208–213. The non-Muslims had to pay several different taxes. Speaking about the Greek Orthodox *millet*, Inalcik argues that these could be 'classified into three categories: Taxes [sic] going directly into the Ottoman treasury, those reserved to the Patriarch and Metropolitans, and those which were exclusively levied for the local clergy

and never mentioned in the Ottoman documents' (212). Taxes going to the Patriarch and Metropolitans were used to 'meet their financial obligations to the state, personal and ecclesiastical expenditures' (210). The 'financial obligations' refer probably to the '*pikshesh*'. Originally a customary offer, the *pikshesh* (from which comes the word *baksheesh*, common in some parts of the contemporary Middle East for 'tip') became a duty.

33. Artinian, *The Armenian Constitutional System*, 11. Artinian, however, recognises that 'the earliest surviving formal ordinance, granting [...] powers and privileges to an Armenian patriarch, dates back to 1764', ibid., 16.

34. Kouymjian, 'Armenia from 1375 to 1604', 11.

35. Ibid., referring to H. Berbérian. 1965. *Niuter K. Polsoi Hay Patmutian Hamar*, Vienna; H. Barsoumian. 1997. 'The Eastern Question and the Tanzimat Era', in Hovannisian, *The Armenian People*, Vol. 2, 175–201. For Artinian, *The Armenian Constitutional System*, 17, 'At first the patriarch's authority extended only over the Armenians of Asia Minor, including Boursa, Aydin, Angora, and Sivas. By the middle of the seventeenth century the empire stretched from Algiers to Armenia, from Budapest to Basra. Consequently, the Armenian dioceses within these geographic boundaries came under his authority'.

36. Barsoumian, 'The Eastern Question and the Tanzimat Era', in Hovannisian, 184.

37. D. Kouymjian, 1994. 'From Disintegration to Reintegration: Armenians at the Start of the Modern Era: XVIth–XVIIth Centuries', *Revue du Monde Arménien*, 1, 9–18.

38. Ibid.

39. Ibid., Kouymjian reports that Armenian *khodjas* played a major role in the trade of Persian silk. *Khodjas* were flourishing in cities like Djoulfa, in Armenia proper, and, particularly, in Aleppo. Some established themselves in Venice, Amsterdam and other European cities.

40. On the *sarrafs*, civil servants and other Armenian notables see Artinian, *The Armenian Constitutional System*, pp. 19–23. Artinian presents a large number of examples of Armenian notables on the payroll of the Sultan, including a physician, an imperial architect, directors of the imperial powder-works, a superintendent of the imperial mint and so forth. Concerning the opportunities granted to the Christians, I refer to the Ottoman practice, common to many pre-industrial societies, to rely on pariah groups for securing the control of strategic sectors of the economy and the bureaucracy. Slightly different seems to be the issue of the employment of Christians in the Empire's so called 'Ruling Institution'. It is indeed true that, as in A.H. Lybyer. 1913. *The Government of the Ottoman Empire in the Time of Suleiman the Magnificent*, Cambridge: Harvard University Press, 36, 'The most vital and characteristic features of this institution were, first, that its personnel consisted, with few exceptions of men born of Christian parents or of the sons of such'; however, on one hand it seems that the Christian personnel was drawn from the Greek Orthodox rather than from the Armenian community

and, on the other, that Christians becoming part of the Ruling Institution had to convert to Islam, severing the link with their original Christian *millet*.

41.  On the *iltizam* tax farm system, see H. Inalcik and D. Quataert (eds.). 1994. *An Economic and Social History of the Ottoman Empire, 1300–1916,* Cambridge and New York: Cambridge University Press, 65: 'A tax farmer had to find wealthy sureties when he made a contract with the government. In the contract he vowed to deliver to the treasury a certain amount of money in regular instalments during the time agreed upon'. It appears that Armenian *sarrafs* were providers of these sureties.

42.  Artinian, *The Armenian Constitutional System*, 24–25, reports that the 'formation of separate guilds for Christians was permitted by the Ottoman authorities' following the deterioration of inter-communal relations after the second-half of the seventeenth century. Artinian does not elaborate on the 'crisis' of these alleged inter-communal problems. Quataert, who rejects as a 'myth' the idea of an 'ethnic division of labour' in the Ottoman empire holds that mixed guilds did not disappear and were still present and functioning in the nineteenth century, albeit mobilization sometimes took place along communal lines. See Quataert, *The Ottoman Empire,* 181.

43.  For Artinian, *The Armenian Constitutional System,* 28, a key date that marked the debut of the *esnafs* in important Armenian affairs is 1725, when the representatives of the *esnafs* of the capital were invited to participate to the election of a new Patriarch.

44.  Artinian, *The Armenian Constitutional System,* 33.

45.  On the history of the Armenian Catholic Church see, among others, Mécérian, *Histoire et Institutions de l'Eglise Arménienne;* Iskandar, *La Nouvelle Cilicie.*

46.  Artinian, *The Armenian Constitutional System,* 35.

47.  Tensions between Apostolic and Catholic Armenians, however, continued; it was not until 1866 that the Armenian Catholic Patriarchal See could be transferred to Istanbul. On the persecutions of Armenian Catholics and on the relations between the Armenian Catholic community and the Ottoman Empire see N.M. Setian. 1992. *Gli Armeni Cattolici nell'Impero Ottomano: Cenni Storico-Giuridici (1680–1867),* Rome.

48.  On the history of the Armenian Protestant Church see L. Arpee. 1946. *A Century of Armenian Protestantism 1846–1946,* New York: The Armenian Missionary Association of America; J.-D. Sahagian. 1986. *Le Mouvement Évangelique Arménien dès Origines à Nos Jours,* Marseille: J.-D. Sahagian; H.A. Chakmakjian. 1985. *The Armenian Evangelical Movement,* Fresno: Rev. Dr. Chakmakjian; Iskandar, *La Nouvelle Cilicie,* 85–86; Artinian, *The Armenian Constitutional System,* 40–44.

49.  Artinian, *The Armenian Constitutional System,* 42. On persecutions of Armenian Evangelicals also see Arpee, *A Century of Armenian Protestantism,* 11: in 1839 Armenian Evangelical priests were 'arrested and cast into the Patriarchal jail [of Constantinople]' and eventually given in charge of the Ottoman authorities and sent into exile.

50. See Artinian, *The Armenian Constitutional System*, 44: 'The Protestants were not a *millet* in full sense. Unlike the Armenian and the Catholic *millet* leaders, the Protestant Agent, who had only nominal authority over all Protestants of the empire, was always an Armenian layman'.

51. D.M. Lang and C.J. Walker. 1987. *The Armenians*, London: MRG, 5.

52. Barsoumian, 'The Eastern Question and the Tanzimat Era', 183.

53. V.N. Dadrian. 1995. *Autopsie du Génocide Arménien*, Bruxelles: Complexe, 31–32.

54. On the 'limits of tolerance' see the useful critical analysis of Masters, *Christians and Jews in the Ottoman Arab World*.

55. Barsoumian, 'The Eastern Question and the Tanzimat Era', 193. Similar observations are contained in C. Issawi. 1980. *The Economic History of Turkey 1800–1914*, London and Chicago: University of Chicago Press, 65–68, who quotes M.S. Lazarev. 1964. *Kurdistan I Kurdskaya Problema*, Moscow, 32–37. The interest of Lazarev's work lies in the reading of Kurdish-Armenian inter-communal conflict in Eastern Turkey through the lens of the concept of class: inter-communal relations were good at the lower-class level.

56. See, for instance, the position of Justin McCarthy in J. McCarthy. 2001. *The Ottoman Peoples and the End of Empire*, London: Arnold, 9–12.

57. See, for instance Quataert, *The Ottoman Empire*, 181.

58. Y. Courbage and P. Fargues. 1997. *Christians and Jews under Islam*, London: I.B. Tauris, 100.

59. Ibid., 58.

60. Ibid., 107. Interestingly, Courbage and Fargues also argue that Christians had a lower death rate during the recurrent waves of infectious diseases, due to their practice of isolating their houses from contacts with the streets (ibid., 65).

61. See K. Karpat, '*Millets* and Nationality: the Roots of the Incongruity of Nation and State in the Post-Ottoman Era' in B. Braude and B. Lewis (eds.). 1980. *Christians and Jews in the Ottoman Empire*, Vol. 1, New York: Holmes & Meier, 141–170.

62. Quataert, *The Ottoman Empire*, 173.

63. Ibid., 179.

64. McCarthy, *The Ottoman Peoples*, 9.

65. Ibid., 8.

66. A full analysis of the Ottoman reforms, of the intentions of their promoters, the scale of the results that they achieved and of the failures of the process is clearly beyond the scope of this book. The reforms were introduced over a long period of time by a number of different rulers and administrators and under a complexity of different internal and international conditions. See Inalcik and Quataert, *An Economic and Social History*, 759–943; Quataert, *The Ottoman Empire*, 61 and following; McCarthy, *The Ottoman Peoples*, Chapter 2.

67. Dadrian, *Autopsie du Génocide*, 36.

68. See the Imperial Rescript (*Hatt-i Hümayun*) issued by Sultan Abdulmecid on February 18th, 1856: 'All the privileges and spiritual immunities granted by my ancestors *ab antiquo*, and at subsequent times, to all Christian

communities or other non-Mussulman [sic] persuasions established in my empire, under my protection, shall be confirmed and maintained'. Translation reported in Artinian, *The Armenian Constitutional System*, 80. On the Tanzimat, see E. Rabbath. 1973. *La Formation Historique du Liban Politique et Constitutionnel*, Beirut: Université Libanaise, 33–46.

69. On the introduction of the new courts, see Quataert, *The Ottoman Empire*, 176.

70. See, for example the effect of the 1839 reforms on Muslim lords in the periphery of the Empire described in Inalcik and Quataert, *An Economic and Social History*, 877–878.

71. Quataert, *The Ottoman Empire*, 146.

72. Ibid., 147–148.

73. Artinian, *The Armenian Constitutional System*, 80.

74. Artinian, ibid., 52–53, provides some examples: 'After the promulagation [sic] of the Hatt-i Sherif and the establishment of the mixed tribunals the civil powers of the millet leaders diminished considerably. The prerogative of sending lay members of the millet into exile at will was lost permanently, and the patriarch's traditional privileges were confined to religious and personal matters such as divorce, fasting and church attendance. [...] After 1840 even the religious prerogatives of the patriarch were limited to some extent'.

75. Quotations are drawn from a proclamation of the Ararat Society released on 7 June 1849, as translated and reported in Artinian, *The Armenian Constitutional System*, 65. On the role of Western education in the formation of a new Armenian elite see ibid., 59–74. On the importance of education in the ideology of the Young Armenians see P.J. Young. 2001. 'Knowledge, Nation and the Curriculum: Ottoman Armenian Education (1853–1915)', Ph.D. thesis, University of Michigan, 76–78. The emergence of the young Armenian laity as a new player in the community was registered politically during the time of the drafting of the Constitution of the Armenian *millet* (1860). In fact, as far as the redefinition of Ottoman-Armenian relations is concerned, the interest of that Constitution lays perhaps less in the contents of the document than in the process of drafting itself. It is in the course of this process that the traditional forces representing the Armenian society, the *Amiras*, the *esnafs* and the clergy, had to acknowledge the presence of the 'young Armenians' as a new political actor within the *millet*.

76. Quataert, *The Ottoman Empire*, 182–183.

77. McCarthy, *The Ottoman Peoples*, 20.

78. On the financial crisis of the Ottoman Empire see Quataert, *The Ottoman Empire*, 71–72 and Walker, *Armenia*, 92–94. In 1881, under the pressure of European governments, the Ottomans had to create a special agency representing foreign creditors, the Public Debt Administration, in order to 'oversee part of the Ottoman economy and use the supervised revenues to repay the debts' (Quataert, *The Ottoman Empire*, 71).

79. For an overview of European powers' efforts to control the Ottomans' treatment of minorities, see Dadrian, *Autopsie du Génocide*, 33–44; according

to Dadrian the first of these arrangements, included in Article 7 of the Treaty of Küçük Kaynarca of 1774 initiated, in international law, the practice of 'humanitarian intervention'.

80. For example 'Patriarch Nerses Varzhapetian issued a pastoral letter calling on his people to work and pray for the victory of Ottoman arms', R.G. Hovannisian. 1997. 'The Armenian question in the Ottoman Empire, 1876–1914', in Hovannisian, *The Armenian People from Ancient to Modern Times*, Vol. 2, Basingstoke and London: Macmillan, 207.

81. Walker, who quotes an 1879 report of a Western official visiting the area, argues that 'numbers of Circassians and Laz from the Russian empire had arrived in the Ottoman empire, and settled themselves at the expense of the local population. The Kurdish tribal leaders, who had fled during the war, reappeared, with apparently limitless licence to rob and kill'. See C.J. Walker. 1990. *Armenia, the Survival of a Nation*, London: Routledge, 123.

82. On the Armenian revolutionary organisations see L. Nalbandian. 1963. *The Armenian Revolutionary Movement*, Berkeley, Los Angeles and London: University of California Press; Hovannisian, in Hovannisian, *The Armenian People*, 212–222; Walker, *Armenia*, 125–131. On the Armenian Revolutionary Federation see H. Dasnabedian. 1988. *Histoire de la Fédération Révolutionnaire Arménienne Dachnaktsoutioun 1890/1924*, Milan: Oemme Edizioni.

83. *Hunchak* is Armenian for *bell*. The name originated from that of a journal of the Russian social revolutionary movement. See Nalbandian, *The Armenian Revolutionary Movement*, 114.

84. See, for example, McCarthy, *The Ottoman Peoples*, 71–72; J. Salt. 2003. 'The Narrative Gap in Ottoman Armenian History', *Middle Eastern Studies*, 39 (1), 19–36.

85. Hovannisian, in Hovannisian, *The Armenian People*, Chapter 7; Walker, *Armenia*, Chapter 5.

86. Hovannisian, in Hovannisian, *The Armenian People*, 227.

87. In support of this, according to Hovannisian, ibid., 217, the Armenian revolutionary organisations found resistance to them within the higher classes of the Armenian community and within the clergy, alarmed by the socialist and anti-clerical elements contained in their ideologies.

88. In the hope of transforming them into a loyal force, Sultan Abdülhamit II enrolled Kurdish forces in newly established auxiliary cavalry regiments (the *Hamidiye* cavalry). In fact, Kurdish raiders – who now wore imperial uniforms – continued to be unruly and to terrorise the defenceless population of the eastern provinces; see Walker, *Armenia*, 133–134. On the formation of the *Hamidiye* regiments see M. Russo. 2001. 'The Formation of the Kurdish *Hamidiye* Regiments as Reflected in Italian Diplomatic Documents', *Armenian Review*, 47 (1–2), 55–77.

89. Reports of Western officials who were eyewitnesses to these events are important for their historical reconstruction. For example, see the report of the British Council in Erzerum mentioned in Hovannisian, *The Armenian*

*People*, 223. Also see on this and further events, S.E. Kerr. 1973. *The Lions of Marash: Personal Experiences with American Near East Relief 1919–1922*, Albany: State University of New York Press.

90. Lepsius established the Deutsche Orient Mission (1895), a foundation in support of Armenian orphans. Figures that he provides include: people killed 88,243; towns and villages plundered 2,493; villages forcibly converted to Islam 456; churches and monasteries desecrated 649; churches turned into mosques 328; see J. Lepsius. 1897. *Armenia and Europe: An Indictment*, London: Hodder and Stoughton.

91. Armenians had already participated to the short-lived First Constitutional Assembly in 1876–1877. See E.Z. Karal. 1982. 'Non-Muslim Representatives in the First Constitutional Assembly, 1876–1877', in Braude and Lewis, *Christians and Jews*, Vol. 1, 387–400.

92. Attacks in Adana took place under the eyes of the British vice-consul in Mersina, Doughty Wylie. The vice-consul's reports highlight Ottoman responsibilities in the events. See Walker, *Armenia*, 182–186.

93. On the personality and political ideas of the components of the so-called triumvirate see H. Morgenthau. 1918. *Ambassador Morghentau's Story*, New York: Doubleday, Page and Company. Morgenthau, US Ambassador to the Ottoman Empire from 1913 to 1916, had the opportunity of meeting extensively and frequently with the most important Ottoman authorities of the time.

94. C.J. Walker, 'World War I and the Armenian Genocide', in Hovannisian, *The Armenian People*, Vol. 2, 245.

95. The thesis of a parallel, covert organisation to carry out the massacres is put forward, among others, by Quataert, *The Ottoman Empire*, 185.

96. A full coverage of all the arguments on both sides is clearly out of the scope of this book. See, for different perspectives: Walker, *Armenia*; Y. Ternon. 1977. *Les Arméniens, Histoire d'un Génocide*, Paris: Seuil; G. Chaliand and Y. Ternon. 1991. *1915, Le Génocide des Arméniens*, Bruxelles: Complexe; Dadrian, *Autopsie du Génocide*; R.G. Hovannisian (ed.). 1999. *Remembrance and Denial: The Case of the Armenian Genocide*, Detroit: Wayne State University Press; K. Gürün. 1985. *The Armenian File: The Myth of Innocence Exposed*, Nicosia and Istanbul: K. Rustem and Brother; Turkey, Foreign Policy Institute. 1982. *The Armenian Issue in Nine Questions and Answers*, Ankara: Foreign Policy Institute; Turkey, Prime Ministry. 1995. *Armenian Atrocities in the Caucasus and Anatolia According to Archival Documents*, Ankara: Prime Ministry State Archives; J. McCarthy and C. McCarthy. 1989. *Turks and Armenians: A Manual on the Armenian Question*, Washington D.C.: Assembly of Turkish American Associations; S.R. Sonyel. 1987. *The Ottoman Armenians, Victims of Great Power Diplomacy*, London: K. Rustem & Brother.

97. On the deportations and the killings see R.H. Kévorkian. 1998. 'L'Extermination des Déportés Arméniens Ottomans dans les Camps de Concentration de Syrie-Mésopotamie (1915–1916): La Deuxième Phase du

Génocide', *Révue d'Histoire Arménienne Contemporaine*, Tome 2; also see R. Jebejian. 1994. *A Pictorial Record of Routes and Centres of Annihilation of Armenian Deportees in 1915 within the Boundaries of Syria*, Aleppo: Violette Jebejian Library.

98.  A critical reflection on the number of the victims is contained in Walker, 'World War I and the Armenian genocide', 271–272.

99.  For a presentation of the several estimations of the Armenian population of Turkey see J. McCarthy. 1983. *Muslims and Minorities*, New York and London: New York University Press, Chapter 3; E. Uras. 1988. *The Armenian History and the Armenian Question*, Istanbul: Documentary Publications, 353–366.

100.  Calculated on the basis of the Turkish census of 1927, as it appears in McCarthy, *Muslims and Minorities*, 123. I accept McCarthy's view that most Christian Catholics and Protestants in Turkey were Armenian.

101.  Kévorkian. 1998. 'L'Extermination des Déportés Arméniens'; also see H.K. Topouzian. 1986. *Suriayi yev Lipanani Haigagan Kaghtojiakhneri Badmoutioun 1841–1946* [History of the Armenian Communities in Syria and Lebanon 1841–1946], Yerevan: Armenian Soviet Socialist Republic's Academy of Sciences, Orientology Institute, 158; Topouzian puts the figure at 70,000–75,000 'in different cities of Syria'.

102.  Kerr, *The Lions of Marash*, 36.

103.  A. Sanjian. 2001. 'The Armenian Minority Experience in the Modern Arab World', *Bulletin of the Royal Institute for Inter-Faith Studies*, 3 (1), 152.

104.  Topouzian, *Suriayi yev Lipanani Haigagan*, 162, provides a breakdown of the 'returns' to Cilicia by 1919. Around 60,000 returned to Adana; 12,000 to Chork Marsban; 8,000 to Hadjn; 3,000–4,000 to Tarsus; 2,000–3,000 to Mersin; 8,000–10,000 to Msis; more than 50,000 to Marash, Aintab, Zeitoun and surrounding villages; around 10,000 Armenian orphans were also gathered and transferred to Cilicia.

105.  A. Sanjian, 'The Armenian Minority Experience'. For an eye-witness report on the 'return' to Cilicia and the new migration see Kerr, *The Lions of Marash*.

106.  R.G. Hovannisian. 1974. 'The Ebb and Flow of the Armenian Minority in the Arab Middle East', *Middle East Journal*, 28 (1), 20.

107.  Walker's data are: Egypt, 4,000; Syria and Lebanon, 90,000; Iraq, 14,500; Palestine, 2,500. Walker refers to the following sources: J. Burtt. 1926. *The People of Ararat*, London, 119, and A. Khatisian. 1968. *Hayastani Hanrapetutian Dsagumn ou Zargatsume* [The Emergence and Development of the Republic of Armenia], Beirut, 369–370.

108.  McCarthy, *Muslims and Minorities*, 125.

109.  Dekmejian, 'The Armenian diaspora', 413–443.

110.  Sanjian, 'The Armenian Minority Experience', 154.

111.  S.H. Varjabedian. 1977. *The Armenians*, Chicago: S.H. Varjabedian, 156.

112.  Topouzian, *Suriayi yev Lipanani Haigagan*, 169. Topouzian mentions, among his sources, E. Rabbath, S.H. Longrigg, archival resources, newspapers, and yearbooks.

# 2

# (Re)constructing Armenia: The Armenians in Lebanon and Syria during the Mandate

## Introduction

At the turn of the 1920s the Armenians of the Levant were largely a community of refugees. Cutting across all layers and backgrounds of Armenian society, the tragedy of war and the Genocide had shattered the foundations of virtually all aspects of the life of the Armenian survivors as it was known before 1914. The damage suffered by the survivors had several dimensions. At the personal level the Genocide produced a gender-imbalanced community of broken families: survivors had lost parents, spouses, children, relatives, with adult men being on top of the list of those missing. Thousands of children had lost their families and were lodged and raised in a number of orphanages that were established along the Lebanese coast and in the main cities of the Levant. For years, parents who had lost their children would search for them across the orphanages of the region.[1] Illness, hunger and deprivation were the daily realities that most of these broken families and individuals had to face. At the larger social level, most of the traditional networks of relations had been destroyed: the working place, the neighbourhood, local or regional spaces of life and identification were lost. The new conditions forced to mix together Armenian refugees from different classes, different cultural and regional backgrounds. Formal communal institutions had also received a major blow. Churches, schools, charities, cultural and political circles had been washed away by the deportations. Lost with them was also a capital of cultural memory of the community: documents, arts, traditions, skills.

From the very start of their new life as refugees, the Armenians worked hard to reconstruct an Armenian world in the post-Ottoman Levant. In the span of a few years this new Armenian world started to emerge in the life of the refugee camps and in the new Armenian residential quarters; a new set of Armenian institutions gradually appeared, catering for the material and spiritual needs of the community.

The commitment and determination of the Armenians to 'reconstruct Armenia' in Lebanon and Syria is interesting from at least three points of view. The first regards the reasons behind this reconstruction effort. Reconstructing, why? Reconstruction had undoubtedly an 'instinctive' component: stranded in a dramatically different environment – at least in part hostile – where locals even spoke a different language, refugees tended to rely on each other, to look for (or to try and reproduce) the traditional communal 'procedures' in dealing with crisis. As a part of this, the refugees regarded dispersion as a threat to their security and preferred to remain concentrated.[2] The experience of the Armenian refugees in this respect could be compared to that of other refugee communities. But the Armenian case could also show that 'culture matters', that different cultures react differently to crises; or, rather, one could apply theories of the impact of war and genocide on communal behaviour: the determination to reconstruct was stemming from the Armenian strong, non-assimilatory communal solidarity,[3] or from the awareness of the fact that the Genocide could have indeed wiped out Armenian culture altogether. A second interesting point of view regarding the reconstruction effort has to do with the contents of it. Reconstructing what? The analysis here could focus on the often thin line distinguishing the preservation and the *ex novo* construction of cultural identities: how much of the reconstruction of the Armenian world was in fact a *construction*? A third area of interest focuses on the actual implementation of the reconstruction effort. (Re)constructing, how? One could observe how Armenian social institutions were gradually re-established: families, churches, schools etc.; one could, for example, identify the agents of this reconstruction and, in particular, determine what contribution the reconstructed institutions themselves brought to the effort; or what role was played by the Armenian pre-Genocide community of the Levant, by the Armenian international diaspora, by the Lebanese and Syrian state, by the international community. Many of these important issues fall beyond the scope and possibilities of this book. What this chapter will do is look at some of these, with a particular attention to *how* the reconstruction of the formal institutional world took place, with the aim of reflecting on the relation between the process of reconstruction and the policies and the evolution of the state.

The type of state in which the Armenians were engaging in the reconstruction effort was, itself, new to the region: it was the colonial French administration of the Mandate. In 1922 France received from the League of Nations a mandate to administer geographical Syria in a move that only came to formalize and acknowledge the consolidation of an area of influence of France in the Levant, as France and Britain had secretly agreed in the Sykes-Picot agreement of 1916. With the exception, broadly, of the Christian Maronite community, the French administration was imposed on the local populations more or less with the use of force and shaped by the strategic priorities of Paris: by 1920 France had established an independent Greater Lebanon and divided the Syrian hinterland in separate territorial units. The form that the French colonial administration took blended French colonial experience (particularly in Morocco)[4] and Ottoman legacy. The constitutional and political formula that resulted created favourable conditions for the Armenians; the community seized them.

The place where the reconstruction of the Armenian world began was the refugee camp. Initially made of canvas tents and later of wooden shacks covered with corrugated sheet-iron, Armenian refugee camps were established on the edge of the main towns of Lebanon and Syria. It was in the late 1920s and in the early 1930s when the refugees could gradually start to move out from these initial shelters and install themselves in new purpose-built popular Armenian quarters. The camps, and later the Armenian quarters, became landmarks in the new geography of the refugees; within these, the Armenian churches were among the first Armenian institutions to be re-established.

## Religious Policy under the Mandate and the Re-establishment of the Armenian Churches

### Ottoman Legacy and Change

For the peoples of Syria and Lebanon the collapse of the Ottoman Empire meant – along with many other things – breaking away from the Ottoman legal system. An important dimension of that epochal change concerned the sphere of the religious life of the citizens: under the new religious policy adopted by the Mandatory, Islam was no longer the religion officially adopted by the state. In sharp contrast with the Ottoman constitution of 1876, which had confirmed Islam as the 'religion of the state',[5] the Lebanese constitution of 1926 did not adopt any official state religion. Article 9 stated that *'La liberté de conscience est absolue. En rendant hommage à l'Etre Suprême, l'Etat respecte toutes les confessions, et en garantit et protège le libre exercice à condition qu'il ne soit pas porté atteinte à l'ordre public'.*[6] Article 9, therefore, was extending the state's protection to all faiths, with the sole limit that they should not prejudice public order. The provision was clearly further reaching than its homologue in the Ottoman constitution of 1876, where the protection was limited to the faiths 'recognised in the Empire',[7] in the framework of the Islamic formula of the *ahl al-dhimma* and the *millet* system. The changes introduced by the

Lebanese constitution, and later by the Syrian constitution of 1930, followed another epochal and far reaching event: in 1924 the new government of Turkey had officially abolished the Caliphate, severing, after centuries, the religious link between Muslim believers and Istanbul.

The clear importance of these changes should not overshadow the fact that the new system of state-religion relations in Lebanon and Syria was characterised by important elements of continuity with the past. Continuity emerges particularly when analysing the changes from two perspectives. The first regards the general position of religion in the new polities organised by the Mandatory. It is true, on the one hand, that the choice of not adopting any official religion 'liberated' the state from being imbued with any specific set of religious values, ways of organising public and private life, and so on; in other words, it is true that the state was in general secularised.[8] On the other hand, by no means did the changes introduce a French-style, separatist model where religious affiliations would be reduced to mere private facts and where a clear distinction was introduced between the concepts of *civis* and *fidelis*. Far from becoming irrelevant, religious affiliation, as determined at birth or acquired by conversion, remained a crucial element in defining the spaces or opportunities of participation in public life of the individuals. In Syria, for example, the constitution of 1930 reserved the office of president of the republic to a Muslim; in Lebanon, the constitution of 1926 recognised the role of religious communities in public life, and Article 95 stated that '*A titre transitoire [...] et dans une intention de justice et de concorde, les communautés seront équitablement représentées dans les emplois publics et dans la composition du ministère, sans que cela puisse cependant nuire au bien de l'Etat*'.[9] In the years of the Mandate religious affiliations became one of the pillars of the construction of the Lebanese constitutional system, based on community-based representation and power sharing. Religious affiliations were thus maintained as necessary, virtually inescapable 'doors of access' to public spaces.[10]

The second perspective which reveals important lines of continuity between old and new is that of the religious freedoms and autonomies enjoyed by non-Muslim religious communities. As far as these were concerned (including the Armenian refugees) the Mandatory did not substantially alter the system of rather vast autonomies that had been established through the centuries of the *millet* experience, particularly in the area of religious affairs and personal status law. Armenian religious and communal institutions – as well as homologous institutions of other faiths – continued to rule autonomously in all issues regarding doctrine and rite, internal organisation, but also on all personal status affairs including inheritance questions. Important moments of the life of the Armenians, such as marriages, divorces, birth registrations, continued to be regulated almost exclusively by Armenian religious authorities, since no alternative secular law was produced. If the legal system of the Mandate *did* make a difference in the daily practice of religions in the Levant, it was perhaps for the minority Muslim confessions (Shi'a, Druze, Alawi and – in Syria only – Ismaili) which had not obtained recognition and protection in the Ottoman Empire; to these confessions the new system granted freedoms and autonomies similar to those that were being confirmed for the non-Muslims.

A separate, important question regards the extent to which the Mandatory actually intended to change the system of autonomies described. French administrators in the Levant surely had to carefully balance the reinforcement of central administration with the need of avoiding measures which could upset the uneasy inter-communal relations or alienate the support of loyal communities.[11] In fact, on a political level, the French were well aware that the religious leadership of the different communities could become a powerful instrument of social and political control and were keen on creating a 'clientele of religious patriarchs'.[12] Legislation in this area of administration had its legal source in the Act establishing the Mandate in 1922. Article 6 of that document stated that *'le respect du statut personnel des diverses populations et de leurs intérêts religieux sera entièrement garanti'*.[13] The provision was further reinforced by Article 9 of the same document, which prohibited *'toute intervention [...] dans la direction des communautés religieuses et sanctuaires des diverses religions, dont les immunités sont expressément garanties'*.[14]

The legislation introduced during the Mandate itself generally reflected these principles. In Lebanon, the constitution of 1926 stated that *'[l'Etat] garantit également aux populations, à quelque rite qu'elles appartiennent, le respect de leur statut personnel et de leurs intérêts religieux'*.[15] The main legislative effort by the Mandatory to regulate the relations between the state and the religious faiths in Lebanon and Syria was made during the 1930s. The *Arrêté* n. 60 L.R. of 13 March 1936 and the *Arrêté* n. 146 L.R. of 18 November 1938 (which amended the first) had two main objectives: the first was to confirm and specify the areas of autonomy granted to the existing religious communities in the countries. The second was to establish the principle that the state had the duty and right to verify that community life did not violate state legislation.[16] The document of 1936 (Article 4) established a procedure to grant legal personality to religious communities, on condition that these submitted to the government *'un statut tiré des textes qui la régissent'*.[17]

The statute that the law requested from the communities was expected, among other things, to specify the structure of communal religious life: this would include hierarchies, jurisdictions, mechanisms of formation and functioning of religious bodies. The introduction of the principle of the governmental right to control the conformity of communal statutes with national legislation represents perhaps the furthest the French authorities decided to go in terms of winning state control over the spaces of autonomy of the religious communities; that is, very little. An exemplary case is that of the legislation on marriage: non-religious legislation allowing civil marriage could not be introduced by the Mandatory as it was going to face fierce opposition from the religious authorities in the country. A partial *escamotage* was found in allowing the official recognition of marriages contracted abroad.[18]

In addition to that, the provisions of 1936 and 1938 remained strictly speaking unfulfilled, in large part due to the break out of the Second World War. None of the statutes was in fact presented to the state by the communities and the legal recognition of religious authorities could not be formalized according to the procedures set out in the law.[19] Nevertheless, the law was important because it established a model of state-community relations that was never discontinued even after Lebanese and Syrian independence. For the Armenian communities the 1936 law was also significant because it included the Armenian Apostolic and Armenian Catholic Churches in a list of 'historical communities' in the country: a politically important recognition for a community which was largely new to the area.[20]

In conclusion, the combination of new and old in the religious policy of the Mandate created a favorable environment for Armenian religious preservation and expression. On one hand the significant secularization of the state had completed the process of elimination of the discriminatory treatment of non-Muslims, something that must have remarkably reassured a population of survivors of genocide. On the other, a certain secularization of the state did not involve any significant loss of autonomy for the Armenian religious authorities, preserving almost in full their position as key communal institutions.

## *The Re-establishment of the Armenian Churches in Lebanon and Syria*

On a practical level, the Armenian Churches during the Mandate had to face the dramatic consequences of the Genocide and re-establish their presence and organization among their own people. In the memories of those who lived in person the experience of the refugee camps, the  churches are often remembered as the first public buildings erected in the camps together with the schools, the first stones in the construction of a new Armenian world for the refugees. Churches were initially hosted in simple wooden shacks, not different from all other makeshift buildings in the camps. Only in the course of the 1930s, when most of the refugees resettled in new Armenian quarters, would churches begin to be rebuilt in a style that interpreted the forms of traditional Armenian architecture, albeit made of the cheap construction materials that the community could afford.[21]

Parallel to the physical reconstruction of the places of worship was the reconstruction of the religious institutions. Of the three Armenian Churches, the one that could perhaps be considered in a comparatively better position was the Catholic Church. Of course, war and the Genocide had hit the Armenians regardless of their religious affiliation; however, the Catholic Church had solid roots in Mount Lebanon and Syria and, when refugees arrived in the Levant, the Church was already able to contribute remarkably in the immediate relief effort. The Armenian Catholic leadership of the convent of Bzoummar was able, for instance, to play a role of mediation with the authorities and with the owners of land needed to set up refugee camps.[22] The main institutional restructuring step within the Church was taken in 1928 when it was decided to relocate the official See of the Armenian Catholic Patriarch from Istanbul and to restore Bzoummar to its ancient role as the centre of Armenian Catholicism. Besides their traditional presence in Lebanon and Syria, Catholic Armenians could count on the support provided by the Holy See. In 1928 Pope Pius XI funded the construction of the urban See of the Armenian Catholic Patriarchate in Beirut-Jeitaoui and of the Cathedral of St. Gregory and St. Elias in Beirut-Centre ville.[23] The support of the Vatican also took the form of the establishment in the Levant of branches of two Armenian religious orders, the Sisters of the Immaculate Conception (in 1927), and the Mechitarist Fathers (in 1937).[24]

The situation of the Armenian Apostolic Church was considerably more complex. With the exception of Aleppo, the presence of the Orthodox Armenians in Syria and Lebanon before the Genocide had been extremely limited. In centres like Damascus or Beirut the Armenian Apostolic communities had been minimal, and the churches had mostly played the role of stations of pilgrimage on the way to Jerusalem. One of the important questions that the Church had to settle was the reorganization of the ecclesiastical territorial jurisdictions, and – in particular – the question of the fate of the Catholicosate of the Great House of Cilicia. The Catholicos of Cilicia, formally the heir of the original Catholicos of the Apostolic Church and – with the other Catholicos of Etchmiadzin and Aghtamar – one of the heads of the Armenian Church, had been based in Sis (Cilicia) since the late thirteenth century.[25] In 1915 the See had to be moved precipitously to Aleppo and then to Jerusalem on order of the Turkish authorities. Briefly reinstalled in Adana after the armistice of 1918, the Catholicosate had to be transferred again following the French-Turkish agreement of 1921 that triggered the new Armenian evacuation of Cilicia. For several years the Catholicosate survived as an unsettled refugee institution while, according to the pre-Genocide tradition, the mass of refugees settling in Lebanon and Syria fell under the jurisdiction of the Armenian Patriarch of Jerusalem. In spite of being politically supported by the French Mandatory,[26] the Catholicos found great difficulty in re-establishing his functions and it was only after 1928, and after he had issued a dramatic Will, that the question was resolved.[27] In 1929 the Patriarch of Jerusalem formally renounced his jurisdiction on the dioceses and properties of Beirut, Damascus and Latakia in favour of the Catholicos, and the following year the Catholicosate of the Great House of Cilicia could find its new permanent See in Antelias, on the coast north of Beirut.[28]

The solution of the question of the Catholicosate of Cilicia was accompanied by the re-establishment of the institutions regulating the internal life of the Apostolic community. These were modelled on the legacy of the Armenian *millet* experience and on the Armenian 'national constitution' of 1863. Dioceses and jurisdictions were adapted to the new context of the Mandate: the Armenian Apostolic community in Lebanon (clergy and laity) would elect an Armenian National General Assembly; the community in Syria would do the same. Each National Assembly would form a Religious Central Council and a Civil Central Council, the religious and secular 'executive organs' of the community, with responsibilities including the organisation of religious life, the direction of the educational and social institutions belonging to the Church, the general management of the Church's finances.

Armenian Evangelical Christianity was very severely damaged by the Genocide, in part on account of the small size of the Evangelical communities: in some areas the Evangelical communities were totally wiped out by the massacres. Moreover, the displacements resulted in the loss of most of the assets that were at the core of the Armenian Protestant movement: the educational and social institutions. On the other hand, the re-establishment of the Church in the new refugee context was made simpler by virtue of the flexible, congregational nature of Protestant Christianity.[29] Re-established Armenian Evangelical Churches were organised in a Union that included, initially, only Lebanon and Syria and then expanded to include other countries in the Near East and beyond.[30]

## Armenian Politics and Public Participation[31] under the Mandate

### From Aliens to Citizens

Armenian refugees displaced to Lebanon and Syria in the 1910s and the early 1920s had initially no title and no ambition to get involved in public affairs in the post-Ottoman Levant. In the years of the military control of the region by the British and the French and in the early phase of the French Mandate they remained a foreign, temporarily hosted community at the very margin of the society. The rise and fall of the ephemeral Arab kingdom of Faysal in Damascus in 1918–1920, the creation of Greater Lebanon, the territorial partitions of Syria,[32] and the first elections organised in 1922–3 to allow the establishment of Representative Councils were events which remained largely alien to the Armenians, whose process of displacement from their lands was continuing and who were struggling with the hardship of life in the refugee camps.

This does not mean that the Armenians always behaved neutrally *vis-à-vis* the political affairs of the region in the new, post-Ottoman order, or that they were perceived by the rest of the inhabitants of the Levant as neutral players. The attitude of the Arab communities towards the Armenians was probably characterized by mixed feelings. It is often remembered that the Sharif Husayn ibn 'Ali of Mecca, publicly condemned the massacres of the Armenians by the Turks and that, in 1917, he 'requested that his son, Faysal, and certain of his associates, protect and support those Armenians who had been driven into the desert'.[33] It has also been documented that many Armenian refugees received life-saving help by Arabs in the dramatic circumstances of the Genocide and beyond.[34] However, as Armenians started populating refugee camps at the margin of the main Lebanese and Syrian cities, they began to be perceived negatively by some.[35]

This was in part related to their condition as foreigners and refugees and to the severe economic and humanitarian crisis that had affected the region since the war. Natural disasters and the blockade of the Lebanese coast since 1915 had disastrous effects on the entire population of Greater Syria: famine and illness killed an estimated 150,000 to 500,000 in the period 1915–1918.[36] In Aleppo alone 35,000 persons might have died of typhus between August 1916 and August 1917.[37] Armenian refugees, who were extremely poor and particularly vulnerable to infective pathologies would become, at times, the scapegoats for all the evils of the period: the spread of diseases, soaring unemployment, or the increase in robbery.[38]

But the Armenians were often also perceived – in part correctly – as protégés and collaborators of the French by Arab nationalists and other opponents of foreign rule. The relation between the Armenians and the French was based upon a convergence of interests. Since the creation of Greater Lebanon in 1920 the French had worked to widen local support for the Maronite-backed separation of Lebanon from Syria and to build religious representative systems in the polities that they were establishing. The events that had involved the Armenians provided the French with the opportunity of enrolling them among those who could assist in the task of controlling the region. Some Armenians, for their part, regarded the French as their 'saviours' from the Turks, providers of protection, humanitarian assistance and jobs and became available for co-operation. Collaboration could hardly be described as involving the community as a whole, nor were the Armenians unified under a solid, defined leadership that could represent them in full. However, regardless of these considerations, cooperation was visible in at least two ways. First, the French administrators contributed remarkably to the early support of the Armenian refugees, providing consistent resources for the relief operations in the camps and establishing food programs and resettlement schemes.[39] Secondly, the French post-war administration was keen on recruiting Armenians and other minority peoples in the public services and in the army and security apparatus with the intention of creating a separation between these bodies and Arab national politics.[40] As soldiers, the Armenians were favoured by some French officers who distrusted the Muslims,[41] even if they won a reputation for unruliness and brutality that created problems for the French Command.[42]

The French strategy of enrolling the Armenians to support their plans for Lebanon and Syria was stepped up in 1924/5, when the Armenians were offered citizenship, creating the condition for their inclusion among the confessional 'families' of the new Lebanese and Syrian political systems. The occasion that opened the doors for the Armenians to become a permanent component of the societies of the Levant and to play a part in its public life was the signing of the Treaty of Lausanne in July 1923. The Treaty, a large document of 143 articles which represented the final peace agreement between Turkey and the states which had emerged as winners in the First World War, addressed, among the several other issues, the question of the nationality of the people who had held Ottoman citizenship.[43] Article 30 of the Treaty stated that 'Turkish subjects habitually resident in territory which in accordance with the provisions of the present Treaty is detached from Turkey will become *ipso facto*, in the conditions laid down by the local law, nationals of the State to which such territory is transferred'.[44]

Article 32 added that 'Persons over eighteen years of age, habitually resident in territory detached from Turkey in accordance with the present Treaty, and differing in race from the majority of the population of such territory shall, within two years from the coming in to force of the present Treaty, be entitled to opt for the nationality of one of the States in which the majority of the population is of the same race as the person exercising the right to opt, subject to the consent of that State'.[45]

The case of the Armenians was left largely unclear by the provisions of Article 30 and Article 32. The Treaty of Lausanne marked the shelving by the great powers of any plan concerning the creation of an Armenian state in historical Armenia. In the absence of any other state where the Armenians could find people of their 'same race', the Treaty seemed to call for the resettlement of the refugees to the Soviet Republic of Armenia, a possibility that was technically and politically complex.[46] It was in this context that, in September 1924, the Mandate administration issued a decree that offered the option of the citizenship 'to all Armenians willing to accept it'.[47] Lebanese citizenship was established officially for all Lebanese – including the Armenians – by another decree on January 1925.[48]

The granting of citizenship to the Armenians was welcomed by Christians, but – not surprisingly – was met with opposition by some Muslim leaders and became another spectacular example of the protection that the French were according to the Armenians. In Lebanon Muslims 'accused the government of deliberately increasing the Christian population in the country'.[49]

## *The Debut of Armenian Public Participation (1925–1929)*

One of the main political consequences of the granting of citizenship was that the Armenians were allowed to participate in elections. From the perspective of the French and their allies this meant that the Armenian collaboration could now be brought formally into the political domain; Armenians were able to support the forces loyal to the French with their votes and – later on – with the votes of their elected representatives. After the granting of citizenship, the French authorities and their allies acted swiftly to reinforce and expand the political spaces reserved for the Armenians in the new confessional systems being established in Lebanon and in Syria.

As for the Armenians, their attitude on what role the community should play in the political systems of the two countries was all but clearly defined. In an attempt to simplify, four main positions among the community could be roughly identified. Armenian collaboration with the French was in general supported by the religious leadership and by a conservative class of the relatively better-off traditionally associated with it and/or linked to the French administrative apparatus. These forces had reasons for considering the French as saviours against the Turks and saw in the association with the new rulers of the Levant the possibility of re-establishing and reinforcing Armenian institutions and their leadership over them.

Alternative to these forces, but initially considerably weaker, were the Armenian nationalist parties. The archives of the Dashnak party, as analysed by Schahgaldian, show that the party regarded the religious leadership of the 1920s as unsuited to lead the community and concerned more about reasserting its hold over it rather than elaborating and pursuing a 'national' strategy. For the Central Committee of Syria and Lebanon of the Dashnaks 'the religious heads, exploiting the mentality of the refugees, [were] continually try[ing] to disrupt and neutralize secular bodies and extend their rule over them'.[50] The Catholicos of Cilicia himself was described negatively as 'not only satisfied with his religious prominence, but also meddl[ing] in politics with local and foreign elements.[51]

The Dashnaks' view on the role the Armenians had to play in Lebanon and Syria appeared initially rather uncompromising: the leadership thought it was wrong for the Armenians to 'meddle in politics with local and foreign elements', that is, it had little interest in getting involved in Lebanese and Syrian politics. True that the party had been already active in Lebanon since 1901[52] and that it had rapidly reactivated its structures in the Levant after the war, but in the early 1920s the Dashnak party's focus of activities was elsewhere. As it was gradually re-establishing itself as a diasporic organisation with a transnational structure and local branches in several countries, the party's core interests were in organising military-terrorist attacks on Turkish officials held responsible for the Genocide, supporting the anti-Turkish struggle of the Kurds, and trying to regain control of the Republic of Armenia that they had lost to the Bolsheviks.[53] Similarly focused on the Armenian question, but ideologically apart was the position of the other Armenian nationalists, the social democrats of the Hunchak party, and the Armenian Democratic Liberals or the Ramkavar (ADL – Ramkavar Azatakan Kusaktsutiun). The latter was a party formed in 1921 by the triple merger of the Armenakan, of a splinter of the Hunchaks, and the Sahmanadir Ramkavar party founded in Cairo in 1908.[54] These formations were, to different degrees, available to work in co-ordination with the Armenian traditional leadership but also with local Lebanese and Syrian movements. More importantly, the Hunchaks and the Ramkavars sharply opposed the Dashnak party, from which they were divided by widening ideological and tactical visions, in particular concerning Soviet Armenia.

A third position was that of the Armenian communists. Originating in 1923 as a student splinter of the Hunchaks, the Armenian communist Spartak group joined forces with Lebanese and Syrian communists and contributed remarkably, in 1925, to the establishment of the Communist Party of Syria and Lebanon.[55] Armenian communists were the only Armenian political group to seek, right from the start, a thorough integration with non-Armenian politics in the Levant: they believed that the Armenian national cause and the interests of the refugees could best be served by supporting the Arab anti-imperialist struggle for independence. During the anti-French Great Revolt of 1925–1927 their leader, Artine Madoyan, developed connections with emissaries of Sultan al-Atrash and was actively involved in the smuggling of arms from Beirut to the Jebel Druze.[56]

Finally, the attitude of the Armenian masses living in the refugee camps was seemingly dominated by apathy, indifference and the prevalence of local interests. Refugees in the camps were to some extent set apart by differences regarding their cultural background, including their regional, social and linguistic origins; many of the Cilician refugees were not primarily Armenian speaking (or could only speak Turkish).

Language and poverty were substantial barriers to participation in affairs that were outside the life in the camps or the sphere of work. Refugees often loosely rallied around regional patriotic unions. These were associations spontaneously created by groups of Armenians from different political creeds who shared the same geographical origin in the homeland. Patriotic unions, named after cities or regions in the homeland (like Marash, Sis, Adana, and so on) played a remarkable role in organising and managing self-help activities in the refugee camps, including the construction of shelters, schools and churches.[57]

In the first phase of Armenian public participation, until the late 1920s, the religious and traditional leadership of the community took a leading, pivotal position and effectively ensured Armenian support for the French. In Lebanon, Armenians publicly debuted in political affairs in July 1925, when they voted for the renewal of the Representative Council, amongst complaints from some local leaders, accusing the community of being alien to the country and of attempting to 'establish a national home in Lebanon'.[58] In the elections of 1925 Armenian co-operation with the French took the shape of the electoral support lent to the Christian Maronites and, notably, to the staunchest ally of the Mandatory, Emile Eddé. In 1929 Maronite-Armenian collaboration resulted in the election, with Lebanese Christian support, of the first Armenian Member of Parliament, Abdallah Ishaq, an Armenian Catholic who took the seat reserved for the representative of the 'minorities'.[59]

In Syria, the debut of Armenian participation in elections took place in 1926, after the French High Commissioner had decided to reshuffle some of the existing Representative Councils.[60] In a pattern similar to that seen in Lebanon in 1925, the Armenian voters sided with the Mandatory and their allies. In Aleppo, the main centre where the Armenian vote was relevant, the nationalist, anti-French leadership of the city boycotted the elections; 'only 23 percent [...] of Aleppo's registered voters participated in the first degree elections, and these were mainly from the Armenian and Syrian Catholic communities'.[61] The popular perception of the collaboration of the Armenians with the French was reinforced by the fact that Armenian fighters were used during French repression of the national revolt against the Mandate. In one of the most dramatic episodes, early in 1926, Circassian and Armenian irregulars were unleashed by the French in the Midan quarter of Damascus where they brought ruthless violence.[62] The association of these Armenian fighters with the French endangered the Armenian refugees who were attacked in their turn: an Armenian refugee camp outside Damascus old city's quarter of Bab Touma was set on fire[63] and, at least in one other occasion, refugees had to leave their shelters and run for their security.[64] These and other incidents resulted in a new flow of Armenian refugees, this time from Syria to Lebanon.[65] An important moment in Armenian participation in public life in Syria occurred in 1928, when the political conditions led the Mandatory to allow the formation of a Constitutional Assembly. On that occasion, an Armenian Catholic, Fathallah Asiun, became the first Armenian member of a parliamentary assembly elected in the post-Ottoman Levant.[66] The political position of the Armenians was strengthened two years later when the Syrian constitution was promulgated. The 1930 constitution formalized political confessionalism, and prescribed that the electoral law must ensure representation for 'religious minorities'.[67]

## The Struggle for Independence and the Armenians (1930–1943)

During the second half of the 1920s the public participation of the Armenians in Lebanon and Syria had been essentially directed and timed by the French authorities. In a second phase, coinciding with the acceleration of the process that led to Lebanese and Syrian independence, the Armenians took a more active role, became gradually more emancipated, and eventually contributed to their own political dédouanement, to legitimize their presence as players on the political scene.

The shift matured in connection with the rise to prominence within the community of the Armenian parties and with the political marginalization of the traditional religious leadership. In the case of the Dashnak, the rise to prominence was the successful result of a political investment made in the 1920s: the evaporation of hopes of an international-supported Armenian state in historic Armenia, the Soviet success in maintaining power in the Republic of Armenia and the initial failure of the party to win substantial support among the refugees had all been factors that had convinced the party's leadership of the need of shifting their attention to the diaspora Armenians and their living conditions as refugees. The party had realized that Armenians must be prepared to live in the Middle East for some time and fight a longer struggle for return. Substantial resources were put into the effort of establishing and/or gaining control of church-affiliated and other communal educational or mobilisation institutions in competition with other parties and with the traditional leadership.[68] As far as participation in Lebanese and Syrian public affairs was concerned the shift of attitude of the Dashnak did not mean that the party became interested in transforming itself into a Lebanese or Syrian political force; however, since the end of the 1920s the party seemingly took a more pragmatic approach and decided that participating in the public affairs of the Levant was a necessary step to win political leadership within the community and establish solid positions from where it could continue the national struggle. The other Armenian nationalist parties followed similar strategies; the result was that Lebanese and Syrian public spaces reserved for the Armenians became increasingly an arena for intra-Armenian competition between parties. From the perspective of the Mandatory, this had the important consequence that, from the beginning of the 1930s, the French could hardly count on a co-ordinated and rather compact support of the community during elections, as they had had in the 1920s. Armenian parties had of course to take into account the need of maintaining good relations with both the Mandatory and the Arab communities; however, besides any ideological consideration, they would pragmatically bargain their support with one or the other side while focusing on the struggle for political supremacy within the Armenian field and the pursuit of their Armenian agenda. As for the Armenian communists, their support for the Arab national movement had never been discontinued: in the 1930s the collaboration with the anti-colonialist Arab left continued on the edge of legality and, more often, beyond.

The new phase of Armenian politics became manifest during the parliamentary elections of 1931/2 in Syria. In Aleppo, where the Armenians formed a large minority of 50,000,[69] the elections within the community were dominated by the split between the Dashnaks and the Hunchaks: the Dashnaks sided with the French-backed 'Liberal Constitutionalists', while the Hunchaks, who 'specifically sought to promote amicable relations with the Arab population' supported the Nationalist Bloc. The Armenian parties were now playing the local political game.[70]

A similar, sharp split between Armenian forces was recorded in Lebanon in 1934, on the occasion of the elections for the third Lebanese Parliament, when the Armenian Apostolic community was for the first time recognised to have the right to a representative of their own in the Chamber. Appeals for a unified Armenian participation failed to materialise. In the course of the negotiations before the elections the Dashnak's position was characterized by a pragmatic bargaining and collaboration with the most important forces on the ground. On one hand, the Dashnak leadership realized that the Armenian candidate for the seat reserved to the Armenians 'must be someone who enjoys the confidence of the mandatory power'.[71] On the other, the party became available to carefully co-operate with the moderate opposition to the Mandate government; eventually, the party ended up supporting a candidate in the list of nationalist leader Abdallah Yafi in opposition to the French-backed candidate Vahram Leilekian, who enjoyed the support of the Hunchaks, of the Ramkavars and of the Apostolic Church.[72] The respective positions were reversed compared to the previous elections in Syria: a fact that seems to confirm that Armenian parties' support for one side or the other in the Lebanese and Syrian political scene had in that phase less to do with ideology than with political opportunity.

By 1935 a series of events in the Levant and in the wider region had given a new push to the struggle for independence against the French

Mandate. The reasons for the opening of a new phase of troubles and nationalist-Mandate confrontations are complex and fall beyond the scope of the present work. It seems, however, worth mentioning two: the Anglo-Iraqi treaty of 1930 – and the Iraqi independence that followed in 1932 – which became a powerful example for the nationalists of Lebanon and Syria; and the deep recession that followed the 1929 Wall Street crash, which had serious consequences on the economic situation of the Levant.[73]

In Syria, the relative truce that had been in place between the nationalists and French from the late 1920s started to deteriorate in 1933 and, early in 1936, a new nationalist strike paralysed the country for several weeks. The French soon realized that they had no other choice than making concessions: elections were held in November and a Franco-Syrian Treaty following the Anglo-Iraqi model was signed the following month. The events in Syria had an effect on Lebanon too: a Franco-Lebanese treaty was ratified in 1936; the Constitution of 1926 was reinstated and new elections were held in 1937. Meanwhile, the Maronite political scene saw the emergence of a split between the pro-French positions represented by the National Bloc – Emile Eddé, advocating a Maronite-dominated Lebanon closely associated with France and the Constitutional Bloc of Bishara Al-Khouri, who believed that the future of Lebanon relied on some form of collaboration with the Muslims. At the same time, part of the Sunni leadership had realized that radical anti-French positions were of no help in bringing about the end of the Mandate and saw the possibility of working in co-ordination with moderate Maronites like Bishara Al-Khouri.

The new developments had an impact on Armenian political participation in Lebanon and Syria. By and large, in the course of the second half of the 1930s the Armenian nationalist parties, while still acting cautiously in their relation with the French, accelerated their emancipation and became increasingly available to provide a contribution to Lebanese and Syrian independence movements. At the same time, developments in the Arab front opposing the French eliminated some barriers and prejudices to work with the Armenians. Armenian parties were looked at increasingly as forces that could provide electoral support. From the Arab perspective, the collaboration with Armenian parties could sometimes be justified on the basis of common ideological traits or, more pragmatically, with the fact that the Armenian parties in the 1930s and beyond appeared as comparatively efficient structures of political mobilization: once their support had been agreed, they were reliable in delivering it to the polling stations.[74]

In Syria, Armenians played their part in the landslide victory of the National Bloc in the elections of November 1936 that brought the nationalists to power. Four Armenian candidates were elected: among these was the Armenian Catholic member of the Constituent Assembly of

1928, Fathallah Asiun, a Western-educated lawyer who had in the meantime joined the 'new generation of angry young nationalists' of the uncompromising League of National Action.[75] In Lebanon, Armenian support to the nationalists took the form of an alliance between the Dashnaks and the Constitutional Bloc Party of Bishara Al-Khouri, representing the moderate wing of the Maronite community. The alliance was sanctioned in the elections of 1937, when the number of parliamentary seats reserved for the Armenian Apostolic community in the new sixty-three-member Chamber were raised to two.[76] In 1938, support for the nationalists became the official policy of the Dashnaks. The 13th World Congress of the party, held in Paris, 'called on the Armenians to support Arab movements for independence in Syria and Lebanon'.[77]

In the last years of French presence in the Levant, Armenian support for the nationalists was reinforced by the French handling of the question of the Sanjak of Alexandretta. The Sanjak, which had a sizeable Armenian population, was eventually reoccupied by Turkey in 1939, resulting in a new flow of refugees. In the Lebanese elections of 1943 a strong Armenian bloc formed by the temporarily-reconciled Dashnak and Hunchak parties supported the candidates of the list led by nationalist leaders Abdallah Yafi and Saeb Salam, in spite of attempts by the French of obtaining Armenian help for their protégé, Sami Al-Solh.[78] A similar support for the nationalists was shown by the Armenians in Syria, where the French had less supporters. The vote in the elections of 1943 confirmed the success of the National Bloc and four Armenian candidates were elected in Aleppo and Damascus.

**Table 2.1. Armenian MPs in Lebanon under the Mandate[79]**

| Election year | Name of MPs | Place of election |
|---|---|---|
| 1929 | Abdallah Ishaq | Beirut |
| 1934 | Vahram Leilekian | Beirut |
| 1937 | Vahram Leilekian | Beirut |
| 1943 | Movses Der Kaloustian | Beirut |
| 1943 | Hratchia Chamlian | Beirut |

**Table 2.2. Armenian MPs in Syria under the Mandate[80]**

| Election year | Name of MPs | Place of election |
|---|---|---|
| 1928 | Fathallah Asiun | Aleppo |
| 1932 | Hratch Papazian | Aleppo |
| 1932 | Movses Der Kaloustian | Antakia |
| 1936 | Bedros Milletbashian | Aleppo |
| 1936 | Hrant Sulahian | Aleppo |

| 1936 | Fathallah Asiun | Aleppo |
| 1936 | Movses Der Kaloustian | Antakia |
| 1943 | Nazareth Yacoubian | Damascus |
| 1943 | Movses Salatian | Aleppo |
| 1943 | Hratch Papazian | Aleppo |
| 1943 | Fathallah Asiun | Aleppo |

## Armenian Associations during the Mandate

The appearance, besides Churches, political parties, and regional patriotic unions, of a number of Armenian associations, was an important component of the process of re-construction of the Armenian world in Lebanon and Syria. First of all, Armenian associations contributed remarkably to the material support of the refugees, providing food, clothing, medical care and other forms of relief in the camps.[81] But the associations also became new reference points for Armenian socialization, contributing to the preservation of cultural traditions and to the perception of the community as a self-contained group which could provide for its own needs.

Many of the early Armenian associations in Lebanon and Syria were charities created in response to the demands of the refugees. A crucial role in establishing and running these charities was played by the Armenian Churches, renewing a tradition of self-aid structures usually co-ordinated at the level of individual congregations. In the case of the Apostolic Church this had become institutionalised in the form of *Aghkadakhnam* (care for the poor) associations: one of these had been operating at the church of Saint Nishan in Beirut since the end of the nineteenth century.[82] Charities were also the expression of the Armenian lay elites, both at the local and at the international, diaspora level.[83] A prominent example of these was the Armenian General Benevolent Union (AGBU). Founded in Cairo in 1906 by a number of Armenian notables, the Union had already established a chapter in Beirut in 1910. Following the arrival of the refugees the organisation participated in the relief efforts and rapidly expanded its activities, opening several other chapters in the main cities of Lebanon and Syria.[84] The Armenian political parties also played a role in the establishment of associations providing relief and social services. In particular, the Armenian Relief Cross, an association founded in Boston in 1910 and dedicated to social welfare, health and education, became – albeit informally – the 'social arm' of the Dashnak party and opened a branch in Lebanon in 1929.[85]

Although limited to Lebanon and not exhaustive, the synopsis that follows should provide a useful insight of the variety of Armenian charities that were operating during the Mandate, showing in particular the coexistence of religious and lay institutions, of local and transnational, diaspora organisations.

**Table 2.3. Synopsis of some Armenian Charities operating in Lebanon during the Mandate[86]**

| Association | Start of activities | Notes |
|---|---|---|
| *Aghkadakhnam* [care for the poor] | end of nineteenth century | Apostolic Church charities based on individual congregations but depending on the Church's authorities. |
| **Armenian General Benevolent Union** | 1906 | Lay institution founded in by Boghos Noubar Pasha and a number of Cairo Armenian notables. Developed as transnational organization, operating in most countries where an Armenian diaspora is found. Opened an orphanage, provided support to Armenian culture and education, sports etc. |
| **Armenian Missionary Association of America** | 1918 | Armenian Evangelical institution. Worked with refugees in camps, provided support for schooling. |
| **Regional patriotic unions** | 1920s | Private benevolent and cultural associations (Konya, Aintab, Zeitoun, Adana, Bitlis, Malatia, Hadjin, Garin, Cesarea etc.) |
| **Old people's home** | early 1920s? | Initiated activities as orphanage in Turkey, funded by Swiss Friends of Armenians (SFA); moved to Ghazir, where it became shelter for widowers and their children; then gradually shifted to care for elderly. Since 1932 in Bourj Hammoud. |
| **Armenian National Sanatorium** | 1923 | Initially specializing in the treatment of TB. Established through the co-operation of the three Armenian Churches in |

| | | |
|---|---|---|
| | | M'aameltein with funding received from Near East Relief. Moved to current location in Azounieh in 1938. Joint Orthodox-Evangelical enterprise. |
| **Saint Ely Beneficent Society** | 1929 | Catholic organization founded by Archbishop Nazlian and leading Catholics. Provided support to Armenian Catholic families with financial problems. |
| **Armenian Relief Cross** | 1929 | Private, voluntary, non-profit women's organization providing social and medical services; unofficially linked to the Dashnak party. |
| **Association of the Holy Saviour** | 1931 | Catholic organization (initially named 'Brotherhood of the Holy Saviour'). Founded by the Catholic Archbishop Nazlian in Bourj Hammoud. |
| **Society of Annunciation** | 1931 | Catholic charity. Also founded by Archbishop Nazlian and operating in Ashrafieh. |
| *Aghkadasiratz* | 1937 | Founded by Armenian ladies to provide support for refugees (clothing, housing, food, education etc.). |
| **Howard Karagheuzian Commemorative Corporation** | 1941 | Private charity founded in New York in 1921 by Armenian-American benefactors; transnational diaspora organization; started operations in 'Anjar and Beirut following the crisis of the Sanjak of Alexandretta. |

Besides the material assistance to the population, Armenian associations were established to cater for the cultural and recreational needs of the community. Churches, political parties, regional patriotic unions, transnational organizations, all engaged in covering these areas of social activity. Armenian youth and sports associations were particularly numerous and successful. Among these were the Homenetmen, the sporting club of the Dashnak party, founded in 1918 in Istanbul; the Homenmen, the Hunchak equivalent, founded in 1921 in Damascus;[87] and the youth group of the AGBU, the Antranik Youth Association, established in 1931. Armenian sports clubs rapidly became prominent on the local scene and by the 1940s they were dominating Lebanese and Syrian football, cycling and athletics.[88]

From the point of view of official relations with the state, Armenian associations were legally subject to the same set of regulations as any other association in Lebanon and Syria. On the issue, the text of the Lebanese Constitution of 1926 simply recognised the right to form associations and referred to ordinary legislation: '*La liberté d'exprimer sa pensée par la parole ou par la plume, la liberté de la presse, la liberté de réunion et la liberté d'association sont également garanties dans les limites fixées par la loi*'.[89]

The Mandatory never developed a specific legislation regarding associations. In its absence, associations in Lebanon and Syria continued to be ruled by the Ottoman law on associations of 3 August 1909. The law defined associations as:

> *Un groupe formé de plusieurs personnes en vue d'unir leur savoir et leurs efforts de façon permanente et dans un but non lucratif. L'association se constitue par la volonté de ses fondateurs: lorsque deux ou plusieurs personnes se réunissent, forment un groupe et informent l'autorité publique, par un récépissé, de l'adresse du groupe ainsi formé, son but, son siège central, les noms des membres qui l'administrent ou qui en ont la gestion. L'autorité doit être saisie aussi des statuts de ces membres, de leur résidence et de deux exemplaires des règlements du groupe formé. Un des membres dirigeants doit être responsable auprès de l'autorité publique (le ministère de l'Intérieur ou ses représentants dans les régions).*[90]

The law, in fact, gave scope to various – liberal or restrictive – interpretations, giving the government the freedom to intervene and effectively control the life of the associations whenever it was considered necessary.

## Armenian Culture and Media during the Mandate

### Literature, Theatre and Cultural Associations

The rebirth of an Armenian cultural world among the refugee communities came up against enormous difficulties. The foremost was, of course, the tragic disappearance of a generation of intellectuals and artists: the Genocide had killed many of the most prominent figures of the

Armenian literary and artistic scene of the time.[91] Together with the intellectuals, a whole system of Armenian cultural institutions (literary circles, publishing houses, theatrical groups, etc.) had also been lost. In addition to that, the harsh reality of the refugee camps left little resources for arts and culture.

Armenian authors who had survived the Genocide were called to the extraordinary task of rethinking their role as intellectuals of an Armenian diaspora, of rethinking the goals and the contents of Armenian cultural production, of giving a sense to it in the light of what had happened. Together with the United States, France and Egypt, Lebanon and Syria soon emerged as two of the centres of rebirth of Armenian literary production. In Aleppo, in particular, Armenian literary life was reactivated by a promising generation of young survivors of the Genocide, including Vahe Vahian, Antranik Zaroukian, and Simon Simonian. Born in the homeland between 1908 and 1914, these authors drew from their experiences as young refugees to reflect upon the tragedy of the Armenian people and on the relation between the refugees and their homeland and cultural heritage.[92] The Lebanese and Syrian literary scene was also influenced by the poet Moushegh Ishkhan, and by an older-generation survivor, the novelist Hagop Oshagan.[93]

In spite of the presence within the Armenian diaspora of an important author like the playwright, poet and novelist Levon Shant, theatre continued to be the poor cousin of the Armenian literary scene.[94] Nevertheless, drama was an important space for expression of the Armenian cultural world among the refugees and one of the few forms of entertainment available in the camps. Stages would often be available within school premises or next to Armenian churches. Information on these early shows is, unfortunately, rather fragmentary. The memories of those who assisted in plays and some pictures dating from the 1930s speak of amateur representations of a popular origin. These had little or nothing to do with the tradition of Armenian Western-style theatre that had been prominent in Istanbul during the late years of the Ottoman Empire. The subjects were drawn from Armenian history or mythology or from recent events, playing with a universe made of kings, princesses, refugees, Turkish officers, Arab bedouins, Armenian priests, etc. Some of the plays were recited in Turkish, the common language of many Cilician Armenians.

Besides their value *per se*, popular theatre, literature, and the arts in general, were also an important tool of Armenian education and socialization. They could play a role in connection or parallel with the churches, the schools, the media, and the charitable associations to build a sense of identity, to promote Armenian culture, language, and values. Armenian political parties quickly realised the importance of becoming players in the process of cultural production and established their own cultural associations. In 1928 a group of Dashnak intellectuals, including Levon Shant and stage director Kaspar Ipekian, founded the party's 'cultural arm', the Hamazkayin (Pan-national) Cultural Association in Cairo.[95] The Hunchak and the Ramkavar parties also established their own cultural associations: respectively the Nor Serount (New Generation) and the Tekeyan. Following the party's structure, these associations could be organised on a transnational basis, connecting the sections of all countries of the diaspora in which they were present.

The development of theatre, of other forms of entertainment in the camps, and – in general – of the Armenian cultural world, happened in quasi isolation from the non-Armenian communities and, apparently, without significant interference from the Mandate authorities. Produced by Armenians, and distributed in Armenian residential areas, the new Armenian cultural production was directed to the community alone.

## Printing Presses, Newspapers and Periodicals

The emergence of new authors was accompanied by the establishment of the first Armenian printing presses and publishing houses. Some of these were independent enterprises competing on the market and available to print anything that was in demand: newspapers, magazines, books, but also cards, stationery, publicity, calendars, etc. Others were institutionally or politically linked to Armenian institutions (churches, parties, associations) and would prevailingly work for these.

The main centre of Armenian printing was initially Aleppo. Two printing presses were established in 1918 and about a dozen others followed starting from the early 1920s throughout the period of the Mandate.

**Table 2.4. Armenian printing presses in Syria during the Mandate**[96]

| Name of printing press | City | Notes | Years of activity |
|---|---|---|---|
| **Hay Tzain** | Aleppo | Founded by Setrag Gebenlian, printed the *Hay Tzain* newspaper. | 1918–1919 |
| **Sebat** | Aleppo | Founded by Hovsep Ajamian, served as a printing press for various newspapers, including Darakir. | 1918–1965 |
| **Souriagan Mamoul** | Aleppo | Hunchak-related press, transferred to Aleppo from Adana. | 1922–1926 |

| | | | |
|---|---|---|---|
| **College** | Aleppo | American college publishing house. Transferred to Aleppo from Aintab. | 1922–1945 |
| **Maranata** | Aleppo | Religious publication of the Spiritual Brotherhood. | 1922–1963 |
| **Arax** | Aleppo | Founded by Puzant Topalian and his brother. Published prayer books, history books, an English grammar. | 1924–1930 |
| **Ararat** | Aleppo | Printed the *Yeprad* newspaper, novels, songbooks. | 1924–1942 |
| **Ani** | Aleppo | Founded by Avedis Ekmekdjian; printed books, newspapers, calendars, personal cards, etc. | 1929– |
| **Der Sahaghian** | Aleppo | Continued the activities of the Arax press. Published 'The Survival of Aintab' (1931); novels in Turkish language with Armenian fonts. | 1930–49 |
| **Rotos** | Aleppo | Founded by Toros Terjanian. | 1934 |
| **Bozoklian** | Aleppo | Founded by Minas Bozoklian; located in the new Armenian quarter of Nor Kur. | 1936–41 |
| **Dickris** | Aleppo | | 1937 |
| **Artzakank** | Aleppo | Published 'The Birth of the Armenian Nation' (1938); 'The Armenian Question' (1938); 'The Golden Age of Armenia'. | 1938–1939 |
| **Jismedjian** | Aleppo | Founded by Taniel Jismejian, who took over from Bozoklian; printed books, flyers, calendars, wedding cards, tickets for events. | 1941 |
| **Yeprad** | Aleppo | Printing press of the Ramkavar party. | 1942–49 |
| **Sevan** | Aleppo | Founded by a group of teachers with interest in literary publications, including Simon Simonian. | 1944–1946 |
| **Nairi** | Aleppo | Founded by Antranik Zaroukian. | 1945–1955 |

In Lebanon one of the first Armenian publishing houses was established in 1924 by Guiragos Doniguian, a refugee from Adana, not far from the main Armenian camp in Medawar.[97] The Catholicosate of Cilicia also started a printing press in 1932, in the premises of the re-established See in Antelias.[98]

Armenian newspapers and periodicals[99] started to appear immediately after the end of the First World War and, with a stronger impetus, after the inflow of refugees in the early 1920s. In Lebanon the first periodical in Armenian appeared in 1918 and the first daily papers, *Pyunig* and *Lipanan*, in 1924. Political parties soon started their dailies and periodicals: the Dashnaks founded *Aztag* in 1927; the Hunchaks and the Ramkavars founded respectively *Ararat* and *Zartonk* in 1937. The Armenian Churches also started their own publications: in 1932, the Catholicosate of Cilicia published the first issue of its monthly, *Hask*, using an old pedal press.[100] By 1944 as many as fifty-seven different Armenian publications had appeared in Lebanon.[101] In Aleppo the first Armenian dailies, *Hay Tzain* (The Armenian Voice) and *Darakir* (The Exiled) appeared in 1918. In 1922 the Hunchak party founded its own newspaper: *Suriagan Surhantag* (The Syrian Messenger), then re-named *Suriagan Mamoul* (The Syrian Press). The Ramkavar followed in 1931 when it took over *Yeprad* (The Euphrates), a journal which had been founded by a number of liberal, upper-class, Aleppine Armenians.[102] By the end of the Mandate about thirty Armenian publications had appeared in Syria, including political newspapers, literary, religious, sports and satirical magazines, and student newsletters.[103]

The attitude of the French authorities towards the Armenian press reflected the more general, uneasy relation of the Mandatory with the Arab Lebanese and Syrian press. Arab newspapers, often mouthpieces of competing local elites, were throughout the Mandate a political space where negotiations – or confrontations – between the French and the nationalists would take place. Beyond formal affirmations of the freedom of the press, as in the Lebanese Constitution of 1926,[104] the French did not hesitate to subsidize newspapers that were promoting their rule and censuring those which were undermining it. The Armenian press was no exception, and it suffered whenever it was perceived as a supporter of the anti-French cause. At times this was the case with the Hunchak Aleppine press, but – most importantly – it was the norm with the Armenian communist press. The communists of the Spartak group had to work clandestinely to publish their journals. After a first attempt in Beirut in 1925, when they printed two issues of *Nor Paros* (The New Lighthouse), they worked between Raqqa and Deir Ez-Zor to produce – in 1927 – a few issues of *Spartak* and *Nor Basdil* (The New Bastille).[105]

## Armenian Education during the Mandate

The opening of Armenian schools in the Levant originated almost entirely as a response to the inflow of refugees after 1915. Not that schools were completely absent before: the Churches, including the Evangelical congregations and the Catholic monastery in Bzoummar, had been running schools for the lay communities since the mid-nineteenth century. In Aleppo the presence of an Armenian school is continuously recorded from 1841; the Armenian Apostolic Patriarchate of Jerusalem opened an elementary school in Damascus in 1849 and another in Beirut in 1859, in the premises of the Armenian Apostolic monastery of Saint Nishan.[106] However, until the Genocide, Armenian educational institutions in Beirut, in Damascus, and even in Aleppo, could be counted of the fingers of one hand.

In the case of Lebanon and Damascus this could be largely explained by the small size of the resident Armenian communities. Further explanations could be possibly found in the fact that the Armenian Catholic community did not feel a strong need for culture-specific education. Many Armenian Catholic families had been settled in Lebanon for generations and had developed some form of cultural integration with local populations and particularly with the Maronites. When it came to education, the Armenian Catholic community of Beirut would send children 'either to French or Maronite schools'.[107] In the case of Aleppo, where the Armenian population was more dense and the economic conditions of the Armenians fairly prosperous, explanations are more complex. Sanjian has observed that, in spite of an increasing inadequacy of the existing Armenian institutions and the availability of resources, the Aleppine community of the nineteenth century rarely invested in education.[108]

The demand for Armenian education in Lebanon and Syria changed dramatically as a consequence of the population displacements which started in 1915. As refugee camps were established in and around the cities of Syria and Lebanon – particularly after 1921 – a major, urgent need of schools emerged. In the numerous orphanages that were set up schooling was, at least in part, provided by international relief agencies like Near East Relief.[109] Most important, however, new Armenian schools were opened in the cities and in the refugee camps. It is fairly difficult to reconstruct a full picture of the number and location of the schools that were opened. Information is often fragmentary, as schools originally established in the camps were later relocated; over the years they sometimes merged with other institutions, or were renamed, or simply discontinued activity. There is no doubt, however, that the inflow of refugees resulted in the rapid, dramatic growth of Armenian education in the main cities of the Levant. A study of Armenian elementary schools in

Syria prepared by Bedian in September 1961 may be a useful means in order to understand the extent of the phenomenon. Out of the fifty-three Armenian schools considered in the study, forty-six were founded after 1919 and thirty-eight in the two decades between 1920 and 1939.[110]

**Table 2.5. Year of foundation of 53 Armenian schools in Syria (after Bedian)**

| Period | Urban schools | Rural schools | Total |
|---|---|---|---|
| Before 1920 | 3 | 4 | 7 |
| 1920–1929 | 14 | 6 | 20 |
| 1930–1939 | 10 | 8 | 18 |
| 1940–1949 | 3 | – | 3 |
| 1950–1960 | 1 | 4 | 5 |

After the first decade of the settlement of the refugees, Armenian schools were present in virtually all cities and villages that had a sizeable Armenian presence. The opening of new schools was often the result of the joint efforts of the refugee population with all those subjects which held some form of authority, or organisation within the community: these, of course, included the Churches, which played the main, pivotal role, but also Armenian political parties (often through their proxy organizations), regional patriotic unions, Armenian welfare organizations, benefactors, and international aid organizations. The following table, drawn from an occasional Armenian Apostolic publication dating circa 1929, provides an interesting snapshot of the newly established system of Armenian schools in Syria.[111]

**Table 2.6. Armenian schools and students in Armenian schools in Syria, ca. 1929**

| N. | Name of the school | Location | Male students | Female students | Total |
|---|---|---|---|---|---|
| 1 | National Haigazian school for boys and girls | Aleppo | 390 | 350 | 740 |
| 2 | Saint Mesrop school for boys and girls (refugee camp) | Aleppo | 247 | 190 | 437 |
| 3 | Sahagian National school (Midan) | Aleppo | 60 | 50 | 110 |
| 4 | Grtasirats school | Aleppo | 329 | 221 | 550 |
| 5 | Guiligian refugee school | Aleppo | 328 | 224 | 552 |
| 6 | Tchersanjak | Aleppo | 100 | 90 | 190 |

| | | | | | |
|---|---|---|---|---|---|
| 7 | Armenyan [sic] school for boys and girls | Aleppo | 60 | 40 | 100 |
| 8 | National school for boys and girls | Alexandretta | 85 | 95 | 180 |
| 9 | Noubarian | Alexandretta | 156 | 159 | 315 |
| 10 | State Armenian school | Soghuk Olouk | 33 | 22 | 55 |
| 11 | National school | Beylan | 35 | 28 | 63 |
| 12 | National school | Kerek khan | 110 | 90 | 200 |
| 13 | National school | Jarablus | 120 | 30 | 150 |
| 14 | National school | Homs | 55 | 40 | 95 |
| 15 | National school | Antakia | 23 | 22 | 45 |
| 16 | National school | Azaz | 65 | 95 | 160 |
| 17 | Sahagian national | Kessab | 70 | 42 | 112* |
| 18 | Ousoumnasirats | Kessab | 40 | – | 40 |
| 19 | Karaderni national Mesrop | Kessab | 60 | 28 | 88 |
| 20 | Karaderni sea shore | Kessab | 18 | 10 | 28 |
| 21 | Kerken United | Kessab | 28 | 24 | 52 |
| 22 | United school of Baljghal | Kessab | 10 | 8 | 18 |
| 23 | Duk Aghatch National school | Kessab | 12 | 12 | 24* |
| 24 | Bitias Armenian national school | Sweidieh | 39 | 26 | 65 |
| 25 | Haji Habibli national kindergarten | Sweidieh | 45 | 20 | 65 |
| 26 | Youghun Olouk national school | Sweidieh | 59 | 36 | 95 |
| 27 | Khedr Beck national school | Sweidieh | 15 | 10 | 25 |
| 28 | Waqf national school | Sweidieh | 24 | 12 | 36* |
| 29 | Qabousieh | Sweidieh | 20 | – | 20 |
| 30 | National school | Bab | 25 | 20 | 45 |
| 31 | National school | Menbidj | 35 | 30 | 65 |
| 32 | National school | Ras el-'Ayn | 27 | 24 | 51 |
| 33 | National school | Raqqa | 38 | 32 | 70 |
| 34 | Hama national school | Hama | | | 40 |
| 35 | Nercessian Varjaran camp school | Aleppo | | | 230 |
| 36 | National school | Arab Pounar | | | 78 |
| 37 | National school | Damascus | | | 375 |
| 38 | Quarter kindergarten | Damascus | | | 70 |
| 39 | Quarter kindergarten | Damascus | | | 60 |
| 40 | Armenian Evangelical school | Damascus | | | 150 |
| 41 | Armenian Catholic school | Damascus | | | 80 |
| 42 | Franco-Armenian school | Damascus | | | 60 |

* = total corrected compared to the original document

The opening of Armenian schools took place amongst the hardest material conditions. Schools in the camps were usually housed in poor, tin roofed, wooden barracks; qualified teachers, teaching materials and – in general – funding were lacking. On the other hand the normative framework regulating education under the French Mandate provided the community with good opportunities. The text of the Mandate called on the authorities to encourage public instruction but it also carefully protected the traditional autonomy of the communities in maintaining their specific educational system. 'The right of each community to maintain its own schools for the instruction and education of its own members in its own language, while conforming to such requirements of a general nature as the administration may impose, shall not be denied or impaired'.[112]

The principle was reflected in Article 10 of the Lebanese Constitution of 1926: '*L'enseignement est libre en tant qu'il n'est pas contraire à l'ordre public et aux bonnes mœurs et qu'il ne touche pas à la dignité des confessions. Il ne sera porté aucune atteinte au droit des communautés d'avoir leurs écoles sous réserve des prescriptions générales sur l'instruction publique édictées par l'Etat'.*[113]

The *prescriptions générales* and the practice of the Mandatory in educational affairs were in general aimed at maintaining some degree of control on schools and requiring the teaching of French. However, this did not undermine the general freedom enjoyed – as among the other communities – by the Armenians, nor to the development of Arab national sentiments.[114] The Armenian community under the Mandate was, thus, considerably free to organize the structure of its educational system and, in particular, to adopt its own school curriculum. Individual school boards or the educational bodies of the Armenian Churches coordinating their respective schools were able to prepare and adopt their own programs.

The definition of the curricula of the Armenian schools was a difficult process and reflected the uncertain situation of the refugees in the first years following their settlement in Lebanon and Syria. The short passage that follows, reported in the book of memoirs of a Near East Relief volunteer, emblematically represents the dilemma that Armenian refugee education was facing, divided between the instinct to preserve Armenian culture and traditions and the pressure to accept some form of cultural integration. 'In Lebanon, some of the teachers thought that the most intelligent pupils should be trained to become literary leaders of the new Armenia. Many of their friends encouraged this idea, but with the help of the exceedingly wise Catholicos, religious leader or the Armenian community, and several of the leading businessmen, we insisted upon teaching the orphans Arabic and trades'.[115]

The dilemma of the relation between Armenian and Arab culture was particularly dramatic in the 1920s, when the Armenians felt the urgent need of providing their youth with the tools to get by in a foreign, alien environment. Besides that, the choices that Armenian educators had to make regarding curricula had to take into account important considerations that concerned the definition of Armenian culture itself. The most important of these, perhaps, was that the Armenian refugees were far from being a culturally homogeneous group. Regardless of their religious affiliations, there were at least two discrete linguistic groups among the refugees.[116] The first included those who had arrived as refugees from Cilicia or from non-traditionally Armenian *vilayets* of the Ottoman Empire: these often used Turkish as their day-to-day language and could not speak Armenian well; some, apparently, could not speak Armenian at all. The second included those refugees who had arrived from Armenian *vilayets*, who were prevailingly Armenian speaking. To these groups one should add the 'local', Levantine Armenians (who, however, were initially not going to attend Armenian refugee schools). Within each of these groups, regional dialects would complicate the picture further. Regional and linguistic groups, differences in class background and lifestyle (peasant, urban) could make one wonder *what* Armenian culture must be adopted and taught.

From the point of view of the Armenian cultural leadership the question was not new. In fact, a process of rationalization and standardization of Armenian education had been on the way since the last decades of the nineteenth century, a period of remarkable development for Armenian schools within the Ottoman Empire. Between 1853 and 1863 the Apostolic community had established and institutionalized a National Education Council (NEC) with the explicit objective of promoting Armenian education. Under the drive of the NEC, a body controlled by laymen elected by the Apostolic community and working in co-ordination with the Apostolic clergy, 'unorganized and highly informal structures consisting of separate educational establishments developed into a unified and systematized method for training the population'.[117] The NEC soon assumed a key role in the preparation of the curricula, of the textbooks and on improving the qualifications of Armenian teachers.

The process of rationalization and standardization of Armenian education initiated by the NEC was revived after the Genocide by the re-established Armenian institutions of the Armenian Apostolic Church. Also, other actors became involved in that process or started parallel processes. These actors included, most notably, the Armenian political parties. The parties had long been aware of the potential that education had in promoting their values and agendas and committed resources to schools, elaborating and adapting their educational policies to the new reality of the refugee condition.

Schahgaldian has observed in particular the role of the Dashnak party in the early development of Armenian education in Lebanon.[118] The party's emphasis on education had its ideological foundations in the view that the Armenian youth was 'wandering' and had lost 'purity' of heart;[119] according to the party it was 'necessary to prepare [the youth] spiritually and mentally, for they must symbolize that revolutionary character which is the party's heritage, for they must always be ever-ready soldiers of the ARF [Dashnak] willing to work everywhere and under all circumstances'.[120]

The party objectives in education were pursued particularly through the opening and running of schools and educational councils. In the words of Schahgaldian, 'the only mission of such schools was the creation of a new breed of Armenians in the image of what the party considered "true Armenians", conscious of their history and culture, well-versed in their mother tongue and dedicated to the ideals of Armenian nationalism'.[121]

## The Socio-Economic Position of the Armenians during the Mandate

One of the consequences of the Genocide was the dramatic social levelling of the Armenian refugee communities. In the span of a few years starting in 1915 the traditional class structure of Armenian Ottoman society was radically broken up and social differences minimized. Class identifications based on property, land and investments were undermined; status-based stratifications were deeply shaken by the rough, equalizing experience of deportation, migration and refugee settlement. The traditional distinction between town and countryside also became confused: the resettlement of the Armenians in Lebanon and Syria resulted in the rapid, abrupt urbanization of a large number of families from peasant backgrounds.

Some form of social stratification, however, persisted, and class distinctions were soon developed and diversified. By the mid-1920s at least three social strata could be roughly identified within the Armenian population of Lebanon and Syria.[122] The first, which represented the majority of the community, consisted of destitute refugees living in camps; often, their only asset – given the circumstances – was their labour. These refugees, at the very bottom of the Lebanese, Syrian and Armenian social ladder, would be available to take any income opportunity that was presented: men would work as labourers in the growing Lebanese construction industry,[123] as workers in factories, and as dockers, and porters; women would seek employment as cleaners or maids or take sewing jobs. Those who possessed craftsmanship skills and had managed to save, or to gather enough capital, would also try to establish a small productive activity of their own in the refugee camps. Pictures taken in the mid-1920s in Aleppo show family workshops arranged in the crammed refugee shacks, where domestic life is almost undistinguished from business. These early enterprises re-established craft traditions in which the Armenians had been prominent in Ottoman times, including carpet making, shoe making, metal and leather works.

A second group of refugees consisted of those who had managed to avoid the experience of life in the camps (or had managed to move away from it) and settled in the cities proper, usually by renting rooms or flats. This group included those refugees who could afford to conduct activities requiring bigger investments, like jewelry workshops, optician's shops, photography and tailor's workshops, and, in general, those who managed enterprises larger than family-size. To the same group of the comparatively well off belonged Armenians who had found employment within the French colonial administration or with foreign firms operating in the region. Finally, there was a small Armenian upper class, initially almost exclusively composed of Armenians who were natives of Lebanon and Syria.[124] This group was economically and socially integrated into the region, but could hardly be considered a local elite: the so called *Arman qadim* (old Armenians) of Aleppo and Beirut had been mostly engaged in trade and crafts and were excluded from extensive land ownership, the main basis of social and political power of the Lebanese and Syrian elites.

The economy of the Levant in the 1920s did not offer a favourable environment for the integration of the newcomer Armenian community. The region struggled to make a full economic recovery from the harsh years of the blockade and war. The difficult recovery of the economy was, in part, the consequence of ill-conceived French policies. In spite of the solemn obligations assumed in accepting the Mandate, the French administration's economic policy soon appeared to be guided by the double priority of reducing the cost of colonial control and creating opportunities for French economic interests. The decision to introduce a new local currency tied to the weak French franc, for instance, resulted in a rise in the cost of imports and contributed to a general, dramatic increase in prices.[125] The customs system, in its turn, did not provide adequate protection for the Lebanese and Syrian industries which were hit by competition from European and Japanese goods; at the same time, high spending on security and the military reduced the budget of the Mandate states for economic development.[126] The economic difficulties put a severe stress on the labour market, which was characterized by a high unemployment rate. The arrival and settlement of the destitute, job-seeking Armenians, a working force available to work for little, further reduced the level of wages, generating animosity towards the refugees.[127]

In the course of the 1930s the Lebanese and Syrian economy suffered from the repercussions of the world economic crisis ignited in 1929. However, under the protection of higher custom duties on imports introduced by the Mandatory,[128] some local industries could emerge, and Armenians were able to take their opportunities, undoubtedly taking advantage of the availability of cheap Armenian labour force and of their strong, communal-solidarity links. The leather sector, in particular, became increasingly an Armenian business, with Armenians specializing in tanning and, most important, in the production of shoes. Shoe manufactures, often employing a family and only a few waged workers, were established in the new Armenian residential quarters on the peripheries of Beirut and Aleppo.[129]

During the Mandate, and in a pattern that continues to date, the involvement of Armenians in the agricultural sector of Lebanon and Syria remained extremely limited. In the second half of the 1920s the Mandatory studied the possibility of establishing Armenian agricultural settlements as a strategy to deal with the issue of the refugee camps. Plans to resettle a sizeable number or refugees from Beirut, Aleppo and Damascus to the Sanjak of Alexandretta and to Tyre were drawn up, starting in 1926. None of these was successful however. In the case of Alexandretta, it is possible that the plans were withdrawn by France in a move accommodating Turkish demands; on the other hand, the plans were generally met with opposition by the Armenian leadership itself, as they were perceived as dangerously dispersing the community.[130] In Lebanon, the one exception to these failures was the foundation, in 1939, of a successful Armenian refugee community in 'Anjar, in the Beka'a valley, to accommodate the Armenian refugees of the Jebel Mousa, following the cession of the Sanjak of Alexandretta to Turkey.[131]

# Notes

1.  Among those many children who had lost their parents was Haroutioun Khoshmatlian, a 9 year-old boy in the spring of 1915. Luckily escaping deportation from his hometown of Palu (in the province of Harpout), he grew up in various orphanages until he was finally found by his mother in 1922. Interview with Mr. Haroutioun Khoshmatlian, Damascus, 4 November 2003.

2.  See T.H. Greenshields. 1981. 'The Settlement of Armenian Refugees in Syria and Lebanon 1915–39', in J.I. Clarke and H. Bowen-Jones (eds.), *Change and Development in the Middle East: Essays in Honour of W.B. Fisher*, London and New York: Methuen, 233–241.

3.  What J. Weulersse in 1940 defined as '*une solidarité ethnique sans rivale au monde*', quoted in Greenshields, 'The Settlement of Armenian Refugees', 235.

4.  See P.S. Khoury. 1987. *Syria and the French Mandate: the Politics of Arab Nationalism 1920–1945*, London: I.B.Tauris, 55–57.

5.  Ottoman Constitution of 1876, Article 4. See E. Rabbath. 1986. *La Formation Historique du Liban Politique et Constitutionnel*, Beirut: Université Libanaise, 97.

6. Lebanese Constitution of 1926, French text in B. Ménassa. 1995. *Constitution Libanaise: Textes et Commentaires et Accord de Taëf,* Beirut: Edition L'Orient, 30.

7. Ottoman Constitution of 1876, Article 11: *'L'Etat protège le libre exercice de tous les cultes reconnus dans l'Empire'*; see Rabbath, *La Formation Historique,* 97.

8. It could be noted, however, that Article 9 of the Lebanese Constitution of 1926 indicates that the state accepts the existence of a single God (*'En rendant homage à l'Etre Suprême'*), which raises questions on the status of non-believers (or non-monotheists). For a theoretical introduction on state-religion relations see C. Cardia. 1988. *Stato e Confessioni Religiose,* Bologna: Il Mulino, 15–109; E. Tortarolo. 1998. *Il Laicismo,* Roma and Bari: Laterza.

9. Lebanese Constitution of 1926, French text in Ménassa, *Constitution Libanaise,* 133.

10. See A. Nasri Messarra. 1994. *Théorie Générale du Systeme Politique Libanais,* Paris: Cariscript, 210–219. Nasri Messarra is correct in pointing out that the meaning of 'religious affiliation' in this context should be limited to the simple 'belonging to a cultural community' and not to the actual participation in the religious life of a community or the sincerity of religious belief. But it can be hardly denied that, in practice, belonging to a cultural community included, at least, the respect of formalities defined and controlled by a specific religious authority; hence the continuing relevance of religion, and of religious leadership in public life. An example of all is that of the registers of civil status, which remained under the exclusive authority of the religious groups.

11. See P. Gannagé. 2001. *Le Pluralisme des Statuts Personnels dans les Etats Multicommunautaires,* Beirut: Université Saint-Joseph, 29. Gannagé quotes High Commissioner Weygand saying: *'On ne touche à ces choses qu'avec beaucoup de doigté et de prudence'*, in reaction to a project of reform of the personal status laws.

12. The expression is used in E. Thompson. 2000. *Colonial Citizens: Republican Rights, Paternal Privilege and Gender in French Syria and Lebanon,* New York: Columbia University Press, 54.

13. Text reported in Rabbath, *La Formation Historique,* 99.

14. Ibid. These obligations, which the international community required of the Mandate, were nothing less than a reiteration of the long tradition of similar guarantees that had been granted by the Ottoman Empire, and under which the recognized non-Muslim communities had enjoyed autonomous administration in a variety of areas. In the nineteenth century, most notably, the *Hatt-i Sherif of Gülhane* of 1839 and the *Hatt-i Hümayun* of 1856 contained similar guarantees, while the Ottoman constitution of 1876, Article 11, stated that *'L'Etat [...] maintient les privilèges religieux accordes aux diverses Communautés, a condition qu'il ne soit pas porté atteinte a l'ordre public ou aux bonnes moeurs'*, ibid., p. 97.

15. Lebanese Constitution of 1926, Article 9, para 2. French text in Ménassa, *Constitution Libanaise,* 30.

16. E. Rabbath, *La Formation Historique*, 102–106. The *Arrêté*, the French word for decree, was the main legal instrument of the Mandate administration; the High Commissioner would issue them without having to consult the elected Lebanese or Syrian representatives and 'rarely depended on directives from Paris'. See Khoury, *Syria and the French Mandate*, 77.
17. Ibid., 103.
18. See Gannagé, *Le Pluralisme des Statuts*, 53–54, referring to the *Arrêté* n. 146 L.R. of 18 November 1938, Article 25.
19. Rabbath, *La Formation Historique*, 102–106. Other reasons contributed to the lack of success of the provision, including a perceived sense of state interference and the objective difficulty of preparing 'statutes' out of laws and practices whose origin was rooted in a corpus of old and non organised traditions.
20. The Armenian Evangelical community was not included in the original list. The *Arrêté* n. 146 L.R. of 18 November 1938 added the Protestant community (including its numerous Armenian components) to the list.
21. An important role in the development of Armenian architecture in Lebanon was played by architect Mardiros Altounian (1889–1958). Born in Boursa but educated in Bulgaria and Paris, Altounian moved to Beirut in 1920. Appointed Architect of the Ministry of Public Works within the French administration, he soon became one of the most prominent and successful architects on the Lebanese scene of the Mandate. In Beirut he designed two symbolic landmarks of the *centre ville*: the Lebanese Parliament and the clock tower in Parliament square. His work for the Armenian community included the construction of the Cathedral of St. Gregory the Illuminator in Antelias (1939–40), and the sanatorium of Azounieh (1937). See A.M. Altounian. Ca. 1997. *A la Recherche du Temps Retrouvé avec mon Père – l'Architecte Mardiros Altounian*, Beirut: Sipan; A. Mangassarian, J. Makhlouf and S. Saade. 1991. 'Eglises Arméniennes du Liban: Relevé Archéologique', *Haigazian Armenological Review* (11), 85–124.
22. Interview with Father Vartan Kazanjian, Convent of Bzoummar, 11 May 2002.
23. A.J. Iskander. 1999. *La Nouvelle Cilicie: les Arméniens du Liban*, Antélias: Catholicosat Arménien de Cilicie, 76.
24. Both institutions were independent from the Armenian Catholic Church and referred to the *S. Congregationis de Propaganda Fide*.
25. Iskander, *La Nouvelle Cilicie*, 93.
26. The authority of the Catholicos of Cilicia within the territory of the Mandate was recognised by the French authorities as early as 1924. See R.P. J. Mécérian S.J. 1961. *Un Tableau de la Diaspora Arménienne*, Beirut: Imprimerie Catholique, 161.
27. In the Will (*gdag*) of February 29, 1928 a disenheartened Catholicos Sahak came to 'pose the question to the nation, about the necessity to continue the Catholicosate', see S. Dadoyan. 2003. *The Armenian Caholicosate from Cilicia to Antelias*, Antelias: Armenian Catholicosate of Cilicia, 88–89.

28. Ibid., 89–90; Iskander, *La Nouvelle Cilicie*, 98.
29. Interview with Rev. Paul Haidostian, Chair of the Central Committee of the Union of the Armenian Evangelical Churches in the Near East, Beirut, 8 November 2002: 'the Armenian Evangelical model was [the Church's] capital. [...] It's congregational, and it's not dependent on tradition nor anything else, it's dependent on the body of believers. [...] Wherever you find believers, that's where the Church is'.
30. Ibid.
31. The concept of participation in political science is not fully straightforward. For the present research, 'participation' is used in a broad sense, meaning taking part in the 'conduct of public affairs', what the UN Committee on Human Rights has recently defined as 'a broad concept which relates to the exercise of political power, in particular the exercise of legislative, executive and administrative powers. It covers all aspects of public administration, and the formulation and implementation of policy at international, national, regional and local levels'. See UN Human Rights Committee. 1996. General Comment 25 (57), *General Comments under Article 40, Paragraph 4, of the International Covenant on Civil and Political Rights, Adopted by the Committee at its 1510$^{th}$ Meeting*, U.N. Doc. CCPR/C/21/Rev.1/Add.7.
32. Initially in the form of the separate states of Damascus and Aleppo in 1920. See Khouri, *Syria and the French Mandate*, 57–60.
33. A. Sanjian. 2001. 'The Armenian Minority Experience in the Modern Arab World', *Bulletin of the Royal Institute for Inter-Faith Studies*, 3 (1), 152.
34. Ibid.
35. In contemporary Armenian collective memory in Lebanon and Syria the original approach of the Arabs towards the Armenian survivors of the Genocide and refugees is often described as 'saving' or 'brotherly' and tends to deny that tensions had ever existed. It is hard to tell how much of this wide perception is traced back to individual family histories rather than being based on a commonly accepted official version of facts.
36. L. Schatkowski Schilcher. 1992. 'The Famine of 1915–1918 in Greater Syria', in J.P. Spagnolo (ed.), *Problems of the Modern Middle East in Historical Perspective: Essays in Honour of Albert Hourani*, Reading: Ithaca Press, 229–258, supports the higher figure. Also see, among others, J.L. Gelvin. 1998. *Divided Loyalties: Nationalism and Mass Politics in Syria at the Close of the Empire*, Berkeley, Los Angeles and London: University of California Press, 22–24; J.G. Chami. 2002. *Le Mémorial du Liban*, Tome 1, '1861–1943 / du Mont Liban a l'Indépendance', Beirut: Joseph G. Chami, 44–45. The famine was caused by a combination of factors, including drought, locust plague and the Entente's naval blockade of the Lebanese coast.
37. E.M. Lust-Okar. 1996. 'Failure of Collaboration: Armenian Refugees in Syria', *Middle Eastern Studies*, 32 (1), 57.
38. Ibid., 57–58. Lust-Okar reports that 'Freya Stark, a British diplomat, noted that for most crimes – the theft of turkeys, a tailor's belongings or goods in a factory – Armenians were suspected "at a venture"'.

39. Ibid., 60. Also see A.A. Keuroghlian. 1970. *Les Arméniens de l'Agglomération de Beyrouth, Etude Humaine et Economique*, unpublished BA thesis, Beirut: Université Saint-Joseph.
40. See Khouri, *Syria and the French Mandate*, 81.
41. Ibid., 71.
42. S.H. Longrigg. 1958. *Syria and Lebanon under French Mandate*, London, New York and Toronto: Oxford University Press, 78. The brutality of Armenian soldiers was apparently at the origin of an early episode of anti-Armenian insurgence in Aleppo in 1919: Armenians had allegedly ill-treated Arab Ottoman soldiers fighting in Cilicia. See Lust-Okar, 'Failure of Collaboration', 62.
43. Until the signing of the Treaty of Lausanne, the peoples residing in the territories controlled by the French, including the Armenians, had maintained the legal status of Ottoman citizens. See Rabbath, *La Formation Historique*, 377.
44. Treaty of peace signed at Lausanne, July 24, 1923, Part I, Section II, Article 30, as published in Carnegie Endowment for International Peace. 1924. *The Treaties of Peace 1919–1923*, Vol. II, New York: Carnegie Endowment for International Peace.
45. Ibid., Article 32.
46. A technical commission nominated by the League of Nations to study the resettlement was dispatched to Soviet Armenia but its efforts ultimately failed due to the lack of financial and political support from the international community. See F. Nansen. 1928. *Armenia and the Near East*, London: Allen and Unwin.
47. M.W. Suleiman. 1967. *Political Parties in Lebanon: The Challenge of a Fragmented Political Culture*, New York: Cornell University Press, 185. The decree in question was the *Arrêté* No. 1805 (19 September 1924), *Journal Officiel du Grand Liban* (Beirut: 3 October 1924), 2.
48. The *Arrêté* No. 15/S of 19 January 1925. See Rabbath, *La Formation Historique*, 377.
49. See Suleiman, *Political Parties in Lebanon*, 185. Also see P. Rondot. 1947. *Les Institutions Politiques du Liban*, Paris: Institut d'Etudes de l'Orient Contemporain, 55.
50. Armenian Revolutionary Federation Central Archives, Central Committee of Syria and Lebanon, file 1548/29, Report of Activities, 1920–1924, 12–13, as reported in N.B. Schahgaldian. 1979. 'The Political Integration of an Immigrant Community into a Composite Society: the Armenians in Lebanon, 1920–1974', Ph.D. thesis, New York: Columbia University, 155.
51. Ibid., 14–16.
52. See H. Bedoyan. 1973. 'Armenian Political Parties in Lebanon', MA dissertation, (Beirut: American University of Beirut, 74–75; also see Schahgaldian, 'The Political Integration', 54.
53. Schahgaldian, 'The Political Integration', 162.
54. Walker, *Armenia*, 354.

55. T. Ter Minassian. 1997. *Colporteurs du Komintern: l'Union Soviétique et les Minorités au Moyen-Orient,* (Paris : Presses de Sciences Po, 154–162; Suleiman, *Political Parties in Lebanon,* 62–63.

56. Ter Minassian, *Colporteurs du Komintern,* 158–159.

57. For an insight into the formation and activity of the patriotic unions see Social Action Committee of the Armenian Evangelical Union. 1970. *A Survey of Social Problems and Needs within the Armenian Community in Lebanon,* Beirut: Armenian Evangelical Union, 91–92. Also see Sanjian, 'The Armenian Minority Experience', 156–160; Greenshields, 'The Settlement of Armenian Refugees', 233–241. At some stage, a federation of patriotic unions was established in Aleppo, see interview with Mr. Sarkis Najarian, Beirut, 15 December 2003.

58. Z.M. Messerlian. 1963. 'Armenian Representation in the Lebanese Parliament', MA thesis, Beirut: American University of Beirut, 61.

59. Ishaq belonged to the pre-1915 Armenian diaspora of Lebanon and was 'linguistically arabized'; see Schahgaldian, 'The Political Integration', 60.

60. Elections did not take place in those areas where martial law was applied – that is Damascus, the Hawran and the Jebel Druze; see Longrigg, *Syria and Lebanon under French Mandate,* 171–172.

61. Khoury, *Syria and the French Mandate,* 186.

62. Ibid., 191–192.

63. Longrigg, *Syria and Lebanon under French Mandate,* 159.

64. Khoury, *Syria and the French Mandate,* 179, referring to the French withdrawal from Bab Touma on October 19, 1925.

65. Greenshields, 'The Settlement', 236. Greenshields mentions an attack to the Kadem refugee camp, located south of Damascus.

66. M.S. As'eed. 2002. *Al-Barlaman al-Suri fi Tatawouru al-Tarikhi 1919–2001,* Damascus: Al Mada, 237. Fathallah Asiun was an Armenian Catholic lawyer whose origins were in the upper-middle merchant class of Aleppo. See Khouri, *Syria and the French Mandate,* Table 15–3, 421. Also see Maktab Al-Dirasat Al-Suriya wa al-'Arabiya. 1951. *Min Houwe,* Damascus: Matba' Al-'Awlum wa al Adab Hashemi Ikhwan, 42–43.

67. Syrian constitution of 1930, Article 37. Quoted in G.H. Torrey. 1964. *Syrian Politics and the Military, 1945–1958,* Columbus: Ohio State University Press, 89.

68. Sanjian, 'The Armenian Minority Experience', 156.

69. Khoury, *Syria and the French Mandate,* 364.

70. Ibid. The French authorities 'even arrested a number of 20 influential Hunchak partisans before the elections, a crude but successful means of intimidation'. In the Armenian camp, the vote resulted in the election of the pro-Dashnak candidates Hratch Papazian (Aleppo; Papazian was an Istanbul-educated journalist, future editor-in-chief of the Dashnak daily *Arevelk*) and Movses Der Kaloustian (Antakia).

71. 'Who must be the Armenian candidate', editorial in *Aztag* (Dashnak-controlled Armenian newspaper published in Beirut), Vol. 7, January 10, 1934, No. 185 (2124), as reported by Messerlian, *Armenian Representation,* 66.

72. See Messerlian, *Armenian Representation*, 64–79.
73. On the issue of the economic crisis in the Levant see Khoury, *Syria and the French Mandate*, 397–399.
74. An example of this seems to be the widely documented, extensive use of party-hired cars on election days to 'pick up' voters from their residences and take them to the polling stations. See, for instance, Messerlian, 'Armenian Representation', 76.
75. Khoury, *Syria and the French Mandate*, 401.
76. In the Armenian sector the elections were marked by the position of declared neutrality of the Apostolic Church and by a bitter confrontation between the Dashnaks and the Hunchaks, in large part reflecting their hostility regarding relations with Soviet Armenia. Voting operations in the Armenian quarters were marked by episodes of violence: Lebanese police forces had to intervene to prevent street battles from taking place. Intra-Armenian clashes were reported by the Lebanese press of the time; see, for instance *La Syrie*, Vol. 19, No. 227 of 26 October 1937, quoted in Messerlian, 'Armenian Representation', 95.
77. Schahgaldian, 'The Political Integration', 183.
78. A number of rumours spread concerning attempts made, between the first and second round of the elections to attract the Dashnak and Hunchak candidates to the list of Sami Al-Solh. See on this, Messerlian, 'Armenian Representation', 109, referring to an interview with Armenian candidate Chamlian.
79. Sources: As'eed, *Al-Barlaman al-Suri*; Messerlian, 'Armenian Representation'; *Tidag* (Beirut), April-May 2003, 12 and 49.
80. Ibid.
81. The relief effort, however, was crucially sustained by non-Armenian institutions. These included the French Mandatory and a number of foreign Christian-inspired charitable institutions, some deliberately created to support the Armenians. Among these, particularly prominent were the the French *Mission d'Arménie*, Near East Relief, the American Red Cross, the Danish Birds' Nest, the Swiss Friends of the Armenians.
82. Social Action Committee of the Armenian Evangelical Union, *A Survey of Social Problems*, 42.
83. On the origins and early tradition of Armenian upper-class charities in the Ottoman empire (particularly in the area of education), see Artinian, *The Armenian Constitutional System*.
84. In Lebanon, AGBU branches were established in Zahleh (1927), Tripoli, Jounieh, Saida, Tyre, Sinn El-Fil (1928), Rmeil (1929), Ghazir (1930), Bourj Hammoud, Nor Hajn, Ashrafieh (1938), Aley, Jbeil, Bikfaya, Merjayoun and Rayak (1939); see AGBU, *A Brief Overview of AGBU in Lebanon*, pamphlet published in 2001, pp. 3–7.
85. Interview with Mr. Hagop Pakradouni, Dashnak party official, Bourj Hammoud, 26 November 2002; interview with Ms. Seta Khadeshian, Bourj

Hammoud, 15 May 2002; Armenian Relief Cross in Lebanon. Ca. 1998. *Together for a Healthier Future*, pamphlet.

86. Compiled with information contained in Social Action Committee of the Armenian Evangelical Union, *A Survey of Social Problems*; various pamphlets; interview with Rev. Robert Sarkissian, Director HKCC, Beirut, 7 June 2002.

87. Homenmen was established in Syria by the joint efforts of the Hunchak Intellectual Youth and the Aintab 'Ararat' football team. '[The] Hunchakian youth were keen in establishing an athletic organization in order to keep the Armenian youth patriotically healthy in mind and body', official Homenmen website, www.homenmen.org, page visited on April 13, 2004.

88. On Armenian sport clubs in Lebanon and Syria see R. Jebejian. 2000. *Malamih min Tarikh al-Haraka al-Riyadiya fi Suriya – Musahamat al-Riyadiyeen al-Arman fi al-Riyada al-Suriya* [Lineaments of history of the sporting movement in Syria – participation of Armenian sportsmen in Syrian sport], Aleppo: R. Jebejian; Homentmen. 1993. *Homenetmen*, pamphlet issued for the 75th anniversary of the club, Beirut; conversation with Mr. Garbis Tomassian, Aleppo, 14 November 2003; interview with Mr. Sarkis Najarian, former President of Homenmen (Lebanon), Beirut, 15 December 2003.

89. Lebanese Constitution of 1926, French text in Ménassa, *Constitution Libanaise*, 31.

90. Text as reported in K. Karam. 2002. 'Les Associations au Liban: Entre Caritatif et Politique', in S. Ben Néfissa (ed.), *Pouvoirs et Associations dans le Monde Arabe*, Paris: CNRS, 58.

91. As far as literature is concerned these included, for instance, Krikor Zohrab (1861–1915), perhaps the best representative of the Armenian realist novel, and Taniel Varoujian (1884–1915), one of the finest Armenian poets of his generation. See. K. Chahinian. 1988. *Œuvres Vives de la Littérature Arménienne*, Antélias: Catholicosat Arménien de Cilicie, 243–247.

92. Interview with Mr. Toros Toranian, Aleppo, 26 November 2003; interview with Ms. Chahantoukhd, Bourj Hammoud, 30 October 2003.

93. Oshagan was born in Broussa in 1883. See Chahinian, *Œuvres Vives*, 315–321.

94. Ibid., 313. Levon Shant (Istanbul, 1869 – Beirut, 1951), was one of the most prominent figures of Armenian culture in the first half of the 1900s. Author and school educator, co-founder of the Dashnak Jemaran Armenian College in Beirut, he was also briefly one of the Presidents of the Parliament of the independent Republic of Armenia in 1920.

95. Hamazkayin official website, http://www.hamazkayin.com/about.htm, page visited on February 11, 2004.

96. Based on information contained in H. Bariguian and H. Varjabedian. 1973. *Badmoutioun Surio Hay Debaranneru* [The History of Syrian Armenian printing houses], Aleppo: AGBU Bibliographical Committee, 18–83.

97. G. Doniguian & Sons printing press, catalogue of the 80th anniversary, 2 January 2004; interview with Mr. Hagop Doniguian, son of the founder and current owner and manager of the G. Doniguian & Sons printing press, Antelias, 23 October 2003.

98. Interview with Father Norayr Ashekian, current director of the printing house of the Catholicosate of Cilicia, Antelias, 24 October 2003.
99. There is a comparatively vast literature on Armenian publications in Lebanon and Syria: see A. Der Khatchadourian. 1971. 'Fifty Years of Armenian Press in Lebanon (1921–1971)', *Haigazian Armenological Review*, 2, 263–296 (in Armenian); A. Der Khatchadourian. 1972. 'A History of the Armenian Press in Syria', *Haigazian Armenological Review*, 3, 195–230 (in Armenian); J. Tanielian. 1973. 'A Short Account of the Armenian Press in Lebanon', *Haigazian Armenological Review*, 4, 237–282 (in Armenian); J. Tanielian. 1977–1978. 'Issues Pertaining the History of Armenian Press', *Haigazian Armenological Review*, 6, 267–320 (in Armenian); J. Tanielian. 1980. 'New Armenian Periodicals of the Armenian Diaspora', *Haigazian Armenological Review*, 8, 301–324 (in Armenian); J. Tanielian. 1981. ' New Armenian Periodicals of the Armenian Diaspora – Part II', *Haigazian Armenological Review*, 9, 253–294 (in Armenian); M. Minassian. 1981. 'New Discoveries of Armenian Periodicals', *Haigazian Armenological Review*, 9, 295–304 (in Armenian).
100. The original press was still in its place, at the Catholicosate of Cilicia in Antelias, in October 2003.
101. Based on information contained in M.A. Babloyan. 1986. *Hay Barperagan Mamoul: Madenakidagan Hamahavak Tzoutzag 1794–1980* [The Armenian Printed Press: Bibliographical List 1794–1980], Yerevan: The Armenian Soviet Socialist Republic Academy of Sciences, 362–364.
102. These included, among others, the owner of the renown Hotel Baron, Armen Mazloumian, and the founder and owner of the Altounyan Hospital, Dr. Asadour Altounian; see *Keghart* (Aleppo), 1996, 88–89.
103. Ibid., 353–354. At least two publications containing text in Armenian fonts had appeared in Aleppo before the Genocide: *Furat* (1868), a trilingual, Osmanli, French and Arabic periodical published by the local governor, and *Aghpur*, an Armenian nationalist newsletter published between 1912 and 1914. See Bariguian and Varjabedian, *Badmoutioun Surio Hay Debaranneru*, 155–161.
104. Lebanese Constitution of 1926, Article 13: '*La liberté d'exprimer sa pensée par la parole ou par la plume, la liberté de la presse, la liberté de réunion et la liberté d'association sont également garanties dans les limites fixées par la loi*', French text in Ménassa, *Constitution Libanaise*, 31.
105. Bariguian and Varjabedian, *Badmoutioun Surio Hay Debaranneru*, 230. Also see Ter Minassian, *Colporteurs du Komintern*, 159.
106. Sanjian, *The Armenian Communities*, 83–92. An Armenian Evangelical school operating in Kessab has recently celebrated 150 years of activity; see interview with Rev. Paul Haidostian, Chair of the Central Committee of the Union of the Armenian Evangelical Churches in the Near East, Beirut, 8 November 2002.
107. Schahgaldian, 'The Political Integration', 52. For Schahgaldian this 'was a factor in the disappearance of their native language'.

108. Sanjian, *The Armenian Communities*, 90. For an alternative perspective on the Aleppine community's attitudes on education see H. Cholakian. 1982–1984. *'Halebi Azkayin Nersessian Oussoumnarane: Aghchegantz yev Mancheru Tebrotzner 1876–1919'* [The National Nercessian School of Aleppo: School for Girls and Boys, 1876–1919], *Haigazian Armenological Review*, 10, 243–266.

109. Kerr, *The Lions of Marash*, xi. Also see J.L. Barton. 1930. *Story of Near East Relief (1915–1930): An Interpretation*, New York: MacMillan Co.

110. A.N. Bedian. 1961. 'A Study of Elementary Schools in Syria, Related to their History, Background and Teacher's Beliefs', MA thesis, Beirut: American University of Beirut, 17. The 53 schools considered represented more than three quarters of all the Armenian elementary schools in Syria. The information used by Bedian in the table is reportedly based on an unspecified survey carried out during the 1950s by the Calouste Gulbenkian Foundation.

111. Fragment of an Armenian Apostolic yearbook (?) published in Syria and dating circa 1929, 112–114. Personal collection of the author.

112. The Mandate for Syria and Lebanon, 24 July 1922, Article 8, *League of Nations Official Journal*, August 1922, 1013–1017, as reproduced in Longrigg, *Syria and Lebanon*, 377–380.

113. Lebanese Constitution of 1926, French text in Ménassa, *Constitution Libanaise*, 30.

114. On French educational policy in the Mandate see Khouri, *Syria and the French Mandate*, 409–410; R.D. Matthews and M. Akrawi. 1949. *Education in the Arab Countries of the Near East*, Washington: American Council on Education; J.K. Ragland. 1969. 'The Free Educational System of the Republic of Lebanon', Ph.D. thesis, University of Oklahoma, 64–67.

115. Kerr, *The Lions of Marash*, xi.

116. See Schahgaldian, 'The Political Integration', 67.

117. P.J. Young. 2001. 'Knowledge, Nation and the Curriculum: Ottoman Armenian Education (1853–1915)', Ph.D. thesis, University of Michigan, 76.

118. Schahgaldian, 'The Political Integration', 165–167.

119. Ibid., 166.

120. Ibid.

121. Ibid, 165.

122. Information on the socio-economic conditions of Armenian refugees during the Mandate is in general scarce and fragmentary. Some elements are contained in Greenshields, 'The Settlement of Armenian Refugees'; Lust-Okar, 'Failure of Collaboration'; Sanjian, 'The Armenian Minority Experience', 149–179; Schahgaldian, 'The Political Integration'; Keuroghlian, 'Les Arméniens de l'Agglomération de Beyrouth'; C. Babikian. 1983. 'L'Evolution du Rôle Politique des Arméniens au Liban de 1945 à 1975', BA thesis, Beirut: Université Saint-Joseph.

123. The construction industry flourished in Beirut in the years of the Mandate under the pressure of urbanisation and the impulse of the new role of the city as the capital of Greater Lebanon. See S. Kassir. 2003. *Histoire de Beyrouth*,

Paris: Fayard, Chapter 12; J. Tabet, M. Ghorayeb, E. Huybrechts and E. Verdeil. 2001. *Beyrouth*, Paris: Institut Français d'Architecture, 13–19.

124. A considerable number of these were Armenian Catholics, on account of the strong presence of that community in the Mount Lebanon and Beirut. See Babikian, 'L'Evolution du Rôle Politique', p. 11.

125. Syria was heavily reliant on imports. See Lust-Okar, 'Failure of Collaboration', p. 58. Khouri reports that between 1920 and 1926 the French franc lost half of its value in relation to the US dollar and two thirds of its value in relation to the British Sterling pound. The Syrian-Lebanese pound was linked to the French franc at a fixed ratio of £S1 to FF20. See Khouri, *Syria and the French Mandate*, 85–86.

126. Khouri, *Syria and the French Mandate*, 91–92.

127. The effect on the labour market of the arrival of the Armenians was made stronger by the fact that the Armenians tended to avoid dispersion in the territory; their mass presence in concentrated areas (Beirut, Aleppo, etc.) significantly affected the local market conditions. See Greenshields, 'The Settlement of Armenian Refugees', 239.

128. Khouri, *Syria and the French Mandate*, 91–92.

129. Interview with Mr. Varoujian Khandjian, current owner and manager of Vivaro shoe manufacturing and sale, Bourj Hammoud, 9 December 2003. Mr. Khandjian's father, an orphan refugee brought up in the Bird's Nest orphanage in Jbeil became an apprentice in one of those early Armenian shoemaking businesses.

130. On the agricultural resettlement plans, see Topouzian, *Suriayi yev Lipanani Haigagan*, 167–168 and 173–175; Keuroghlian, *Les Arméniens de l'Agglomération de Beyrouth*, 15–16.

131. The refugees of 'Anjar were assigned plots of land in proportion to the size of families. The agricultural dependency of 'Anjar was also provided with an articulated irrigation system. See notes from a visit to 'Anjar on 24–25 October 2003 and interviews with Mr. Sebouh Sekayan, 'Anjar, 25 October 2003; Mr. Vahe Ashkarian, 'Anjar, 24 and 25 October 2003; Mr. Movses Herguelian, 'Anjar, 24 and 25 October 2003.

# 3

# Coping with Political Change: The Armenians in Lebanon and Syria during the First Two Decades of Independence (1946–1967)

## Introduction: The Armenians and the Post-Mandate States of the Levant

By the time the last French troops left the Levant in 1946 the Armenians were not an alien community in Lebanon and Syria any longer. Many of them were still living in refugee camps on the edge of towns, or could hardly communicate in Arabic, but the continuation of the Armenian presence in the cities and villages of the Levant had become a broadly accepted *fait accompli* and the community had found ways to integrate itself in the economy and society of the region. The Armenian population had also grown demographically: figures at the closing of the Mandate put the Armenian community in Syria at nearly 125,000 and the community in Lebanon at around 75,000.[1] Politically, the Armenians had become a marginal but identifiable player in the Lebanese and Syrian arenas, particularly in Beirut and Aleppo. Carefully balancing a policy of good relations with the French with the support provided to their nationalist opponents, the Armenian nationalist parties had managed to make Armenian communal solidarity a political asset that was potentially useful to any Arab political groups. Other Armenian political actors, including the Armenian communists, had also contributed to the legitimisation of the community's position by providing extensive co-operation to local forces.

The *fait accompli* of the Armenian presence, on the other hand, contrasted with the uncertainty concerning the future of the community's coexistence as a diverse ethno-cultural group in the two newly independent countries. The approach that the new states were going to adopt in regulating the presence of ethno-cultural diversity, and in particular the impact that independence was going to have on the Armenian strategy of cultural reconstruction, were questions that could not be separated from the broader debate on the form that the new, post-Mandate institutions of the Levant would take. Independence marked for Lebanon and Syria the beginning of a phase in which the political and cultural identity of the two states was repeatedly and sometimes radically renegotiated, if not openly fought over through *coups d'état* and street battles. The main datum of the previous quarter of a century, the French presence, had gone; Lebanon and Syria had emerged as two independent 'semi-liberal oligarchic republic[s] resting on a 'feudal' social base',[2] dominated by large landowners, clan leaders and urban notables.[3] In the course of the following two decades the oligarchic, post-Mandate order was repeatedly challenged and its serious weaknesses were exposed. The boundaries of the two countries, imposed by the great powers, thwarted the Arab nationalists' ambitions to create a vast and united Arab state and undermined the legitimacy of the new territorial entities; the social bases of the new states remained remarkably thin; the pattern of economic development fuelled latent social tensions and led to class conflict.[4] A number of key policy issues were once again brought to the fore: the question of the relation between state and religion, the question of public education, of the role of the state in the economy and in the provision of social services, of the position of women in society and public life, and so on. The outcome of the challenge to the oligarchic order, in the 1950s and 1960s, was dramatically different in the two countries: in the case of Lebanon the oligarchic order substantially survived (in particular overcoming a serious crisis in 1958); in Syria the system repeatedly tottered, lost some of its components, and eventually ended when the Ba'th Party seized power in 1963.

The question of the relation between the state and culturally diverse groups, and thus the position of the Armenians, must be understood in the context of this phase of tension and conflict over the identity of the state. In the case of Lebanon the oligarchic arrangement, which drew from the Ottoman legacy and from the French Mandatory's approach to ethno-cultural diversity, provided an all but ideal environment for the development of the Armenian project of reconstruction; its capacity to overcome crises played in favour of the consolidation of that strategy. In Syria, on the contrary, the challenge to the system radically transformed the official position of the state on the question of ethno-cultural diversity: officially adopted Arab and Syrian national discourses became tools to make up for the lack of loyalty to the state and the precariousness of the institutions. Armenian diversity, and in particular the system of Armenian formal institutions, was severely damaged by change.

The present chapter is dedicated to analysing the position of the Armenian community in Lebanon and Syria during what I have described as a phase of struggle over the identity of the state in the first two decades of independence. There are two main perspectives of the analysis that I propose: the first looks at any political role the Armenians had in this struggle – in other words, it observes if and how the Armenians 'took sides' on the question of the identity of the state; the other focuses on the effects of the struggle on the spaces of Armenian public participation and on Armenian society as a whole, and in particular the impact they had on Armenian institutions and the process of 'reconstruction' as it had emerged during the years of the Mandate.

## Armenian Politics and Armenian Public Participation in Lebanon and Syria (1946–1967)

### The Armenians in the Early Years of Independence

The struggle over the identity of the state briefly sketched above saw, in general, little participation from the Armenian community. The role of the Armenian parties, of Armenian civil society, or individuals in the crucial events that shaped the political life of Lebanon and Syria in the mid 1940s and beyond was marginal, if not negligible. Attempts at analyzing the 'political marginality' of the Armenians should take into account a combination of factors, in part related to the Lebanese and Syrian context, in part to certain features specific to the Armenian community.

A first important observation in this analysis is that the political integration of the Armenians in Lebanon and Syria was problematic. To begin with, ethno-cultural diversity played a key role as a barrier to political integration. Existing internal and external pressures to the community fostered communal solidarity and discouraged individual, cross-cutting initiatives. Internal pressures included in particular those emanating from the Armenian political leadership: in the 1940s and 1950s the Armenian nationalist parties progressively emerged as the uncontested leaders of the community, increasingly able to speak in the name of the Armenians, efficient at mobilizing (or intimidating) the public and monopolizing political activities. External pressures were no less discouraging of cross-communal initiatives: in a context where ethnic connections were key to political access and networking, community 'defectors' had to be ready to face and overcome formal and informal obstacles to political participation. In addition to this, the language barrier of Arabic still hindered the credentials of the Armenians as full members of the Lebanese and Syrian political scene.

Besides these ethnic factors, the political integration of the Armenians was also made difficult, or at least not encouraged, by factors of class and ideology. The main actors of the Lebanese and Syrian political scene were in general socially and ideologically distant from the Armenians. Armenians were not part of the (mostly Sunni or Maronite) elite oligarchy in power nor could they aspire to join it. At the same time, they did not share much with the radical middle class who formed the backbone of the Ba'th or the Syrian Nationalist Party; ideologically, the Armenians could hardly be attracted by the emerging Syrian or pan-Arab, populist discourse of leaders like Antoun Sa'adeh, Akram Hawrani or Michel Aflaq. Nor did the Armenians represent a significant part of the agricultural working class or of the military. At the end of the Mandate their presence in the army, police, and security services was limited to a few long serving, respected individuals of a past generation.[5]

If, on the one hand, the Armenians as individual citizens were difficult to integrate with the existing political actors, on the other, they were not sufficiently numerous, powerful, interested, or willing to project themselves as a new, distinct group actor in the political struggle over the state. Among the traits of Armenian politics that had appeared from the early days of the diaspora was a strong predominance of Armenian, communal and national concerns over Lebanese and Syrian concerns. Armenian politics focused mostly on the interests and problems of the Armenian people, both at the level of individual diasporas and at the higher, global level. The organization of political activities itself had a distinct transnational character: nationalist parties had reconstructed their transnational networks, and the elaboration of the core political programs always took place at the higher, transnational level. Armenian politics was also characterized by sharp divisiveness. The divide between the nationalist parties, in part ideological (notably in the case of the Ramkavar party), in part explained in terms of struggle to win political control over the diaspora, absorbed considerable political resources. However, common to most Armenian political parties and actors, appeared the predominance of the nationalist themes over other components of their ideology.

The approach of the Armenian nationalist parties towards Lebanon and Syria was generally one of sincere loyalty, combining a sense of gratitude to the countries and peoples which had in some way provided a new home to the Armenians and an interest in maintaining a system of institutions that offered a number of advantages for Armenian communal life. Stemming from this was a moderately conservative political position vis-à-vis radical reforms of the Lebanese and Syrian political systems. During national parliamentary elections the nationalist parties would enter the local political game and build alliances with the main Arab political forces in government or in the opposition. However, Armenian co-operation with these forces tended to be aimed at pursuing intra-Armenian political confrontations and could hardly be stretched to the point of contributing to challenge the pillars of a political order that ultimately benefited the community. This perceived predominance of Armenian concerns resulted in recurrent accusations of non-commitment, of insincerity, if not of disloyalty, from sectors of the Lebanese and Syrian political spectrum.[6]

Within this general picture of the lack of political integration of the Armenian community two main exceptions stand out: the Armenian communists and a section of the (mostly Lebanese) Armenian Catholic community. The communists, arguably the most politically-integrated of the Armenians, continued their co-operation with the Lebanese and Syrian left and became important supporters of the emerging Soviet strategy in the Middle East. The reinforcement of Soviet Armenia, the promotion of the positions of the USSR in the Middle East, the struggle against western imperialism and the de-confessionalisation of the political systems in the Levant were some of the central themes of their political activity. In the case of the *Arman qadim*, pre-Genocide Catholic community of Lebanon and Syria, linguistic and social integration with other Christians was a common fact; in Lebanon the years of independence saw the reinforcement of a tradition of co-operation between the Armenian Catholics and Maronite political forces, most notably the Kata'ib of Pierre Gemayel.

## *The* National Pact *and the Armenians in Lebanon (1943–1951)*

In Lebanon the first outcome of the local 're-negotiation' over state identity was the *mithaq watani* (national pact) of 1943. Often referred to as the defining moment of independence and of the creation of a 'Lebanese formula' of coexistence, the national pact was an inter-communal unwritten compromise 'in the pure tradition of Mount Lebanon'.[7] The pact had two cornerstones: externally, the commitment to preserve a distinct Lebanese Arab identity within the larger framework of an Arab family of states; internally, a renewed consociational agreement to regulate access to public positions in a form that would respect the proportions between the different confessional groups in the country.[8]

The circumstances in which the *mithaq watani* was reached are not known in full detail. What is generally accepted is that the pact was the fruit of the negotiation between Bishara Al-Khouri and Riad Al-Solh, the leading representatives of the Christian Maronite and Sunni Muslim communities, '*respectivement situées aux avant-postes opposés de la tension islamo-chrétienne*'.[9] For what is relevant here, there is no indication that any of the Lebanese communities – including the Armenians – was at any stage collegially involved in the process that led to the pact.[10] Armenians were nevertheless important, insofar as they were counted *ex officio* in the Christian front, and their demographic 'weight' was used to forge a political balance in which the Christians were going to have a position of pre-eminence: in the confessional make up of the Lebanese parliament the ratio of Christian versus Muslim-Druze representatives continued to be 6 to 5. From the point of view of the Armenians, their inclusion in the confessional balance of the national pact had the value of the official blessing of the new independent state on the continuation of their presence in the country. The preservation of the 1926 Constitution and the Lebanese formula of coexistence which emerged with the national pact reinforced the political and juridical bases of their communal spaces of participation and of their strategy of reconstructing of an Armenian world in Lebanon. The requirements of participation in the public life of the country remained fairly limited and the Armenians could continue to engage in a parallel, Armenian political ring.

The first general elections after independence, held in 1947, were a significant indicator of the dynamics of Armenian participation in Lebanese politics. The national political scene was characterized by a heated confrontation over the extension of the presidential mandate of Bishara Al-Khouri. The Armenian camp, however, in the run-up to the elections was dominated by issues all Armenian: the position of the diaspora vis-à-vis the USSR, and, in particular, the question of the repatriation of Armenian refugees to Soviet Armenia.

The resettlement of Armenian refugees in the Soviet Armenian Republic had been the object of plans and considerations before, but it only became a viable possibility in 1945 when the USSR decided to revive the idea and to back it with financial resources. The repatriation campaign was launched in June 1945 on the occasion of the election of the new Catholicos of all Armenians and following the reconciliation between the Armenian Catholicosal See of Etchmiadzin and the Soviet state.[11] By February 1946 practical arrangements were under way and repatriation committees were established in several countries of the diaspora; on June 23, 1946 the first migrants sailed from the port of Beirut.[12] For most Armenian refugees of Lebanon and Syria the repatriations could hardly be described as a home-coming, as their regional origins were far away, in Anatolia or Cilicia. Repatriations, however, offered to many the chance, or the illusion, of bringing to an end their experience as refugees and of contributing to a 'territorial solution' of the Armenian question.[13] Some of the Armenian press drew parallels between the repatriations to Soviet Armenia and the *aliyah* of the Jewish people *'dont les pionniers mettent en valeur le territoire de la patrie d'origine, la Palestine'*.[14]

Armenian parties had initially put aside differences and joined forces in co-operating with the repatriation programs. However, the criteria in the formation and management of the committees, dominated by Armenian communists or communist-sympathizers and hostile to the Dashnaks, soon alienated the support of the latter. The exclusion of the

Dashnaks from the management of the repatriations had a divisive effect on the community and precipitated an internal crisis within the Dashnak party: the right-wing, neo-Dashnak faction could hardly tolerate being outpaced by the party's adversaries on its own Armenian nationalist terrain and eventually won the control of the organisation's leadership.[15] The Armenian political spectrum was again sharply divided between an anti-Soviet, Dashnak side and a front of anti-Dashnaks, including the Hunchaks, the Ramkavars and the Armenian communists. As early as August 1946 the Dashnak mouthpiece in Syria, *Arevelk*, denounced the repatriations presenting them as a new Genocide: 'another 24th of April is coming'.[16]

The electoral alliances established between Armenian and Arab parties in the elections of May–June 1947 were largely based on the intra-Armenian divide over the question of Soviet Armenia. The neo-Dashnaks, headed by Movses Der Kaloustian, were the best qualified and more able to side with the strong list of the majority in government and won both parliamentary seats assigned to the Armenian Apostolic community.[17] The Hunchaks, the Ramkavars, the communists and a number of patriotic unions joined the opposition ranks and formed a Lebanese-Armenian Democratic Front which was included in the electoral list led by former president Alfred Naccache along with Amin Beyhum and Mustafa Aris. The elections and their aftermath were characterized by allegations of fraud, tension and violence in the Armenian quarters: by the end of 1947 'about two dozen party members, mostly neo-Dashnaks and Hunchaks had already been assassinated in the streets of [Beirut]'.[18]

At the close of the repatriation programs in 1948 an estimated 32,000 Armenians had migrated, mostly from Syria.[19] Migrants had left behind a situation of increasing divisiveness and conflict in which Armenian sides were establishing paramilitary organizations and using blackmail and intimidation 'in internal party life and in interparty relations within the administrative apparatus of the community'.[20]

In August 1950 a reform of the electoral law brought the number of parliamentary seats from 55 to 77; the Armenian quota was adjusted accordingly and the Apostolic community was granted the right to elect 3 representatives, while the Armenian Catholics were, for the first time, assigned one seat. The elections of 1951 saw, once again, the Armenian parties divided. The neo-Dashnaks sided with the list of the government and obtained the re-election of their incumbent candidates but failed to obtain the third Apostolic seat mostly due to internal rivalries with an opposing Dashnak faction. The opposition front was also weakened by internal dissent; in this context the Catholic Church arranged an electoral alliance with the Kata'ib party and obtained the election of Joseph Chader, an Armenian Catholic who had become a prominent member of the Falange.[21]

**Table 3.1. Armenian MPs in Lebanon, 1947–1951**[22]

| Election year | Name of MPs | Place of election |
|---|---|---|
| 1947 | Movses Der Kaloustian | Beirut |
| 1947 | Melkon Hairabedian | Beirut |
| 1951 | Movses Ter Kaloustian | Beirut |
| 1951 | Melkon Hairabedian | Beirut |
| 1951 | Dickran Tospat | Metn |
| 1951 | Joseph Chader[23] | Beirut |

## The Armenians in Syria and the First Challenges to the Oligarchic Order (1947–1954)

In Syria the end of the Mandate placed the political control of the country in the hands of the nationalist Syrian elite that had led the opposition to the French. The narrow-based, 'democratic in form but oligarchical in practice'[24] parliamentary system established by the constitution of 1930 continued to be in place. As a part of it, the political approach that granted spaces of autonomy and group representation in the access to public offices to the many diverse ethno-religious communities of the country was also maintained. The Syrian political system in the early period after independence, however, did not overcome its weaknesses and its institutions were soon radically shaken; in the context of the dramatic changes which took place, the relation between the state and culturally diverse groups became one of the disputed issues of the national political debate.

The first round in the re-discussion of that issue took place in the run-up to the parliamentary elections of 1947 and, in particular, in the context of the heated confrontation between the National Bloc and the opposition on the reform of the electoral law. One of the issues at stake was, in fact, the question of the representation of minorities. The constitution of 1930 prescribed that a mechanism of representation for the '*minorités religieuses*' be included in the electoral law.[25] However, 'when applied to Christians, the words *minorités religieuses* could be interpreted in two ways. The first interpretation would imply that there would be seats apportioned to the Christians as a group, while the second would define the term as applying to each of the confessional minorities'.[26] The leaders of the main opposition bloc, the People's Party, opposed the allocation of seats to minorities on grounds that reserved quotas and similar arrangements were violating the constitutional principle of the equality of all citizens, granting a privilege to some. In 1947 the debate was resolved in favour of the maintenance of confessional representation: a presidential decree issued on June 4, 1947 set the number of parliamentary seats at 140; of these, two were allocated to the Armenian Apostolic community and one to the Armenian Catholics.[27]

The elections of 7–8 July 1947, the first after the departure of the last French troops from Syria in the spring of 1946, saw the political spectrum divided on two fronts: on one side the supporters of the government, roughly represented by the Nationalist Bloc, on the other a varied opposition mainly identified with the Liberal/People's Party – an alternative, but equally 'oligarchic' formation. The Armenians, caught in their own debate over the issue of the repatriation to Soviet Armenia, were also divided: the Dashnaks sided with the Nationalist Bloc, the Hunchaks with the opposition. The run-up to the elections was marked by incidents in the Armenian quarters resulting at least in one casualty.[28]

A second phase in the re-discussion of the question of the representation of diverse groups was prompted by the turbulent events of 1949. The military coup carried out by Colonel Husni Al-Za'im on 30 March, the counter-coup by Colonel Mohammed Al-Hinnawi in August, and the third coup conducted by Colonel Adib Shishakli in December produced a substantial break of continuity in Syrian politics: they marked the debut of the army as an actor in the political scene, they represented a first strong rejection of the oligarchic class in power, and saw some form of participation of representatives of the new radical opposition present in the country.

The issues that triggered the coups and the *milieu* in which they had been conceived were essentially at a remove from the Armenian community.[29] The crisis of 1949 had, conversely, a negative impact on the community, as it marked a turning point for minority representation in the country, and – more in general – for civil liberties. In the elections for the Syrian Constituent Assembly of 1949 the representation of Christians was simplified along the lines that had been anticipated in the debate of 1947: the number of seats allocated to minorities was reduced and the Christian representatives were elected without distinction of their specific confessional community.[30] But it was not until the late phase of the regime of Adib Shishakli that the conditions of the Armenians suffered the first serious setback of their experience in Syria. During the first two years following his coup, Shishakli had kept away from direct participation in government; after his 'second coup', in November 1951, the regime increasingly took the character of an open military dictatorship. The measures of the autocratic regime of Shishakli were arguably directed at suppressing opposition; however, they tended to assume a 'chauvinistic [...] tone' and 'were aimed at curbing the influence of foreigners, religious leaders, and minority racial groups'.[31] The Armenian system of communal institutions, including schools, churches, clubs, etc., was deeply affected by change. In April 1952 Armenian parties suffered from the general, national ban on political parties. In the course of 1953 Shishakli started a process of institutionalization of the regime. In a plebiscite dominated by himself as a single candidate Shishakli was elected president and obtained the approval of a new constitutional text; new parliamentary elections were called for October.

The new electoral law passed at the end of July included provisions to prohibit political associations whose membership was based on ethno-religious groups; a measure that, once again, hit the Armenian political parties. However, it appears that Shishakli did not wish to eliminate Armenian representation in the parliament altogether. The new parliament, elected under strict control of the army and security forces, included one Armenian representative, Judge Krikor Eblighatian.[32] The memories of Eblighatian offer a clear indication of the nature of the Syrian regime and of the constraints imposed on Armenian politics.[33] In 1953 Eblighatian was a young judge in Latakia. It was Shishakli who handpicked him as the representative of the Armenians in the parliament, in part – apparently – for trivial reasons, in part for reasons of substance. As for the trivial reasons, Shishakli used to spend weekends in Kessab, an Armenian village and holiday resort in the north of Syria, next to the border with the Sanjak of Alexandretta; Eblighatian, who was also often in Kessab, had been introduced to Shishakli. Eblighatian recalls that: 'chez les Arméniens [Shishakli] ne connaissait que moi'.[34]

The reasons of substance included the fact that Eblighatian combined the skills and capacities of a trained lawyer (including a perfect command of Arabic), with his formal independence from Armenian nationalist parties. Eblighatian remembers having received strong encouragement within the Armenian community itself, as some were hoping that his appointment could serve as a channel of communication between the community and the government and reverse the restrictive measures that were hindering communal activities: 'on m'a presque obligé a quitter mon travail de juge'.[35]

Another Armenian, the veteran Syrian nationalist Fathallah Asiun, was appointed by Shishakli to a short lived cabinet formed in July 1953. Asiun, however, a fully assimilated Catholic Arman qadim, could hardly claim to be a representative figure among the Armenians; arguably, Shishakli's choice was based on Asiun's credentials as an independent old nationalist.[36]

**Table 3.2. Armenian MPs in Syria, 1947–1953**[37]

| Election year | Name of MPs | Place of election |
|---|---|---|
| 1947 | Fred Arslanian | Damascus |
| 1947 | Dickran Tchradjian[38] | Aleppo |
| 1947 | Abdallah Fettal | Aleppo |
| 1949 | Dickran Tchradjian | Aleppo |
| 1949 | Fathallah Asiun | Aleppo |
| 1953 | Krikor Eblighatian | Aleppo |

Table 3.3. The evolution of confessional parliamentary representation in Syria, 1947–1943

| Confessional group | 1947 elections[39] | 1949 elections[40] | 1953 elections[41] |
|---|---|---|---|
| All Muslims | (121) | 100 | 73 |
| All Christians | (19) | 14 | 9 |
| Tribal representatives | 10 | – | – |
| Sunni Muslims | 94 | – | – |
| Alawis | 11 | – | – |
| Ismailis | 1 | – | – |
| Druzes | 5 | – | – |
| Greek Orthodox | 6 | – | – |
| Syriac Orthodox | 2 | – | – |
| Armenian Apostolic | 2 | – | – |
| Greek Catholic | 2 | – | – |
| Syriac Catholic | 1 | – | – |
| Armenian Catholic | 1 | – | – |
| Maronites | 1 | – | – |
| Other minorities | 3 | – | – |
| Jews | 1 | – | – |
| Total MPs | 140 | 114 | 82 |

## *Armenian Politics in Lebanon and Syria and the Rise of Nasserism (1952–1961)*

In the course of the 1950s the domestic political order of Lebanon and Syria was increasingly put under pressure by regional and international developments. The Egyptian revolution of 1952 and the rise of a charismatic Arab leader like Nasser severely tested the notion of Lebanon's regional 'separateness' and opened new perspectives for Arab political integration. On the international level, the decade was characterized by the process of the redefinition of the regional strategy of the big powers after the Second World War. The redefinition took place in the context of the emergence of the cold war, with the effect of providing national and regional actors with external sources of political support.[42] In the Levant, regional and international factors of destabilization interacted with existing internal tensions and precipitated national crises in which the identity of the state was radically re-discussed: in Lebanon this amounted to the first breakdown of the national pact during the crisis which peaked in the events of 1958; in Syria it led to the experiment of political union with Nasser's Egypt from 1958 to 1961.

Throughout this phase, the prime determinants of Armenian politics in Lebanon and Syria remained essentially questions regarding the Armenian community and its political divisions: the Armenian political debate remained largely removed from the issues at the core of the Lebanese and Syrian political crises. The local, regional and international pressures, however, had a significant impact on the Armenian political parties and on their pattern of participation in the political life of the region: on one hand they contributed to sharpen the intra-Armenian political divide (most notably as the Dashnak party reinforced its positioning within the so-called 'free world', pro-Western camp); on the other, they indirectly provided a new potential for co-operation between Armenians and local Arab politics, as the Arab political scene was increasingly adopting a cold war discourse. This potential, however, could only be used in Lebanon, where the overlap between the Armenian internal and local national struggles resulted in the dramatic increase in the involvement of Armenian political parties in Lebanese affairs. In Syria, on the contrary, political developments severely restricted the spaces for Armenian public participation.

## The Struggle for the Armenian Apostolic Church: The Armenians and the Lebanese Crisis of 1958

In Lebanon, the early 1950s were characterized by the deepening of the intra-Armenian political crisis. In an atmosphere of violent radicalization, the Dashnak party and its opponents engaged in a struggle to obtain the political control of existing diaspora institutions, and in particular of the Apostolic Church. The 'struggle for the Church' had some ideological bases. From a Dashnak perspective the control of the Church was justified with the imperative of rescuing it from Soviet tutelage, as it had become apparent that the 'Soviet authorities [intended] to use [the Catholicosal See of] Holy Etchmiadzin as an instrument to control the Armenian communities in the Diaspora'.[43] In 1953 the Dashnak-controlled *Armenian Review* wrote that

> the Armenian churches must be rescued from Soviet agents, and this is possible only if and when the throne of the Cilician Catholicosate is occupied by a man who is capable and courageous, independent-minded, and completely free of Soviet influence, to assume the spiritual leadership of the Armenian people. Once such a man is found, the churches for the Dispersion can sever their relation with Etchmiadzin for the time being and rally around the Catholicos of Antilias [sic] (Cilician See) who will be in a position to protect the interests of the Armenian church in the free world without the Soviet's intervention[44]

In a sense, the defence of the Church and of the Catholicosate of Cilicia in Antelias was a battle for the core values of the Dashnaks: the Church was surely a central component of the 'Armenianness' that the party claimed to protect. However, besides any ideological consideration, obtaining the control of the Church and of all the social and educational institutions that it controlled meant winning the possibility of reinforcing the party's base in the Armenian community, or – conversely – to prevent the opposing side from doing the same.

The acute phase of the struggle for the Apostolic Church began in 1952, when the Catholicos of Cilicia, Karekin I died after a long illness.[45] During the following four years the Armenian political parties could not agree on the name of the new Catholicos and all attempted elections failed. Soviet interference was made clear in February 1956, when the Catholicos of Etchmiadzin Vazken I, in an unprecedented move, travelled to Beirut and became involved in the electoral process.[46]

During the crucial days of the election, and in the troubled aftermath, the Dashnak party obtained the support of President Camille Chamoun. The political co-operation between Chamoun and the Dashnaks was not new: in the elections of 1953 the party had joined the government's list and contributed to obtaining a large victory.[47] The level of co-operation, however, had been stepped up by the mid-1950s: on one hand, the sharp divide among Armenian political forces between supporters of Soviet Armenia and a pro-Western camp was increasingly in tune with Lebanese national political debate, as the question of the relation between Lebanon, Egypt and the Arab world assumed the tones and discourse of the cold war; on the other, the 15th World Congress of the Dashnak party, under the impulse of the fiercely anti-communist neo-Dashnak faction, had removed any hesitation and expressly called for the party's 'cooperation and alliance with all anti-communist and anti-Soviet forces'.[48]

On February 19, 1956, when it became apparent that the disputed election would result in the enthronement of the Dashnak candidate – Bishop Zareh of Aleppo – Catholicos Vazken I formally asked President Chamoun to suspend it. Chamoun, on the contrary, deployed the gendarmerie in the Catholicosate and allowed the vote to take place.[49] The following day, the election of Catholicos Zareh I marked the victory of the Dashnaks, but had the effect of breaking the religious unity of the Apostolic community and further radicalising intra-Armenian confrontation. During the following days and months the anti-Dashnak front denounced the election and attempted a resistance: a coalition of Hunchaks, Ramkavars, independents and other community representatives challenged the authority of the new Catholicos and elected a *locum tenens*, unsuccessfully seeking official recognition from the Lebanese government as a new independent community. Armenians had to get used to a new political geography of the Armenian Apostolic churches, as some became 'loyalist' to the new Catholicos and others sided with the opposition. The Lebanese government intervened again with public force to seize the monastery of Bikfaya from the opposition and hand it over to the Catholicos of Cilicia.[50]

Tension, violence and Armenian collaboration with Arab political groups reached a peak in 1957 and 1958, when the intra-Armenian struggle overlapped with a crisis of the Lebanese national institutions. In the heated elections of 1957, the Armenians were again split between a Dashnak/pro-Western front, allied with Chamoun and the Kata'ib, and an anti-Dashnak front, siding with the leaders of the national opposition, which included Abdullah Yafi and Saeb Salam. The run-up to the election saw a rare example of Armenian participation in joint demonstrations side to side with the national opposition. On 30 May 1957, the security forces opened fire against opposition demonstrators, killing eight persons and arresting five hundred; twelve of the arrested were Armenians.[51] In the following months, Armenian supporters of Chamoun obtained important recognition when the *falangiste* Joseph Chader became the first Armenian to be appointed minister in a Lebanese cabinet.[52]

When the Lebanese crisis developed into an insurrection in May 1958, the Armenian quarters of Beirut became the theatre of open armed confrontation between opposing Armenian sides. The Hunchaks were mostly based in Nor Hadjin, Khalil Badawi and Charchabouk; the Dashnaks were on the opposite side of the Nahr Beirut, in Bourj Hammoud. Small groups of gunmen would cross the river and attack their opponents.[53] In the hysteria of those days Armenian society became radically polarised: a number of Hunchak-supporting families left their residence in Bourj Hammoud in fear of violence, as Dashnak supporters also left from the other side of the river. In the words of Schahgaldian 'intermarriage or even ordinary interpersonal relations between the two [opposing camps] ceased altogether. The schools, churches, clubs and other public centers of one faction were closed to members or sympathizers of the other faction. Entire Armenian neighborhoods in Bayrut [...] were sealed off to members of the opposite camp'.[54]

The hostilities in the Armenian quarters continued beyond the end of the national conflict and it was not until December 1958 that an agreement between the parties could be achieved through the mediation of the new Minister of the Interiors, Raymond Eddé.[55]

**Table 3.4. Armenian MPs in Lebanon, 1953–1957**

| Election year | Name of MPs | Place of election |
|---|---|---|
| 1953 | Movses Ter Kaloustian | Beirut |
| 1953 | Dickran Tospat | Bourj Hammoud |
| 1953 | Joseph Chader | Beirut |
| 1957 | Movses Der Kaloustian | Beirut |
| 1957 | Khatchig Babikian | Beirut |
| 1957 | Dickran Tospat | Bourj Hammoud |
| 1957 | Joseph Chader | Beirut |

## The United Arab Republic and the Crisis of the Dashnak in Syria

For Syria, the fall of Colonel Adib Shishakli following a military coup in February 1954 marked the return to the parliamentary institutional system that had been established by the constitution of 1950. A phase of recovery of civil liberties followed the end of the Shishakli regime. The new parliamentary elections, held in September-October, were regulated by the electoral law of 1949 and were arguably free and fair.[56] The Armenian political parties, sharply divided along cold war lines, made electoral alliances with Arab contenders. In Aleppo, the Hunchaks obtained the election of the Armenian Protestant Dickran Tchradjian.[57]

Beyond the regained freedom of public life, however, the Syrian parliamentary system remained weak. The elections confirmed the traditional elite as the main social force in the renewed parliament, but the vote was marked by the success of radicals like the Ba'th party, reflecting the crisis of legitimacy of the traditional ruling class and growing social tensions within the country. The army, temporarily confined to its barracks, remained highly politicized and dangerously divided in a number of factions. It was the rise of Nasser as a charismatic regional leader, in the context of the great powers' 'struggle for the Middle East', that precipitated a new crisis of the system early in 1958. In the face of a difficult regional situation, and under pressure from an enthusiastic, mobilized public opinion, Syria entered an ill-planned political union with Egypt.[58]

The Armenians, alien to public enthusiasm for pan-Arabism, and – on the other hand – not strong enough to engage in national political battles, played an unsurprisingly marginal role in the political phase that led to the union. In the second part of the 1950s the Armenian parties were largely caught in the intra-Armenian confrontation and in the struggle for control of the Armenian Apostolic Church. The tensions and episodes of violence that had marked the election of Catholicos Zareh I to the See of Antelias were paralleled by similar events in Syria, and so was the tactical interaction of the Armenians with some of the local political groupings. In one episode, an Armenian Dashnak activist was shot dead in a café in central Damascus. The assailants, allegedly Hunchak militants, took refuge in the left-leaning Apostolic prelacy of Bab Sharqi, which became the object of attacks.[59] If, in Lebanon, the struggle for the Apostolic Church had seen the almost total success of the Dashnaks, in Syria the outcome was dramatically different. The Church effectively split: while the prelacy of Aleppo remained loyal to the Catholicosate of Cilicia, the prelacy of Damascus, politically controlled by the Hunchaks, placed itself under the authority of the Catholicosate of Etchmiadzin.

The evolution of the state during the union was once again severely restrictive for civil liberties and considerably damaged the system of Armenian communal institutions. The regime became a 'bureaucratic apparatus with the charismatic leader at the top, legitimised by Arab nationalist ideology, and resting on a network of military and police control and on Nasser's vast but unorganised mass support'.[60] Under the control of Nasser's proconsuls in Syria, and particularly of Abdel Hamid Sarraj, the powerful head of the security apparatus, the country was turned into a 'police dictatorship'.[61] Secret police control was omnipresent, arbitrary arrests and torture became a common practice, freedom of expression was curtailed. Political parties were dissolved and the elected parliament was substituted with an appointed chamber; judge Krikor Eblighatian became once again the neutral, representative figure that Nasser and his men chose to represent the Armenians.

Within a situation in which the whole Armenian community suffered from the new liberty-suppressing regime, the Dashnak party was, perhaps inevitably, the one most affected, on account of its pro-Western stance. The crisis between the Dashnaks and the regime reached its peak in 1961 when the police seized a certain amount of light weapons, arrested several party activists, and charged them with sedition and espionage. The arrested were accused of forming a 'spy ring', of having relations with the CIA, with Israel and even with Turkey; some were tortured and died in detention. Tension between the community and the state rose high on the occasion of the funeral of one of the victims of torture. The governor of Aleppo demanded in vain that the funeral be held at night to avoid incidents. The army and security services were deployed in the Armenian quarter where the ceremony took place.[62] The crisis of Dashnak-state relations eventually resulted in the migration of hundreds of Armenian-Syrian families to Lebanon and the position of the Dashnak party in the country was severely weakened.

Table 3.5. Armenian MPs in Syria, 1954–1961[63]

| Election/appointment year | Name of MPs | Place of election or appointment |
|---|---|---|
| 1954 | Dickran Tchradjian | Aleppo |
| 1958 (appointed) | Krikor Eblighatian | Aleppo |

## Establishing Dashnak Hegemony: The Armenians in Lebanon in the Era of Chehabism

The crisis of 1958 marked in many ways a turning point in the evolution of Armenian politics in Lebanon and in the participation of the Armenians in the Lebanese political system. A first important aspect of change involved the balance of forces within the Armenian political spectrum. Besides any conciliatory agreement, or formula, that could be employed to bring peace to the Armenian streets, the Dashnaks emerged as the substantial winners of the long confrontation between the opposing camps. In the course of the 1960s, relying on its control over the Apostolic Church and over many of the communal institutions depending on it, the Dashnak party was able to gradually establish itself as the hegemonic political force among the Armenians of Lebanon. The Armenian left, numerically weakened by repatriations to Soviet Armenia of many of their cadres and supporters, never recovered a position from which it could credibly challenge Dashnak supremacy.

Secondly, the end of the 1958 crisis coincided with a major shift in Dashnak political ideology: the party began to drop its strong anti-communist stance and significantly departed from the cold war logic that had characterized it for most of the 1950s. The shift reflected a change of leadership: at the 17th World Congress the neo-Dashnak faction was defeated, and the party's new politburo, dominated by the Lebanese diaspora, brought new perspectives.[64] The backstage details of the Dashnak's shift are perhaps still not entirely known, but the ideological turn seems to have happened in connection with a combination of factors: the rejection of an approach that had led to intra-Armenian violence and to many moderate Armenians being turned away from politics; an element of influence from the relative success of the non-aligned movement; and the emergence of new possibilities of co-operation with the USSR on the advancement of Armenian issues.[65] Whatever element was the most significant, the Dashnak ideological turn was important insofar as it contributed to a certain legitimization of the party's acquired leading role in the Lebanese diaspora and to the opening of a phase of *détente* between the Armenian parties.[66]

Thirdly, the crisis of 1958 and its aftermath marked the deepening of Armenian integration into the Lebanese political system. This was not really because the Armenian parties had participated – however marginally – in the 'national' events of 1958: their involvement in 'Lebanese' issues remained remarkably superficial, as the Dashnak's political shift reveals. Nor was it because of the consolidation of a certain tradition of co-operation of the Armenians with the Maronite right: it is true, for instance, that many young Armenians were attracted by the Kata'ib, but their number was never significant to the point that it would affect the Armenian national parties' monopolisation of the Armenian community's political life.

Rather than that, the deepening of Armenian integration lay in the fact that the Armenian parties had consolidated their understanding and mastered the rules of the Lebanese political system. In fact, the crisis of the late 1950s was perhaps the final episode of a process in which the Armenian parties, and particularly the Dashnak and the Hunchak parties, established themselves as new urban *zu'ama'* (local leaders, bosses, sing. *za'im*) on the Lebanese scene. It was during the events of 1958 that the parties stepped up the territorialization of their control over the Armenian residential areas in a way that paralleled that of other non-Armenian patrons. In a way, the breakdown of the state helped the Dashnaks and the Hunchaks to carve out their own 'feudal' spaces in Lebanese politics and society. Of course, the Armenian 'fiefdoms' would not be ruled by a traditional *za'im*, but by a collegial party leadership instead; however, the leadership in charge would be equally able to distribute patronage, intervene in business, play a mediating role within the community and with the authorities, ensure employment, and use *qabadays* (strong-arm men) to maintain security and order.[67]

The emergence of the Dashnak as the hegemonic *za'im* among the Lebanese Armenians – and of the Hunchak as a minor *za'im* – took place against the background of the mandate of President Fouad Chehab. The mandate of Chehab marked for Lebanon the beginning of a period of peace and reconciliation based on the restoration of the national pact of 1943. Externally, Chehab established Lebanon as a neutral player on the regional scene, disavowing the Eisenhower doctrine and moderately re-orienting the country towards the Nasserist camp. Internally, he successfully negotiated the closing of the institutional crisis of 1958 on the basis of the return to the power-sharing formula that had ruled the country before, a solution that was captured by the popular slogan: "no winners, no losers".[68]

In reality, the re-establishment of the consociational system under Chehab was not a mere return to the past. The old order came in a new breed; a formula that, introduced during the mandate of Chehab and continued by his political heir, President Charles Helou (1964–1970), became known as *chehabism*. At least two aspects made the Chehabist formula distinctive. First, it acknowledged the legitimacy of Muslim demands for a better representation in the administration: legislative decree No. 112 of 13 June 1959 provided for the equal division between Christians and Muslims of appointments in the public administration.[69] Secondly, the mandate of Chehab was characterized by an extension of the powers and range of activity of the state apparatus, a development that included an increased role of the bureaucracy, but also of the military, police, and security forces in Lebanese public life. It has been pointed out that the combination of these aspects was highly contradictory: on the one hand, in order to consolidate the allegiance of the different components of the Lebanese society, *chehabism* reinforced the confessional system, providing indirect support to the traditional networks of confessional and regional clienteles which controlled it. On the other, by developing a stronger central state, Chehab challenged the power of those very same networks.[70]

The position of the Armenians regarding *chehabism* reflected this ambiguity. On the one hand, the Armenian leadership remained suspicious of the state-building dimension of the regime of President Chehab, in the same way as a large part of the Lebanese traditional establishment: however beneficial for the social and economic development of the country, governmental action had the potential to undermine the community's acquired position in the system. On the other hand, however, the Armenians benefited from the re-establishment of the national consociational agreement: as the framework in which state-diversity relations were organized was confirmed, the Armenians were able to maintain their exclusive social and cultural spaces and to consolidate their communal strategies. Also, the process of national reconciliation conducted by Chehab was politically useful because it kept at bay a dangerous destabilization, neutralized external pressures on the Armenian community, and offered the Armenian parties the opportunity to disengage from local, Lebanese issues and to autonomously re-plan their strategy.

For the Dashnaks, the leading force in the Armenian camp, the tactical outcome of these considerations was a policy of support for the Chehabist governments in charge – the formal guarantor of the confessional system – and of moderate co-operation with their programme of national reform and development.[71] As a result of this choice, the parliamentary elections of 1960 saw a blatant reversal of the previous Armenian affiliations with Lebanese political forces: the Dashnaks sided with the Chehabist government and against the Chamounists. The elections, in which the Armenians were allocated five seats,[72] were characterized by success for the Dashnak party, which elected all of its four Apostolic candidates. The incumbent, Kata'ib-affiliated Catholic candidate, Joseph Chader, retained his post with the support of the Dashnaks. In the following parliamentary elections, held in 1964, the Dashnak political dominance grew even stronger: in the electoral districts of Beirut the electors were presented with no alternative to the four Dashnak-supported candidates. In the Metn district, the Armenian entrepreneur André Tabourian, presented in the strong, efficiently organised Dashnak-Kata'ib list, had no difficulty in defeating his opponent, former MP Dickran Tospat.[73]

Dashnak co-operation with Chehab was also taken into the Cabinet when, in August 1960, the Armenian MP Khatchig Babikian became Minister of State for Administrative Reform. Babikian, a Dashnak-supported independent, was a respected lawyer and an advocate of Armenian participation in the reform program of *chehabism*.[74]

**Table 6.6. Armenian MPs in Lebanon, 1960–1964**

| Election year | Name of MPs | Place of election |
| --- | --- | --- |
| 1960 | Movses Ter Kaloustian | Beirut |
| 1960 | Khatchig Babikian | Beirut |
| 1960 | Souren Khanamirian | Beirut |
| 1960 | Joseph Chader | Beirut |
| 1960 | Vartkes Chamlian | Metn |
| 1964 | Movses Ter Kaloustian | Beirut |
| 1964 | Khatchig Babikian | Beirut |
| 1964 | Souren Khanamirian | Beirut |
| 1964 | Joseph Chader | Beirut |
| 1964 | André Tabourian | Metn |

## The Ba'thist Takeover of Power and the Retreat of Armenian Participation in Syria (1961–1966)

The gap between the political fate of the Armenians in Lebanon and those in Syria had previously never been as wide as in the 1960s. While the Armenian community in Lebanon was consolidating its participation in the Lebanese consociational system, and its political leadership was assuming a role of pre-eminence among Armenian diasporas worldwide,  in Syria the political evolution of the country accelerated the forced retreat of Armenians from public life.

 The end of the union with Egypt marked for Syria the return to an independent parliamentary system. The military junta which took power in September 1961, a 'handful of conservative Damascene officers'[75] who supported the political restoration of the traditional bourgeoisie, soon called for new elections and for the drafting of a new constitution. The elections, held in December, saw the Armenian parties intent on resuming their activities and two Armenian candidates were elected in Aleppo: the Dashnak-supported Krikor Eblighatian, while the Hunchaks facilitated the election of the retired General Aram Karamanoukian.[76] However, the new regime brought only a partial recovery of Armenian political participation. Under the emergency laws in force, political parties remained officially banned. The Dashnaks, moreover, still suffered from the effects of the 'spy ring' crisis of 1961: the trial of eighteen Dashnak activists arrested under the United Arab Republic (UAR) continued until 1962, in a climate that encouraged further migration to Lebanon.[77]

Outsiders in the bourgeois regime that had replaced the UAR, the Armenians were also unconnected with the main forces of the opposition, both civilian and military. Not surprisingly, the Armenians were mere observers of the *coup d'état* that brought to power an insecure coalition of Ba'athist and Nasserist officers in March 1963. The community, not represented within those forces, remained substantially alien to the coup and to the following struggle for power that opposed the two factions. Similarly, the Armenians had no role in the following Ba'th internal struggle that led the radicals to power in 1966.

The consequences of those events, on the other hand, were far reaching, and their impact on the community was pronounced. The coup represented the closing episode of the experience of the oligarchic parliamentary republic in Syria: the events of 1963 and 1966 radically transformed the Syrian state and brought to power a 'whole new political elite of distinctly plebeian, rural lower middle class "ex-peasant" social composition'.[78] The new regime engaged in a 'revolution from above',[79] a vast program of top-down reforms of state and society. The nature and the effects of the reforms introduced by the Ba'th in the political economy, in education, in the relations between the state and civil society, will be sketched in the following sections of the present chapter. As far as political participation is concerned, under the new leadership's authoritarian rule and its radical semi-Leninist[80] version of Ba'th ideology, the country's constitutional structure was suppressed and civil freedoms were again suspended. As a result, the Armenians lost their parliamentary representatives, a situation which prevailed until 1971. The Armenians virtually disappeared from public life. The activities of the Armenian nationalist parties were strictly forbidden and could only be continued in secrecy.

## Religious Policy and the Armenians in Independent Lebanon and Syria (1946–1967)

### The Debate on the Religious Policy of the State

The question of the role and space of religion within the state, and the question of the regulation of the relations between the state and the plurality of religious communities present in the Levant formed an important dossier in the debate over the 'redefinition of the identity' of independent Lebanon and Syria that I have briefly sketched in the introduction to this chapter. For the Armenians, the determination of the religious policy of the two newly independent states was of crucial importance in defining the conditions of the continuation of their presence in the region, as the outcomes of the debate were bound to affect key aspects of their identity.

In Syria, the inherited French Mandate policy, based on state neutrality and – simultaneously – on the concession of a system of autonomies to recognised confessional communities, came under challenge soon after independence. Calls for reform originated from opposing fronts: one side, which included the Muslim Brotherhood and a number of *'ulama'* (Muslim scholars), actively supported the recognition of Islam as the religion of the state; the other side, including the communists and the radical populist parties like the Ba'th and the Syrian Socialist Nationalist Party (SSNP) of Antun Sa'adah was in favour of further secularisation of the state.[81]

The first major political confrontation between these opposing views took place on the occasion of the drafting of the constitution of 1950. The months and weeks that preceded the constituents' discussion on the issue were marked by a crescendo of mobilisation and public participation: *'ulama'* would include the question of the Islamisation of the state in their Friday sermons and distribute tracts supporting the cause; public demonstrations were organised in the streets of Damascus and Aleppo by the Muslim Brotherhood. Christians would mobilize too: in February 1950 a delegation of clergy representing the Catholic communities in Syria met with the Syrian Prime Minister presenting its position, and in July a Christian conference prepared a memorandum 'which requested that the new constitution include no mention of a special religion for the state'.[82] The draft constitution initially accepted Islam as the state religion, while declaring other 'heavenly religions' to be 'respected' and 'sacred';[83] but the constitutional debate, which lasted one week, resulted in a compromise: the recognition of Islam as the religion of the state was rejected but the formula which had characterized the constitution of 1930 – by which the head of state must be a Muslim – was retained, and Article 3 of the new constitution added that 'Islamic Law shall be the main source of legislation'.[84] This compromise formula lasted until the 1960s, when, under the secularising Ba'th regime, any explicit reference to Islamic law was eliminated from the constitution.[85]

In Lebanon, the political debate over religious policy never touched the core question of the religious neutrality of the state. The different confessional balance, with the country divided almost equally between Christians and Muslims, and the nature of the political system, could not tolerate alternative arrangements. Nevertheless, calls for reform did emerge in the 1950s and 1960s, when they focused on issues regarding personal status and family law, touching the question of the relation between the exclusive jurisdictions of the different religious communities and the jurisdiction of the state. As a general trend, and reflecting similar developments in a number of other Arab countries, the 1950s and 1960s saw a number of attempts by the state to reduce, or to regulate and supervise the areas traditionally assigned to the exclusive competence of the religious authorities. The trend originated in the context of the general modernisation of the state and the society: it represented, for instance, a response to demands for better protection of women in questions regarding personal status and children; it defended a new concept of citizenship which called for equality of treatment; it pledged to protect individuals against abuses by their own communal leadership.[86]

In general, as during the Mandate, the expansion of the role of the state in questions of personal status and family law was met with strong opposition by the religious leadership of the communities, and the Lebanese state in most cases was too weak to enforce change; as a result, little of the autonomy of the religious communities was eroded. An emblematic example of the state's failure to make substantial advances in the field of personal status was the question of the institution of civil marriage: in spite of a number of attempts, this was never achieved.[87] A good example of the uneasy relation between the state and the communal jurisdictions which concerned the Christian communities, including the Armenians, is represented by Law 2 April 1951, the most important regulatory effort on the issue of communal autonomies introduced during the second mandate of President Bishara Al-Khouri. The law reiterated the Mandate's effort to ensure the conformity of communal exclusive legislation to national Lebanese law.[88] It reconfirmed the official recognition of the religious authorities representing the communities that composed the Lebanese 'family', and required them to submit to the Ministry of Justice, within one year, codes regulating their communal jurisdictions. The Ministry would then grant its 'approval' of the codes within six months of their submission, after having verified their conformity.[89] Codes were in fact submitted, and, in some cases, the lack of conformity of parts of the codes with national legislation prevented the state from granting the approval; the impasse, however, was never resolved and communities continued to apply the unapproved codes.[90]

In Syria, under the pressure of radical secularising ideologies, and backed up by an authoritarian, stronger state apparatus, incursions of the state in the spaces traditionally reserved for the religious communities were occasionally deeper. This affected the Armenians too. Under the United Arab Republic, and after, a number of Armenian prelates were reportedly forced to leave the country, or prevented entry, on account of their alleged sympathies with Western powers.[91] More importantly, relations between the Armenian Churches and the state became strained when the government waged a campaign to suppress the autonomy of Armenian schools.[92] However, on a formal level, the general framework of the relations between state and religion was not changed and the principle of the recognition of exclusive jurisdictions for non-Muslim minorities was never abandoned. In particular, the reform of personal status law introduced in 1953, which represented an effort to rationalize and unify the existing norms, maintained a system of exceptions: Christians and Jews retained the right to apply their own specific family law regulating engagement, marriage and annulment, dowry, alimony, and fosterage.[93]

In conclusion, the debate on the redefinition of the religious policy of the state in Lebanon and Syria was conducted by different actors and under different conditions, but eventually resulted in similar outcomes: an essentially neutralist and secularist approach of the state[94] coupled with modest advances in the rationalisation and secularisation of the areas of traditional exclusivity of the religious jurisdictions. In the framework of this outcome, the Armenians could preserve valuable spaces of communal autonomy, a fact that acquired particularly important significance in Syria, where the community was forced to retreat from political participation and from other sectors of organised social life: the Armenian Churches increasingly returned to being focal points of Armenian communal activity.

## The Completion of the Re-establishment of the Armenian Churches

The framework of religious policy described in the previous paragraph played in favour of the consolidation and completion of the Armenian effort to re-establish their Churches in Lebanon and Syria. Under the existing legislation the Armenian Churches were able to expand their networks of religious institutions. The construction of Armenian churches accompanied the development of Armenian residential areas in the major cities of Lebanon and Syria and completed a process that had started in the 1930s; in Lebanon, the Catholicosate of Cilicia constructed the Patriarcal residence of Bikfaya, in a building complex that included the new theological seminary and the church of the Mother of God (1952).[95]

More problematic was the development of the internal organization of the Apostolic Church, mostly on account of the bitter political divide between the Dashnak party and its rivals which had culminated in the struggle for the Catholicosate of Cilicia at the end of the 1950s. In spite of the intra-Armenian political *détente* that intervened in the course of the 1960s, the deep rifts in the community did not disappear: Armenian churches continued to be divided on the basis of the new political geography of the community. In Beirut, churches in the quarters of Nor Hadjin, Khalil Badawi and Nahr continued to be pro-Hunchak, those in Bourj Hammoud generally pro-Dashnak; the Ramkavars found themselves rallying around the church of St. Nishan, next to the Serail. In Damascus, the church and prelacy of Bab Touma continued to be pro-Hunchak and to consider itself under the jurisdiction of Etchmiadzin rather than Antelias.

## Armenian Education in Independent Lebanon and Syria (1946–1967)

### *The Development and Consolidation of the Armenian Educational System in Lebanon*

In the early years of Lebanese and Syrian independence the effort of reconstruction of a system of Armenian schools was well under way. The provision of basic Armenian primary education to the community, both in the major centres and in the villages where Armenians had settled, was arguably an achieved result. Schools and kindergartens, together with churches, were becoming part of the urban landscape of the new Armenian quarters that were under construction at the periphery of Aleppo and Beirut; the number of schools, pupils and teachers was rising, reflecting the community's demographic growth and the slow but generally steady improvement of its material conditions.

Nevertheless, much had to be done. In the course of the 1950s, many Armenian schools still had to cope with inadequate, unhealthy premises: in 1958 about one in every six Armenian elementary schools in Lebanon was hosted in tin-roofed barracks and most of them had insufficient space for classrooms, play-grounds and services.[96] The quality of teaching was also generally poor: a study conducted by the Calouste Gulbenkian Foundation in Syria in the school year 1958–1959 showed that more than 40 per cent of the Armenian teachers had only received elementary education.[97] Secondary education institutions, furthermore, were highly insufficient for the increasing demands of the community.

The task of completing and consolidating the development of the Armenian educational system had to be carried out in the context of the new independent states and of the national educational policies introduced by their governments. In Lebanon, the regulatory framework in which schools operated continued to provide the Armenians with the opportunity to develop their autonomous educational system and pursue their strategy of cultural preservation. The post-independence educational policy of the Lebanese state continued to be structured on the principles expressed in the 1926 constitution: the regime of substantial freedom that the state had traditionally granted to confessional communities in matters regarding schools was not altered. At the same time, the consociational nature of the political system led the government to renounce its development of the public educational system as an instrument of state building: contrary to the prevailing trend in the Middle East, the bigger share of the educational needs of the country continued to be catered for by the private sector and – even if it is true that public education did expand – the role of the Ministry of Education remained more that of bridging the gaps left by the communities than offering alternative educational options.[98]

The main pieces of legislation relevant to Armenian schools in Lebanon were the Ministerial Decree 1436 of 1950, which regulated the sector of private education, and the Law of 15 June 1956 (*Tandhim al-hayah al-ta'allimiyyah fi al ma'ahid al khassah*), which set rules for the teaching bodies. With the exception of prescriptions regarding the teaching of the history of Lebanon and of the Arab world, the law merely established forms of moderate state supervision over private schools, mostly in order to offer protection to citizens from unscrupulous and under-qualified principals and to guarantee a certain quality of education.[99]

Taking full advantage of this framework, Armenian education developed remarkably throughout the 1950s and 1960s. A first dimension of development consisted in the slow but steady improvement of the material conditions of the schools, through the efforts of the local community and donations from organizations of the Armenian diaspora. In 1951, following a visit to the region, the US branch of the Armenian General Benevolent Union (AGBU) organized a fund-raising campaign to support Armenian schools; by the summer of 1953, with nearly $250,000 collected, AGBU was allocating funds for the replacement of old buildings.[100]

Secondly, the system expanded to cover secondary and higher education, ideally bringing the process of re-foundation of Armenian education in Lebanon to a completion. Secondary schools grew in number and attendance: by 1958, fifteen Armenian schools, out of a total of sixty-three, were offering different types of secondary courses. Besides these, the establishment of a small number of institutions offering higher education degrees had a special significance for the depth they lent to Armenian culture in the region. The first to be established, and in many respects the most notable of these, was Haigazian University. Haigazian College – in its initial denomination – was founded in Beirut in 1955 through the joint effort of the Armenian Missionary Association of America (an Armenian Evangelical diaspora institution) and the Armenian Evangelical Union of the Near East.[101] In the absence of state legislation regulating the sector of higher education, Haigazian College opened and registered with the Lebanese Ministry of Education as a high school, but *de facto* operated undisturbed as an American-styled 'Junior College', teaching students up to the *sophomore* level: students were then able to join the final year courses of foreign universities in the country, such as the American University of Beirut or the Université Saint-Joseph.[102] As for the contents of the courses, the Haigazian College was able to enjoy the virtually complete freedom granted by Lebanese legislation on private education. Subjects of instruction, which originally focused on Armenology and Armenian religious studies, developed through the years to cover a wide range of non Armenian-specific topics. When, in 1961, the Lebanese government adopted legislation regulating higher education, Haigazian was rapidly able to obtain recognition as an institution of 'higher learning' and, in 1966, the Lebanese government recognized Haigazian's Bachelor degrees as equivalent to the Lebanese *Licence*.[103] Other higher education institutions included the Dashnak/Hamazkayin-organized Palandjian College and the Hussissian College, the latter being the result of AGBU efforts; a chair of Armenology was also activated at the Université Saint-Joseph.[104]

The establishment of higher education institutions became functional to a third, important dimension of the development of Armenian education: the improvement of the quality of teaching. The new generations of Armenian teachers would receive technical instruction and would hold certificates that qualified them to teach in Armenian schools.

The main agents of the process of expansion and consolidation of the Armenian educational system were the Armenian Churches, the political parties and a number of Armenian associations. The Churches undoubtedly played the main role: each of the three Churches organized and managed a network of schools through an independent board of education in which both clerics and laity would be represented. Parties would also establish and run their own institutions, while – among the associations – the AGBU soon emerged as the most important player. The following table provides a snapshot of the situation of Armenian education in Lebanon in the school year 1952–1953.

**Table 3.7. Number of Armenian schools in Lebanon by affiliation, 1952–1953**[105]

| School affiliation | Number of schools |
| --- | --- |
| Armenian Apostolic Church* | 25 |
| Armenian Catholic Church** | 14 |
| Armenian Evangelical Church | 12 |
| AGBU | 2 |
| (Dashnak party) | 1 |
| (Hunchak party) | 1 |
| (Ramkavar party) | 1 |
| Church of the Brethren | 1 |
| Adventist Church | 1 |
| School for the Blind | 1 |
| Birds' Nest Danish orphanage | 1 |
| Total | 60 |

\* The figure includes one seminary
\*\* The figure includes four seminaries

The political polarization of Armenian Lebanese society during the 1950s had an impact on the schools too. Schools, like churches, became identified with one or the other side and sometimes were the object of tensions and controversies, particularly after the Dashnak party extended its influence on the Apostolic Church. Armenian families were often caught in a logic of 'bloc affiliation': an ideal Dashnak-leaning family would live on the Bourj Hammoud side of the Armenian areas, send children to a Dashnak-friendly school, attend a Dashnak-friendly church, read a Dashnak newspaper, support the Homenetmen sports club, attend Hamazkayin cultural events, etc. Hunchak families would affiliate with their own sets of institutions, and so on. In this framework, the AGBU schools and social institutions, that many described as Ramkavar leaning, were perceived by others as offering a form of affiliation alternative to the political parties.

Arguably, the most important question that the Armenian leadership had to debate with regard to the schools was that of the curricula and of the relation between the teaching choices of the Armenian educators and the realities and needs of the new generations of Armenians having to live their lives in Lebanon. Again, the Lebanese regulatory framework left the Armenians remarkably free to decide what to teach in their schools. This meant that, if they were prepared to renounce obtaining Lebanese officially recognized diplomas, school boards had the freedom, for example, to teach the entire curriculum in Armenian.

Indeed, even in 1960 a number of Armenian elementary schools taught all, or most subjects in Armenian.[106] However, in the course of the 1950s and 1960s, the Armenian educational leadership increasingly made efforts to adapt programs to the national standard curricula, so that Armenian students could develop a sense of belonging to their 'second motherland' or – more practically – could obtain recognized diplomas, crucial for gaining access to universities and careers. In an interview given in 1971, a member of the Armenian Apostolic Education Commission, observed that:

> *Au début, l'enseignement de l'arabe n'avait pas, dans nos écoles, toute l'importance qu'il y a de nos jours. Ce n'est en effet qu'à partir de 1950 qu'une prise de conscience s'est opérée. Les programmes officiels libanais ont remplacé les anciens programmes qui étaient conçus dans une optique différente et les efforts des dirigeants se sont de plus en plus orientés dans ce sens.*[107]

He also reflected that:

> *Les jeunes se mêlent de plus en plus à leur camarades libanais et c'est une chose excellente [...]. Mais s'intégrer ne veut pas dire que l'on cesse d'être arménien. L'enseignent et le développement de la culture arménienne restent donc essentiels et les efforts que nous faisons pour améliorer nos instruments de formation et de culture ne peuvent s'affaiblir. Les Arméniens ont besoin d'être eux-mêmes pour être libanais ; le Liban ne pourra d'ailleurs qu'y gagner en richesse.*[108]

These passages suggest that through the 1950s and 1960s a change of perspective on the role of Armenian education had matured. The whole educational project of the Armenian schools was not simply that of preserving (or developing) Armenian culture any more, and not even that of providing the new Armenian generations with the mere survival tools to live in the diaspora, but had grown more ambitious: it was about preparing a new generation to be Armenian and Lebanese at the same time. In practical terms, this involved the adoption of the national Lebanese curricula and their integration with a selection of Armenian subjects, a solution that placed a heavy burden on Armenian pupils, as they had to attend a number of extra classes compared to their Arab Lebanese colleagues.

## The Crisis of Armenian Education in Syria

The development of Armenian education in Syria was remarkably different, mostly on account of the different evolution of the state and of its educational policy. Contrary to what happened in Lebanon, the Syrian state soon assumed a leading role in education. The Syrian constitution adopted in 1950 placed a significant emphasis on the duty of the government to provide education and on the importance of education as a tool of national social and economic progress. The constitution proclaimed the right to education for all citizens; elementary education was made compulsory and the government undertook the task of giving 'priority in the budget for the spread and expansion of elementary, rural, and professional education'.[109]

Public education was also assigned the task of contributing to building national cohesion under the flag of Arab identity. Article 28 of the constitution defined the aims of national education as 'the creation of a generation strong in body and mind, full of faith in God, endowed with moral virtues, proud in the Arab heritages, equipped with knowledge, aware of its duties and obligations, working for the general welfare, imbued with the spirit of collaboration and fraternity among all citizens'.[110]

The appearance of Arabism as one of the components of Syrian identity that schools must help to forge was culturally rooted in an Arab nationalist tradition that had solid bases in Syria. In particular, the organization of the national educational system of post-independence Syria was deeply influenced by the ideas of Sati' Al-Husri. In sixteen reports written between March and July 1944, when he was working for the government as an advisor, Al-Husri had condemned the French-styled educational policies of the Mandate as 'attempts to isolate Syria from the mainstream of Arab nationalism through the imposition of French language and culture' and had urged 'the complete Arabization of the educational system'.[111]

In policy terms, these principles were specified in the sense of an increased role of the state in the supervision of all levels and types of educational institutions through a governmental Board of Education.[112] In particular, all elementary schools had to follow a curriculum determined by the Government. This had an important consequence for Armenian schools: while in Lebanon schools were left alone in deciding what to teach and in what language to teach it, in Syria the Ministry of Education prescribed programs to the private schools.

The question of the curricula did not represent the sole area of interference of the government in Armenian schools. During the last phase of the leadership of Adib Shishakli, the schools were affected by the regime's hostility towards minorities, religious leadership and foreigners: support for Armenian schools from the international Armenian diaspora became subject to governmental control.[113]

However, in spite of these limitations and of other occasional crises, Armenian education remained fully functional throughout the 1950s and the early 1960s. As far as curricula were concerned, the Syrian authorities did take into account the special needs of Armenian students and included hours of Armenian language and culture in the programs prescribed to Armenian private schools. The following table suggests that – albeit in the framework of an imposed schedule – the accommodation of the cultural needs of the Armenians was, in the academic year 1960–61, remarkably generous. The combination of the Arab Syrian curriculum with Armenian subjects was, in conclusion, similar to the solution adopted, voluntarily, by school boards in Lebanon.

**Table 3.8. Subjects taught and respective weekly periods in Armenian elementary schools, Syria, 1960–1961**[114]

| Subjects taught | 1st class | 2nd class | 3rd class | 4th class | 5th class | 6th class |
|---|---|---|---|---|---|---|
| Arabic language | 12 | 11 | 10 | 10 | 8 | 8 |
| Arithmetic (Arabic) | 3 | 3 | 3 | 5 | 5 | 5 |
| Social sciences (Arabic) | – | – | 1 | 2 | 5 | 5 |
| Science (Arabic) | 1 | 1 | 1 | 3 | 3 | 3 |
| English | – | – | – | 3 | 3 | 3 |
| Singing | 2 | 2 | 2 | 1 | 1 | 1 |
| Drawing & handicrafts | 4 | 4 | 4 | 3 | 3 | 3 |
| Physical training | 2 | 2 | 2 | 2 | 2 | 2 |
| Armenian language | 8 | 9 | 9 | 8 | 7 | 7 |
| Arithmetic (Armenian) | 3 | 3 | 3 | – | – | – |
| Science (Armenian) | 1 | 1 | 1 | – | – | – |
| Armenian Religion | 2 | 2 | 2 | 3 | 3 | 3 |
| *Total periods per week* | 38 | 38 | 38 | 40 | 40 | 40 |

At the same time, governmental control and interference did not result in the interruption of the international diaspora's support for Armenian schools in Syria, nor did it disrupt the community's effort to expand and consolidate the existing network of schools. Considerable resources, raised through AGBU and donated by the Gulbenkian Foundation, were spent in Syria for the construction of new schools, for the purchase of buildings or for repairing and extending existing ones.[115] The following tables, based on a report by the Gulbenkian Foundation, offer a glimpse of the network of Armenian schools in Syria at the end of the 1950s.

Table 3.9. Armenian schools, students and teachers in Armenian schools, by religious denomination, Syria, 1958–1959[116]

| School religious denomination | No. of schools | No. of students | No. of teachers |
| --- | --- | --- | --- |
| Armenian Apostolic | 41 | 8,734 | 531 |
| Armenian Catholic | 15 | 5,744 | 231 |
| Armenian Evangelical | 12 | 1,456 | 104 |
| Total | 68 | 15,934 | 866 |

Table 3.10. Geographical distribution of Armenian schools in Syria, 1958–1959[117]

| Location | No. of schools | No. of students | No. of teachers |
| --- | --- | --- | --- |
| Aleppo | 29 | 11,263 | 559 |
| Damascus | 7 | 1,113 | 74 |
| Latakia | 1 | 187 | 12 |
| Homs | 1 | 124 | 8 |
| Kessab | 3 | 240 | 25 |
| Karadouran | 3 | 82 | 7 |
| Koerkune | 1 | 24 | 3 |
| Ekiz Olouk | 1 | 10 | 1 |
| Baghjaghaz | 1 | 6 | 1 |
| Ayn el-'Arab | 2 | 253 | 15 |
| Derik | 1 | 85 | 3 |
| Qamishli | 3 | 1,764 | 78 |
| Amouda | 1 | 41 | 4 |
| Hasakeh | 2 | 628 | 20 |
| Derbesie | 3 | 215 | 16 |
| Ras el-'Ayn | 1 | 84 | 5 |
| Afrin | 1 | 15 | 2 |
| Yacoubieh | 1 | 50 | 5 |
| Azaz | 1 | 62 | 5 |
| Tel Abiad | 1 | 110 | 4 |
| Raqqa | 1 | 135 | 7 |
| Deir ez-Zor | 1 | 30 | 3 |
| Jarablus | 2 | 163 | 9 |

It was not until the mid 1960s that the turbulent political evolution of Syria severely affected Armenian education. The radicalization of pan-Arab discourse in the Middle East and within the political forces which gained control of Syria had a substantial impact on the educational policies of the state. The question of the role and importance of the Arabic language in national education became an important issue in the debate over the state. In the context of post-UAR Syria the main contenders for power, the Ba'th and the Nasserists shared the view that 'Arabic [was] the principal centripetal force of Arab unity capable of countering the centrifugal power of the territorial state';[118] Article 9 of the so-called constitution of the Ba'th party of 1962 declared that the 'official language of the [projected Arab] state, as well as that of all the citizens, is Arabic'. The article further added that Arabic 'alone is recognized in correspondence and in teaching'.[119] These principles assumed a crucial importance after the Ba'th seizure of power in 1963. The 6th National Congress of the Ba'th party (5–23 October 1963) marked a shift in the party's ideology towards more radical socialist doctrines; within that framework, education was called to play a role in empowering people to participate in a program of revolutionary transformation of the social order.[120]

In 1965, in the context of an open state policy of Arabization, the authorities decreed that Armenian schools should abandon their Armenian names and adopt Arab names instead.[121] The following table reports a few examples of name changes.

**Table 3.11. Names of five Armenian schools in Aleppo, before and after 1965**

| Original school name | New school name |
| --- | --- |
| Sahaghian | Dar As-Salam |
| Haigazian | Al-Amjad |
| Zavarian | Dijleh |
| Gulbenkian | As-Sharq |
| Mesropian | Bethlehem |

The events affecting Armenian education took a dramatic turn following the Syrian defeat in the Arab-Israeli conflict of 1967. The 9th National Congress of the Ba'th party, which opened in Damascus on 4 September 1967, called for the 'mobilization of all resources' and for armed resistance to liberate the occupied territories.[122] Schools were included in the 'mobilization' plans and a decree issued on September 9, 1967 established that 'all contracts between proprietors of private schools and their teachers and administrative personnel would be annulled and that management of the private schools be transferred from the owners to the Ministry of Education'.[123] On the basis of the decree, the Armenian community would have lost control over its schools and the teaching of Armenian language and culture in the country would have been discontinued.

The seizure of schools was met by opposition from the owners of private schools, in particular when Churches were involved. On September 18, 'fifteen leading Christian clergymen notified the government that schools operated by their organizations would not open unless the government repealed the September 9 decree'.[124] During the following days and weeks, in a series of meetings between representatives of all the Christian communities concerned, a rift began to emerge. Part of the Christian religious leadership, including the Armenian Catholic bishop and the Roman Catholic apostolic delegate, maintained its resolute refusal to bow to the governmental diktat. Another part, including the Armenian Apostolic representative, was willing to seek some form of compromise with the government. As far as the Armenian Apostolic schools were concerned, a solution to the crisis was negotiated in October between the Minister of Education and Judge Krikor Eblighatian, representing the Apostolic Prelate.[125] The compromise was a hard blow for Armenian educational autonomy: the curriculum restricted the number of periods that could be dedicated to non-Arab subjects to a mere 3 weekly periods for 'religion' and 4 weekly periods for 'language of the religion'. Furthermore, the schools would be presided over by a government-appointed director. On the other hand, the compromise rescued a certain autonomy in the internal management of the schools: a new figure, the 'representative of the ownership' would act as the executive and didactic director of the school, with the governmental appointee limiting its role to supervision over the application of the national curriculum. The control of the budget and of the admission policy would remain in the hands of the Armenian community, represented by its religious leadership. The compromise reached by the Apostolic community later became a model for the other Armenian schools: these too managed to avoid the brutal takeover of the premises and interruption of the activities that was suffered by other, 'hardline' Christian communities.[126]

## Armenian Cultural Production between Flourishing and Decline: The 1950s and the 1960s

### Armenian Literature, Publishing, and Media

The publication and distribution of books, newspapers and periodicals represented the dimension of Lebanese and Syrian cultural production which most directly reflected the different political evolution of the two states after independence. During the 1950s and 1960s Lebanon emerged as a culturally liberal model of modernity in the Arab world; its economic prosperity, laissez-faire economic policy and remarkable freedom of expression were at the origin of the emergence of Beirut as the 'Mecca' of the publishing industry in the entire Middle East and as a rare haven for a comparatively free media and literary life.[127] By the end of the 1940s Lebanon already published some 39 dailies and an overall 137 titles of periodicals in three languages;[128] the reform of the law regulating the press, in October 1952, further extended the bases of freedom of expression. In 1956 the first book fair in the Arab world was held in Beirut and, by 1962, as many as 95 publishers and 251 printing presses were officially registered in the country.[129] A number of Arab authors, leaving Palestine or the authoritarian regimes that were emerging in Egypt, Syria and Iraq, found refuge in Beirut, contributing to the vitality of its intellectual life. Syria, by contrast, became increasingly inhospitable for many of its intellectuals. Strict limitations on the freedom of opinion and press accompanied the frequent regime changes of the 1950s and 1960s. Newspapers and periodicals suffered from numerous closures as the control of public information and the suppression of dissent became an important part of the strategy of any force bidding for the political leadership of the country.

The different evolution of the state's cultural and information policy in Lebanon and Syria had a tremendous impact on Armenian cultural life and contributed to its development in the two countries along two separate courses. For the Armenian diasporas of the region, and beyond, Beirut became a flourishing cultural hub, a safe haven for Armenian media, literature, theatre, music, and plastic arts. On the contrary, the limitations imposed on cultural exchanges and the frequent restrictions on freedom of expression in Syria encouraged the migration of Armenian intellectuals and artists (in large part towards Beirut) and indirectly triggered a process of gradual decline of Armenian cultural production in the country.

As far as the literary scene is concerned, the second half of the 1940s and the early 1950s saw the rapid transfer of a whole generation of prominent Armenian authors from Aleppo to Beirut. With a few exceptions,[130] most of the leading figures of Syrian Armenian literary circles moved to Lebanon: Antranik Zaroukian, Vahe Vahian, Simon Simonian, Zareh Melkonian, Karnig Attarian, all resettled in Beirut, taking with them the crème of the Armenian Aleppine literary movement of the time. Zaroukian and Vahian, in particular, transferred to Lebanon the influential literary periodicals that they had edited in Syria: *Nairi* and *Ani*. These two periodicals, later joined by Simonian's *Spurk* and by *Pakin*, became the focus of Armenian literary and intellectual life in the region throughout the 1950s, 1960s and beyond.[131] The literary circles of Beirut, enriched by the contributions of the Syrian Armenian authors, continued their reflections on the theme of the Genocide, of its persisting consequences on the survivors, and on their shattered material lives and identities. In 1955 Zaroukian published a successful account of his personal experience as an orphan child-refugee in *Des Hommes sans Enfance*.[132] At the same time, the publication of *Spurk* (Diaspora), in 1959, anticipated, and perhaps contributed to a process of rethinking of the Armenian experience in the Levant, marking a shift from the idea of the Armenian communities as nations in exile to a new conception of them as 'permanent' transnational diasporas.[133]

If certain Syrian Armenian publications, like *Nairi* and *Ani* could be relocated to Beirut, a far larger number were simply discontinued over the years. By 1955, when as many as twenty-five periodicals were published in Beirut, in Syria there was less than half that amount.[134] Particularly significant for the Armenians of Syria was the loss, one after the other, of their daily political newspapers. *Yeprad*, the paper that represented the interests of the Ramkavar and the Armenian Aleppine liberal upper class, fell victim to intra-Armenian political violence: its director was attacked on November 29, 1947 and the premises of the newspaper burnt down by alleged Dashnak activists.[135] *Suria*, an independent (and later Hunchak/Ramkavar-supported) daily founded in 1946, discontinued publication in 1960. Finally, *Arevelk*, the Dashnak daily, was abruptly closed in March 1963, when the Ba'th revolution suppressed all existing newspapers. By 1965 only a handful of Armenian publications survived in Syria, while the number of titles published in Lebanon had climbed to fourty-four, including four daily papers.[136] Of the several Armenian printing presses that had been established in Syria during the mandate, only *Ani* and *Yeirikian* survived, sharing the market with a few smaller presses. On the contrary, the Armenian Lebanese industry prospered, taking advantage of the growing Armenian population and winning a share of the Lebanese and Arab market.[137]

## The Âge d'Or *of the Armenian Lebanese Theatre*

The 1940s and 1950s marked a turning point in the quality of Armenian theatre in the Levant and prepared the ground for the opening of a very prolific era which lasted until the breakout of the civil war in 1975. In Beirut, the arrival of Kaspar Ipekian brought a new impetus to the Armenian theatrical movement. Ipekian, who took charge of the Hamazkayin troupe, brought professionalism, fresh ideas, and connections with theatrical circles and traditions abroad. Under the direction of Ipekian and of his successor George Sarkissian, the Hamazkayin group started offering to the Armenian public the plays of Levon Shant, but also the high-culture tradition of European theatre, including plays by authors like Chekhov, Ibsen and Miller, all of which were translated into Armenian.[138] In Aleppo a similar approach was attempted by Vartan Bariguian and his group. Bariguian, the director of the Hunchak-Nor Serount theatrical troupe Antranik, would stage a selection of classics of Armenian theatre, like the national saga *Vartanank*,[139] but also works by Shakespeare (*Hamlet, Othello*), Goldoni and others, drawing on the translated repertoire of the Armenian theatre in Istanbul.[140]

These developments placed Armenian theatre among the *avant-garde* in Lebanon and Syria: while Armenian troupes in Beirut and Aleppo were staging Ibsen or Shakespeare, Arab Lebanese and Syrian theatre was still in its infancy. It is true in fact that, at least in Beirut, there had been experiments with classic Western theatre since the mid nineteenth century; however these had remained inconsistent, and until the 1950s the Arab public was only offered rather trivial, if not dubious shows that combined Arab songs or belly-dancing with single-act improvisations.[141]

By the end of the 1950s, Armenian high-quality theatre in Lebanon had become more diversified, developing – as had happened with schools and associations – along the lines of traditional Armenian political divisions. The arrival, in 1951, of the actor and director Berge Fazlian enriched the scene with a prominent, emerging figure. Fazlian, an openly leftist artist educated in Istanbul, worked with the Armenian communist Literary Circle and then formed in 1958 the AGBU theatrical group Varant Papazian. Competition between the two more professional Armenian groups on the scene, the Kaspar Ipekian (Dashnak-Hamazkayin) and the Varant Papazian (AGBU), had a positive impact on the quality and depth of the movement; by the early 1960s Armenian troupes were able to deepen their exposure to the most advanced international theatre, and other groups were formed. Some figures undertook periods of study and tours abroad: Varoujian Hadeshian and Krikor Satamian studied in London, Zohrab Yacoubian in the United States, while a number of others took courses in Armenia; some formed their own groups upon their return to Lebanon.[142]

The successful Armenian Lebanese theatre of the 1960s also deserves credit for having contributed to boosting the rapidly emerging Lebanese Arab theatrical movement: media and intellectuals became acquainted with the until then neglected Armenian Lebanese theatre, and Armenian professionals started teaching at the newly established Académie d'Art Dramatique or other, university-based drama schools. These developments offered, in turn, new opportunities: Berge Fazlian became the first Armenian artist to become involved in a major Arab Lebanese production, as he was called to a collaboration with the Rahbani brothers and to work side to side with the star singer Fairouz. In 1962, in the framework of the Festival des Cèdres, he staged *Biya' al-Khawatem* (The ring seller), a would-be classic of Lebanese popular culture. In the same year, Fazlian initiated a collaboration with Antoine Moultaqa, one of the leaders of the new Arab Lebanese theatre, and staged Shakespeare's *Comedy of Errors*, which he set in a 'thousand and one nights' atmosphere.[143]

In Syria, Armenian theatre never reached the peaks of the Lebanese movement. In a cultural environment generally less open to foreign influences and dominated, particularly after 1967, by the state as a cultural producer and patron, Armenian theatre could make no exception. Damaged, since the 1950s, by the migration of Armenian Aleppine intellectuals to Lebanon or Western countries, Armenian theatre gradually declined and lost its position of local pre-eminence in favour of the Syrian national theatre, created at the beginning of the 1960s.

## The Flourishing of Armenian Figurative Arts in Lebanon

The development, since the late 1940s, of a tradition of Armenian figurative arts in Lebanon filled a gap in the reconstruction of an Armenian cultural world in the country and enriched the image of Beirut as a hub of Armenian culture in the diaspora.

In painting, the Armenian-Lebanese artistic movement arguably began with the arrival in Beirut of a young, Jerusalem-born son of refugees: Paul Guiragossian. Initially self-taught, and then artistically educated in Italy, Guiragossian managed to elaborate a personal style that drew inspiration from the European tradition of authors like Goya, Daumier, Van Gogh but also from the Oriental tradition of Mesopotamia, Egypt, Byzantium and Armenia, and rapidly imposed himself as one of the most promising artists on the Lebanese scene. Life in the Armenian camps and quarters (*Baraque, camp Amanos*, 1948; *Funerailles à Bourj Hammoud*, 1948; *L'Eglise St. Joseph, Bourj Hammoud*, 1949), the 1915 deportations and his own family life (*Juliette et Mano*, 1955; *La famille*, 1957), were the main themes of his work, all bound together by the experience of the Genocide.[144]

In sculpture, the talent of Zaven Hadeshian stood out. Born in Beirut in 1932 from a refugee family, he was educated in Paris at the Ecole Supérieure des Beaux Arts. The author of a conspicuous statue erected in Bikfaya to commemorate the Genocide, 'Zaven' partially drew his inspiration from classical and Phoenician mythology.[145]

Together with Guiragossian and Zaven, a thriving generation of artists came to animate the cultural scene of Armenian figurative arts in Beirut in the 1950s and 1960s. This included Armenian Lebanese authors like Haroutioun Torossian, Sophie Yeramian, Guv, Rosevart Sisserian, Shart, Dickran Dadrian, Toros Der Agopian and Lucy Tutundjian; but also Armenian painters from other diasporas, including the Aleppine Karzo and Galents. The Armenian figurative movement had a strong influence on Lebanese arts, particularly as the elite of the Armenian movement started to teach in the local universities and art schools.

# Armenian Associations and the State in Lebanon and Syria from Independence to the 1960s

## Developing Armenian Self-Help

By the time Lebanon and Syria obtained full independence in 1946, the network of Armenian associations established during the Mandate was going through a phase of transformation and expansion. As the Armenians were slowly but steadily improving their living conditions, the associations could increasingly shift their focus from the provision of emergency relief towards longer term, community development activities, and cover other areas of social life. During the first decades of independence the role of the associations and their presence within the social fabric of the Armenian communities developed steadily, to the point that they would become part of the daily life of most Armenian families, be it because of involvement in social welfare schemes or because of participation in sports, scouts or cultural events.

Among the associations, patriotic unions remained important structures of self-help, socialization and cultural preservation. Their role was initially important in the continuing effort to solve the problem of housing. In Lebanon, the resettlement of the Armenians from the refugee camps and the provision of proper housing had started in the second half of the 1920s and the 1930s, but the construction of new Armenian residential areas was only achieved in the following two decades, particularly as new immigrants moved in from Alexandretta and the Jabal Mousa, from Palestine, and from Syria. In the 1950s and until the 1960s a significant number of Armenian families was still living in refugee shacks in the area of Karantina or in the so-called Sanjak and Charchabouk camps.[146] Some of the patriotic unions were also involved in education and managed to run a school and a program of cultural activities.[147]

Armenian political parties, for their part, confirmed their leading role in organising and running associations in the framework of a strategy to promote their values, develop tools for the mobilization of the society, and enlarge their base of support. During the 1940s and 1950s, and as a dimension of their political confrontation, the parties significantly intensified efforts to obtain the control of Armenian social spaces and institutions; their competing, all-embracing networks including schools, sports and recreational clubs, cultural associations, media, and so on, were expanded and reinforced. The Dashnak party, in particular, increasingly extended its influence on the institutions co-ordinated by the Apostolic Church, notably through the control of appointments to the institutions' boards.

The politicization of social spaces, however, was far from complete. The networks of social institutions related to the Catholic and Evangelical

Churches, for instance, were in fact to a large extent able to preserve their autonomy from the parties' influence, and could provide the community – or at least part of it – with alternative opportunities of socialisation. So also was the case with a number of transnational organisations of the Armenian diaspora which ran projects and associations in Lebanon and Syria. These included in particular the Howard Karagheusian Commemorative Corporation (HKCC), the Jinishian Memorial Program, and the Calouste Gulbenkian Foundation. These organisations, whose head offices and boards in the United States and Portugal could provide substantial amounts of funding, played a crucial role in the development of medical care, family and child care and education. A position of autonomy also characterised the AGBU, although many of its members were considered to be close to the Ramkavar party.

The following table, which is limited to Lebanon, presents an overview of the main associations and organisations running activities among the Armenian community by the second half of the 1960s. Although it is non exhaustive, it should offer a view of the variety of actors which were involved in the Armenian NGO scene of the time.

Table 3.12. Armenian associations in Lebanon and areas of activity, late 1960s[148]

| Association(s) | Affiliation | Notes |
|---|---|---|
| Adana, Aintab, Amanos, Berejik, Hadjin, Kilis, Konia, Malatia, Marash, Ourfa, Sassoun, Tigranakert, etc.[149] | Independent patriotic unions | Housing improvement support, scholarships, school support, food and clothes distribution, regional cultural preservation, income generating projects; some had transnational structure |
| Armenian Relief Cross | Party-affiliated | Dashnak 'social arm'; medical services, community development |
| Hamazkayin | Party-affiliated | Dashnak 'cultural arm'; cultural events, publishing, education, arts promotion |
| Homenetmen | Party-affiliated | Dashnak athletic club |
| Zavarian | Party-affiliated | Dashnak student association |

| | | |
|---|---|---|
| **Homenmen** | Party-affiliated | Hunchak athletic club |
| **Dekhrouni** | Party-affiliated | Hunchak student association |
| **Nor Serount** | Party-affiliated | Hunchak 'cultural arm'; cultural events, publishing, education, arts promotion |
| **Armenian Educational Benevolent Union** | Party-affiliated | Hunchak 'social arm'; dispensaries, support to education |
| **Tekeyan** | Party-affiliated | Ramkavar cultural association |
| **St. Ely Beneficent Society, Association of the Holy Saviour, Society of Annunciation, Catholic** *Akhkadakhnam*, **Catholic summer camps for boys and girls, Armenian Catholic Sisters' orphanage** | Church-affiliated | Catholic charities; material and spiritual support to the destitute |
| **Apostolic** *Akhkadakhnam* | Church-affiliated | Apostolic charities; material and spiritual support to the destitute |
| **Armenian Evangelical Home and Family Committee, Armenian Evangelical Social Action Committee, Armenian Missionary Association, Trad Social Center** | Church-affiliated | Evangelical charities; material and spiritual support to the destitute; support to education |
| **Armenian National Sanatorium (Azounieh)** | Church-affiliated | Jointly supported and run by the Churches (notably, Apostolic and Evangelical) |
| **AGBU** | Independent transnational diaspora | Support to education and cultural preservation; sports club; support to the destitute |

| | | |
|---|---|---|
| **Calouste Gulbenkian Foundation** | Independent transnational diaspora | Support to education |
| **Howard Karagheusian Commemorative Corporation** | Independent transnational diaspora | Based in the USA; medical care, family and child care; support to housing projects, income-generating projects |
| **Jinishian Memorial Program** | Independent transnational diaspora | Based in the USA and connected to the US Presbyterian Church; family care, health care and counselling |
| **Philibossian Foundation** | Independent transnational diaspora | Support to education |
| **Danish Birds' Nest** | Foreign charity | Danish missionary association; education and care of orphans |
| **Hilfsbund** | Foreign charity | German evangelical charity; education, medical care, training in 'Anjar |
| **Institute for the Blind, Deaf and Mentally Retarded** | Foreign charity | Established by the Swiss Friends of the Armenians; run jointly with the Apostolic and Evangelical Churches |
| **Old peoples' home** | Foreign charity | Established by the Swiss Friends of the Armenians; run jointly with the Apostolic and Evangelical Churches |

## The Armenian Associations and the State: The Crisis of the Associations in Syria

The table presented above indicates that, by the end of the 1960s, the process of establishing a system of Armenian self-help associations in Lebanon had reached an advanced stage. The number, variety and range of activity of the associations arguably amounted to the establishment of a full system of communal self-care that, partially through competing networks and partially through co-operative efforts, was able to provide the Armenians with support in virtually all dimensions of their material and cultural well being and progress.

Such an achievement, over the span of four decades, had been facilitated by the Lebanese political and legal framework: in the absence of a strong centralised state which could lead the task of constructing a system of social services for its citizens, the Lebanese communities were not only allowed, but also expected to provide for the needs of their own confessional family. Even during the age of *chehabism*, when the state abandoned its traditional policy of maintaining budgetary surpluses and engaged in programs of development of infrastructures and national services,[150] the role of the communal system of social services and safety nets was not undermined. The legal framework in which associations operated remained that of the constitution of 1926 and although the *chehabist* administration did encourage the emergence of a new type of (non-confessional) developmental association, the principle that each community was ultimately responsible for its own 'social care' was never abandoned.[151]

In Syria, by contrast, the demise of the liberal democratic system that started in 1949 and the emergence of authoritarian regimes had a heavy impact on Armenian associations: their development suffered a number of halts, backlashes and restrictions. The Armenians were affected on two levels: on the one hand, Armenian associations were hit along with other associations in the country as part of a strategy to undermine any form of potential organised opposition; on the other, Armenians were victims of the climate of hostility towards foreign and non-Arab cultures that had pervaded the state's changing approach on education.

In 1953, under the regime of Adib Shishakli, Armenian associations suffered a first wave of restrictions: closures by decree were accompanied by new regulations aimed at preventing associations from maintaining 'all suggestion of an exclusive confessional or racial membership'.[152] As a matter of fact, Armenians abandoned the Armenian names of their associations and adopted Arab names instead: the Damascus chapter of Hamazkayin was registered with the Syrian authorities on May 20th, 1953 under the name of Jam'ayat Al-Taraqqi Al-Thaqafi;[153] the Hunchak's cultural association Nor Serount (the new generation) adopted the Arab translation of its name: Jam'ayat Al-Jil Al-Jadid; the AGBU was registered under the name of Jam'ayat Al-Khairiya Al-'Oumumiya al-Armaniya; and so on. The union with Egypt in 1958 brought further troubles to Armenian associations. The Nasserist regime repealed the Ottoman law of 1909 that had continued to regulate associations after independence; the recent Egyptian law of association of 1956 was assimilated with the Syrian Law 93 of 1958, introducing severe restrictions on the freedom of association: the Law introduced, among other things, the requirement of a highly discretional governmental authorization to establish associations, security checks on the founders, and the possibility for representatives of the government to participate in meetings. Furthermore, governmental approval was only granted when there was clear correspondence between the organisation's aims and the 'public social needs' described by a governmental plan of action.[154]

In 1963, following the Ba'th rise to power, the definition 'from above' of social needs was further radicalized and the autonomy of association increasingly limited. The new regime suppressed autonomous centres of power and engaged in organising corporatist-like mass organizations[155] entrusted with the task of creating social mobilization that could support the new leadership. Finally, in 1969, the government introduced new restrictions, reinforcing the possibility for the executive to dissolve associations, in particular when their activities were deemed to create inter-communal tensions.

It is understandable that the evolution of events sketched above resulted in a series of major setbacks for Armenian associations in Syria. However, against the odds, and making the best of a political and legal framework increasingly hostile, Armenian associations in Syria were to some extent able to survive through the crises of the 1950s and 1960s. At the cost of limiting the contents of their cultural diversity – and certainly the exterior appearance of it – the Armenian communities of Syria were able to develop a system of Armenian institutions similar, at least in its theoretical structure, to the one in Lebanon. As it will become clear later in this work, a key role in shielding the associations during the crisis was played by the Churches, which could offer some degree of protection to the community's cultural needs.

## Political Economy and the Social Position of the Armenians in Lebanon and Syria from Independence to the End of the 1960s

The material conditions and the social position of the Armenians improved slowly but steadily during the first decades of Lebanese and Syrian independence. Economic improvement arguably involved all social strata of the Armenian communities and contributed to a certain degree of upward social mobility both within Armenian society and in relation to Lebanese and Syrian society at large.

At the bottom, the destitute refugee lower class that was formed in the 1920s and 1930s gradually shrank, as working class Armenians increasingly managed to abandon employment as unskilled workers and to find more regular or better paid work opportunities. In part they moved on to offer skilled labour to a growing Armenian manufacturing sector; in part they were absorbed into an expanding Armenian middle class, the emerging driving component of Armenian economy and society.

The middle class, for its part, was characterised by what could be defined as the chief trait that marked the evolution of the socio-economic position of the Armenians for most of their experience as a community in Lebanon and Syria: the inclination to avoid involvement with government-related jobs and the ambition to seek self-employed positions as urban craftsmen, skilled artisans, repairers, retailers, importers, distributors, and so on. During the 1950s and 1960s the success of these small and medium size entrepreneurs provided the Armenians with a solid economic basis in the Lebanese and Syrian economies and contributed to reverse early negative perceptions of the community. As the Armenians established their shops and workshops in Beirut, Aleppo, Damascus, and all other major centres, they became known and respected as hard-working, reliable businessmen.

Among the areas of activity of these Armenian enterprises, two particularly continued to stand out for specialisation and excellence: the manufacture and sale of shoes and jewellery. In Lebanon, throughout the 1950s and 1960s, the production and marketing of shoes largely remained in Armenian hands: according to Keuroghlian, in 1967 more than three quarters of Lebanese shoe manufacturers employing five workers or more were owned by Armenians and employed Armenian labour. Keuroghlian went on to estimate that about half of the population of Bourj Hammoud made their living from the production and sale of shoes.[156] Jewellery seemed to be an art equally dominated by the Armenians, who could count on their Bourj Hammoud workshops and often family-connected network of retail points: Armenians were estimated to control 80 per cent of the market.[157] Other areas of activity in which Armenians acquired a certain specialization included tailoring and the trade in quality clothes, photography, the sale and repair of spectacles and watches, and the trade in carpets.

The Armenians, on the contrary, were underrepresented in the traditional middle class occupations offered by the public sector. In Lebanon, where the appointment of employees in the public sector was subject to rules of confessional proportionality, Armenians hardly filled their quotas. By 1970 Armenian public servants numbered only 132, a mere 1.26 per cent of a total of 10,445, considerably less of the community's 5 per cent share of the seats in the parliament.[158]

The most successful among Armenian middle class businessmen became large scale entrepreneurs and rose to the social status of the Armenian upper class, which also included native *Arman qadim* families, medical doctors and professionals. A number of these successful, self-made Armenian entrepreneurs were involved in the import-export trade, as in the case of the steel importer and trader Demco Steel, run by the Demirdjian family. Founded as a blacksmith workshop in Aleppo in 1922 by a refugee from Aintab, the business expanded to Lebanon in 1947 and developed into one of the largest steel companies in the country.[159] Similarly, the Ayanian firm was founded in 1928 by a young refugee from Cesarea who had been displaced to Aleppo in 1921. It pioneered the import and distribution of electrical equipment in Lebanon and in the early 1960s the firm held profitable agencies of European and Far Eastern manufacturers and, from its base in Bourj Hammoud, re-exported to the entire Arab world.[160]

Other Armenian entrepreneurs participated and contributed to the industrial development of Lebanon and Syria. Typically, small enterprises that had been founded in the 1920s or 1930s developed to an industrial size during the Second World War period of growth and further expanded in the 1950s, when a technically educated second generation was sometimes involved in the business. In Lebanon, by 1967, 260 industrial enterprises – or more than 12 per cent of all registered industrial businesses – was run by Armenians.[161] Sectors of activity of Armenian industrial entrepreneurs included, in particular, metalwork, knitwear, and tanning. A few examples could help in sketching a picture of these areas of Armenian economic activity. The Dantziguian firm, active in metalwork (metal frames, windows, gates, etc.) was founded in Beirut in 1924 by Kegham Dantziguian, a young refugee from Istanbul who had moved with his family to Aleppo during the Genocide. By the 1930s Dantziguian was able to bid for contracts with the Mandate administration; in the 1950s and 1960s – when the second generation joined the management – the firm was a solidly established business, able to introduce aluminium products into the Lebanese market and to bid for some of the largest contracts in the country, including the construction of the prestigious Hotel Phoenicia-Intercontinental.[162] The Etablissements Abroyan, producing knitwear, were founded in Lebanon in 1920; taking advantage of the block on imports during the Second World War, the firm emerged as a leading business and – by the end of the 1960s – it managed two large production plants supplying the Lebanese and Arab markets.[163] The Kassardjian Foundries, producing pipes, pipe joints, taps, sanitary fittings, and such like, were established by Ohannes Kassardjian, a self-made entrepreneur who had begun life as a simple worker at the age of twelve. Initially based in Aleppo, the firm was re-established in Beirut in 1939 with an initial workforce of about 15 persons; by 1970 it employed nearly 700 workers.[164]

A discussion of the reasons behind the general inclination of Armenians toward non-governmental, self-employed occupations (questions of cultural and linguistic barriers to access? Or of culturally-transmitted traditions, approaches to work?) falls outside the scope and possibilities of this book. What is important to note here, however, is that the Armenian approach to entrepreneurship was more at ease in the *laissez-faire*, deregulated political economy of Lebanon than in the increasingly interventionist and *dirigiste* Syria, particularly after the radical, leftward turn the country took in 1963.

Not that the Lebanese economic system after the Second World War represented an ideal economic setting for Armenian businesses. The Lebanese economic model which emerged after the Second World War was chiefly designed to bring benefits to the interests of the mercantile-financial elite of the country, with regards to which the Armenians remained outsiders. A certain specialization of the Armenians, in manufacturing most notably, was not encouraged by the turn that the political economy took after the end of the Mandate, as Lebanon became a 'service oriented open economy'.[165] The Lebanese political economy of the late 1940s and 1950s neglected industrial development: it dropped import tariffs and provided manufacturers with token assistance, only to 'placate influential industrialists or to preserve labour relations'.[166] Besides the dropping of import tariffs, many Lebanese industrialists were hit by the breakup of the customs union with Syria in 1950; these included some Armenians, like the already mentioned knitting business of Abro Abroyan and the Tchatalbachian tanneries, which lost access to important markets and had to reduce production.[167] In the long run, however, many Lebanese industrialists, including Armenian entrepreneurs, were able to react to the crisis: they increased their competitiveness and successfully reoriented their production towards exports, in spite of the constraints imposed by the overvalued Lebanese pound.

The economic conditions and the political economy in Syria were less favourable to the Armenians, particularly where industrial enterprises were concerned. If the Armenians were able to develop their traditional small urban trades (retailing, tailoring, crafts, photography, repair shops, etc.), larger businesses were affected by the drastic interventionism undertaken by the radical regimes of the 1950s and 1960s. Under the so-called 'socialist decrees', introduced by Nasser in 1961, banks, insurance companies and a number of industrial enterprises were nationalized, triggering a wave of disinvestment.[168] A few years later, under the Ba'th regime, a new wave of nationalizations took place, this time affecting a larger number of enterprises: many Armenian businesses were affected, and entrepreneurs often re-located their activities to Lebanon.[169]

It should be noted that the Ba'th 'revolution from above' was aimed at breaking the power of the traditional upper class of Syria, and thus did not chiefly, or directly affect the Armenians.[170] The economic sectors where the majority of the Armenians made their living, including retailing and small crafts, remained, for instance, under private control. The negative effects of the nationalizations on the economy, however, had an impact on smaller businesses too, and became a constraint on the economic development of the community.

# Notes

1. Based on A.H. Hourani. 1946. *Syria and Lebanon: A Political Essay*, London, New York and Toronto: Oxford University Press, Appendix B, Table II, 386. The table puts forward the following data: in Syria (figures for 1943; total population 2,860,411) 101,747 Armenian Apostolic, 16,247 Armenian Catholic, 11,187 Protestants (including Armenian Protestants); in Lebanon (figures for 1944; total population 1,126,601) 59,749 Armenian Apostolic, 10,048 Armenian Catholic, 10,440 Protestants (including Armenian Protestants); I have here accepted the view that about half of the Protestants were Armenians, see Hovannisian, R.G. 1974. 'The Ebb and Flow of the Armenian Minority in the Arab Middle East', *Middle East Journal*, 28(1), 26, footnote 20.

2. The sentence is used by Raymond Hinnebusch to describe Syria in R. Hinnebusch. 2001. *Syria: Revolution from Above*, London and New York: Routledge, 21.

3. See A. Hourani. 1976. 'Ideologies of the Mountain and the City', in R. Owen (ed.), *Essays on the Crisis in Lebanon*, London: Ithaca Press, 35.

4. Hinnebusch, *Syria: Revolution from Above*, 18–27; T. Petran. 1972. *Syria: A Modern History*, London and Tonbridge: Ernest Benn, 82–86.

5. Two names, particularly, stand out : General Aram Karamanoukian and Hrant Maloyan. 'Hrant Bek', as he was known, was an Armenian Catholic born in Istanbul in 1896. Becoming a commissioned officer in 1922, he served in the Syrian army and in the gendarmerie, and then fought with distinction against the French at the close of the Mandate. A figure highly respected for his neutrality, he rose to the position of head of the gendarmerie after independence. See P.P. Atamian. 1964. *Histoire de la Communauté Arménienne Catholique de Damas*, Beirut : Institut Patriarcal de Bzoummar, 153–157.

6. A joke is circulated in Lebanon concerning an unspecified 'first Armenian Member of the Lebanese Parliament'. The MP remains silent for several months of parliamentary activity. Never a comment, never a word. When, after nearly a year of silence, he asks the speaker of the Chamber to be given the floor everyone is astounded and freezes, ready to listen his opinions. Complete silence descends and the Armenian MP says, in a mix of Arabic and French: '*Sakkaru as-Shubbak, fi courant!*' ('Close the window, there is a draught!').

7. E. Rabbath. 1973. *La Formation Historique du Liban Politique et Constitutionnel*, Beirut: Université Libanaise, 550.

8. Ibid., 547. Contrary to a widespread opinion, the pact did not establish the confessional distribution of the offices of President of the Republic (to a Christian Maronite), President of the Council of Ministers (Sunni Muslim) and Speaker of the Chamber (Shi'a Muslim), which emerged from constitutional practice instead. However, the negotiations that led to the pact did include an agreement on the question of the renewal of political confessionalism. See, in

particular, the account of the second meeting of Aley between El-Kouri and El-Solh reported in Rabbath, *La Formation Historique*, 547.

9. Ibid.

10. Ibid., p. 550: '*il est loin d'être prouvé que les autres communautés, ou que même les masses maronites ou sunnites, aient jamais été consultées ou appelées a y acquiescer*'.

11. The Apostolic Church had been tolerated by the Soviet authorities during the 1920s but it suffered from attacks during the purges of the 1930s. See C.J. Walker. 1990. *Armenia: the Survival of a Nation*, second edition, London: Routledge, 341 and 368. Concerning the reasons at the origin of the Soviet 'repatriation' initiative, many Lebanese and Syrian Armenians believe that it was motivated by the need for labour in Soviet Armenia, particularly after the Second World War, in which Soviet Armenia was said to have lost more than 200,000 young men. Some recall that the promoters of the repatriation had suggested that a failure to reach a large number of returning migrant would result in the Soviet Armenian Republic being suppressed and its territory absorbed into one of the neighbouring Soviet Republics. Interview with Mr. Sebouh Sekayan, Mayor of the *Baladiat* Haoush Musa, 'Anjar, 25 October 2003; interview with Mr. Krikor Eblighatian, former Member of the Syrian Parliament, Aleppo, 12 November 2003.

12. *Joghovourti Tzain*, 23, 25 and 28 June 1946. Also see Z. Messerlian. 2002. 'Armenian Participation in the Lebanese Legislative Elections during the Presidency of Bishara Kouri 1943–1952', *Haigazian Armenological Review*, 22, 271–305 and 273: "[a]ll returning Armenians would automatically become Soviet citizens. Their families would get a government loan of 30,000 rubles each to construct their new houses"; also see H.K. Topouzian. 1986. *Suriayi yev Lipanani Haigagan Kaghtojiakhneri Badmoutioun 1841–1946* [History of the Armenian Communities in Syria and Lebanon 1841–1946], Yerevan: Armenian Soviet Socialist Republic's Academy of Sciences, Orientology Institute, 263.

13. T. Ter Minassian. 1997. *Colporteurs du Komintern: l'Union Soviétique et les Minorités au Moyen-Orient*, Paris: Presses de Sciences Po, 300.

14. Ibid.

15. N.B. Schahgaldian. 1979. 'The Political Integration of an Immigrant Community into a Composite Society: the Armenians in Lebanon, 1920–1974', Ph.D. dissertation. New York: Columbia University, 200–204.

16. *Arevelk*, 24 August 1946, quoted in Topouzian, *Suriayi yev Lipanani Haigagan*, 263. For Topouzian "[t]he Dashnak were doing everything they could to make the repatriation fail".

17. The pro-government list included personalities like Sami Solh, Abdullah Yafi, Hussein Oweyni, and Habib Abi Chahla.

18. Schahgaldian, 'The Political Integration', 199–200. On the incidents also see Messerlian, 'Armenian Participation', passim.

19. Ter Minassian, *Colporteurs du Komintern*, 303. Topouzian puts the figure for Lebanon and Syria at 40,000 and the overall figure for repatriation at 105,000;

see Topouzian, *Suriayi yev Lipanani Haigagan*, 263. Schahgaldian puts the figure of migrants who left Lebanon at 9,000–11,000; see Schahgaldian, 'The Political Integration', 248, note 33.

20. Ibid., 204–205.
21. Ibid., 208. Joseph Chader was the son of a refugee from Diarbekir, Antoine Chader, who had been active in the 'patriotic union' of Diarbekir. Interview with Mr. Sarkis Najarian, Beirut, 15 December 2003.
22. Sources: Messerlian, *Armenian Representation*, passim; interview with Mr. Hagop Pakradouni, Bourj Hammoud, 14 November 2002.
23. Armenian Catholic.
24. G.H. Torrey. 1964. *Syrian Politics and the Military, 1945–1958*, Columbus: Ohio State University Press, 28.
25. Article 37 of the constitution of the State of Syria, 1930.
26. Torrey, *Syrian Politics*, 89.
27. Ibid., 116, note 33.
28. Ibid., 94.
29. For instance, the Armenians had, at this stage, only a token presence in the Syrian army and security forces. The respected Armenian commander of the gendarmerie, Hrant Bek, was temporarily dismissed days after the Hinnawi coup. From 1949 many other officers of the 'old guard' formed during the Mandate were retired and substituted with young nationalists. See P. Seale. 1965. *The Struggle for Syria: A Study of Post-War Arab Politics*, Oxford, New York and Toronto: Oxford University Press, 119.
30. See G. Haddad. 1950. *Fifty Years of Modern Syria and Lebanon*, Beirut: Dar al-Hayat, 112: 'In the elections for the Syrian Constituent Assembly on November 15, 1949 the number of deputies was reduced, and the deputies were elected to represent either the Moslems or the Christians in each *mohafazat*. On a total of 114 deputies there were 100 Moslems and fourteen Christians'. The seat allocated to the Jewish community was suppressed.
31. Seale, *The Struggle for Syria*, 121.
32. The new parliament was formed by 82 deputies: 69 Muslims, 9 Christians and 4 representatives of tribes. Seale, *The Struggle for Syria*, 129.
33. Based on an interview with Judge Krikor Eblighatian, Aleppo, 12 November 2003.
34. Ibid.
35. Ibid.
36. Seale, *The Struggle for Syria*, 129.
37. Sources: M.S. As'eed. 2002. *Al-Barlaman al-Suri fi Tatawouru al-Tarikhi 1919–2001*, Damascus: Al Mada; Messerlian, *Armenian Representation*; *Tidag*, April-May 2003, 12 and 49.
38. Armenian Protestant, elected for the seat allocated to the 'minorities'.
39. Torrey, *Syrian Politics*, 116, note 33. 'Only 136 members ever sat – 117 Muslims and 19 non-Muslims'.
40. Haddad, *Fifty Years*, 112.

41. Torrey, *Syrian Politics*, 237, note 47.

42. For a perspective on how Lebanese and Syrian actors were affected by and sometimes made use of these international sources of support, see P. Seale. 1997. 'Syria', in Y. Sayigh and A. Shlaim (eds.), *The Cold War and the Middle East*, Oxford: Clarendon Press, 48–76; F. Gerges. 1997. 'Lebanon', in Y. Sayigh and A. Shlaim (eds.), *The Cold War and the Middle East*, Oxford: Clarendon Press, 77–101.

43. S.B. Dadoyan. 2003. *The Armenian Catholicosate from Cilicia to Antelias*, Antelias: Armenian Catholicosate of Cilicia, 95; also see Ter Minassian, *Les Colporteurs du Komintern*, 318, speaking of the Soviet strategy regarding the Church: '*créer par l'intermédiaire de l'Eglise une image consensuelle de l'Arménie soviétique. En même temps, il s'agit bien de réaffirmer la primauté spirituelle d'Etchmiadzin, seule garante de l'unité de l'Eglise apostolique et du peuple arménien'*.

44. R. Darbinian. 1953. 'In Retrospect: A Glance at the Last Thirty Years', *Armenian Review*, 6 (3–23), 62.

45. Karekin I Hovsepiants, elected to the See in 1943, had been at odds with the Dashnak party, which blamed him for his frequent relations with the Soviet embassy in Lebanon; see J. Mécérian, *Un Tableau de la Diaspora Arménienne*, Beirut: Imprimerie Catholique, 164.

46. Ibid., 164–8; also see S. Kalpakian. 1983. *The Dimensions of the 1958 Inter-Communal Conflict in the Armenian Community in Lebanon*, unpublished MA thesis, Beirut: American University of Beirut; K.D. Kouyoumjian. 1961. *The Recent Crisis in the Armenian Church*, unpublished MA thesis, Beirut: American University of Beirut.

47. A reformed electoral law introduced in 1952 reduced the number of deputies from 77 to 44. In the new communal allocation of seats, the Armenians were granted the election of two representatives from the Apostolic community. The Dashnaks, siding with Chamoun and his allies, obtained the election of both their candidates: Movses Ter Kaloustian and Dickran Tospat. Joseph Chader, the incumbent Armenian Catholic MP and vice-president of the Kata'ib, was re-elected as representative for the seat of the 'minorities'. On the 1953 elections in the Armenian community see Messerlian, 'Armenian Representation', 192–214.

48. Schahgaldian, 'The Political Integration', 208, quoting the *Excerpts from the Decisions of the 15th ARF* [Dashnak] *World Congress* (Paris: 1951), ARF Central Archives, File 1581/81, 28.

49. Mécérian, *Un Tableau de la Diaspora*, 166.

50. Messerlian, 'Armenian Representation', 218 ff.

51. Ibid., 234. The elections, in which the Armenian Apostolic community was allocated three seats, saw the success of the incumbents Ter Kaloustian, Tospat and Chader and of a young, independent lawyer supported by the Dashnak, Khatchig Babikian.

52. Chader was Minister of Planning in a short-lived Solh cabinet, between March 14 and September 24, 1958.

53. Kalpakian, 'The Dimensions', 63.
54. Schahgaldian, 'The Political Integration', 221.
55. The agreement was signed by the representatives of the three nationalist parties (Kabakian for the Dashnak; Jerejian for the Hunchak; and Aharonian for the Ramkavar); see Kalpakian, 'The Dimensions', 90–91.
56. On the elections see Seale, *The Struggle for Syria*, 164–185; Torrey, *Syrian Politics*, 252–263; Petran, *Syria: A Modern History*, 107–108.
57. *Tidag*, March-April 2003, 49.
58. Hinnebusch, *Syria: Revolution from Above*, 42. Seale, *The Struggle for Syria*, 186–326; Torrey, *Syrian Politics*, 347–383; Petran, *Syria: A Modern History*, 106–127.
59. Interview with Ms. Hasmig Khanikian, Damascus, 4 November 2003.
60. Hinnebusch, *Syria: Revolution from Above*, 43.
61. Petran, *Syria: A Modern History*, 147.
62. Interview with Mr. Krikor Eblighatian, Aleppo, 12 November 2003.
63. Sources: As'eed, *Al-Barlaman al-Suri*; *Tidag*, April-May 2003, 12 and 49.
64. Schahgaldian, 'The Political Integration', 238.
65. G. Minassian. 2002. *Guerre et Terrorisme Arméniens*, Paris : Presses Universitaires de France, 18. Red Army officers would have approached Dashnak cadres as soon as 1957; the USSR would offer the annexation of Mountaineous Karabagh to the Soviet Republic of Armenia in exchange for the Dashnaks' dropping of their pro-US position.
66. The peak of intra-Armenian violence at the end of the 1950s left long lasting, deep wounds in the Armenian society of Lebanon. Among these was the problem of the difficult demobilisation of the militarised party youth. After 1958, a handful of young activists – like 'Asmer Artine' and 'Garo' – maintained armed gangs at the margin of the parties and became involved in various types of crime. Garo's story as a fugitive criminal was represented in a film realised in Lebanon by the Armenian director Gary Garabedian (1965).
67. On the concept and practice of the Lebanese *zu'ama'* see A. Hottinger. 1961. 'Zu'ama' and Parties in the Lebanese Crisis of 1958', *Middle East Journal*, 15 (2), 127–140; A. Hottinger. 1966. 'Zu'ama' in Historical Perspective', in L. Binder (ed.), *Politics in Lebanon*, New York, London and Sydney: John Wiley and Sons, 85 ff.; on urban *zu'ama'* see A. Hourani. 1976. 'Ideologies of the Mountain and the City'.
68. Rabbath, *La Formation Historique*, 568–573.
69. Ibid., 570. The decree introduced the so-called 'fifty-fifty' principle as a rule of administrative law; until then, the proportional allocation among the confessional groups of posts in the public administration had been guided by a simple political recommendation under Article 95 of the constitution. The decree raised doubts of constitutionality.
70. See, for instance, R. Owen. 1976. 'The Political Economy of the Grand Liban, 1920–1970', in R. Owen (ed.), *Essays on the Crisis in Lebanon*, London: Ithaca Press, 23–32.

71. See M.C. Hudson. 1968. *The Precarious Republic: Political Modernization in Lebanon*, New York: Random House, 139–141.
72. The new electoral law of April 20, 1960 assigned four seats to the Armenian Apostolic community and one to the Armenian Catholic community, out of an enlarged chamber of ninety nine members. The law was also important for the Armenians because it changed the boundaries of the electoral districts: in some of these, Armenian electoral co-operation became a crucial component of any successful bid to the parliament, a fact that enhanced the political importance of the community. See Schahgaldian, 'The Political Integration', 240.
73. Ibid., 249.
74. Hudson, *The Precarious Republic*, 139–141; Interview with Ms. Christine Babikian-Assaf, daughter of Khatchig Babikian, Beirut, 8 November 2002.
75. Hinnebusch, *Syria, Revolution from Above*, 43.
76. Interview with Mr. Krikor Eblighatian, Aleppo, 12 November 2003.
77. Ibid; Eblighatian was defending counsel of some of the accused.
78. Hinnebusch, *Syria, Revolution from Above*, 47.
79. Ibid., Chapter 3.
80. Ibid., 52.
81. For Sa'adeh 'the idea of political and religious inseparability [was] incompatible with the concept of nationalism in general and Syrian nationalism in particular', quoted in Torrey, *Syrian Politics*, 173.
82. Ibid., 173–174.
83. M. Khadduri. 1951. 'Constitutional Development in Syria, with Emphasis on the Constitution of 1950', *Middle East Journal*, 5 (2), 152–153.
84. Ibid., 153.
85. B. Botiveau. 1996. 'Il Diritto dello Stato-Nazione e lo Status dei Non Musulmani in Egitto e in Siria', in A. Pacini (ed.), *Comunità Cristiane nell'Islam Arabo: la Sfida del Futuro*, Turin: Fondazione Giovanni Agnelli, 133.
86. See P. Gannagé, 'Statut Personnel et Laïcité au Liban et Dans les Pays Arabes', lecture given at the Université Saint-Esprit of Kaslik, 23 March 1969, in P. Gannagé. 2001. *Le Pluralisme des Statuts Personnels dans les Etats Multicommunautaires: Droit Libanais et Droits Proche-Orientaux*, Bruxelles and Beirut: Bruylant and Presses de l'Université Saint-Joseph, 15–27.
87. One of these attempts was conducted, in 1959, by the Minister of Interior, Raymond Eddé.
88. The *Arrêté* n. 60 L.R. of 13 March 1936 and the *Arrêté* n. 146 L.R. of 18 November 1938, see Chapter 2 of the present book. Within this general context of uneasy relations between state and communal jurisdictions, an exception stood out: the successful introduction of a reform of inheritance law applying to the Christian communities; the law was promulgated on June 23, 1959, see J.G. Chami. 2002–2003. *Le Mémorial du Liban*, Vol. 4, Beirut: Chami, 44.
89. P. Gannagé. 1966. 'Les Conséquences du Défaut d'Approbation des Codes de Statut Personnel des Communautés non Musulmanes', extrait des *Etudes de Droit Libanais*, 211 ff., reprinted in Gannagé, *Le Pluralisme des Statuts*, 55 ff.

90. Ibid., 55–63, with specific reference to Article 215 of the Code of the Catholic communities, including the Armenian Catholic community.
91. Hovannisian, 'The Ebb and Flow', 27.
92. See further in this chapter.
93. Botiveau, 'Il Diritto dello Stato-Nazione', 130.
94. In Syria with the two important exceptions mentioned above: the reservation of the position of Head of State for the Muslim communities and the recognition of Islam as the main source of legislation – the latter proposition, however, remained fairly hollow.
95. A.J. Iskandar. 2002. *La Nouvelle Cilicie: Les Arméniens du Liban*, Beirut: Catholicosat Arménien de Cilicie, 109.
96. K.M. Kaloustian. 1958. *A Study of Armenian Schools in Lebanon*, unpublished MA thesis, Beirut: American University of Beirut, 34.
97. Quoted in A.N. Bedian. 1961. 'A Study of Armenian Elementary Schools in Syria, Related to Their History, Background, and Teacher's Beliefs', MA thesis, Beirut: American University of Beirut, 31.
98. In 1945 the public sector accounted for a mere 20.8% of the total school enrolment. By 1961–1962 the figure had climbed to 39.5%, but remained small compared to the 95.1% recorded in Iraq, 80.8% in Syria, 72.2% in Egypt, and 69.5% in Jordan; calculated on the basis of data contained in R.D. Matthews and M. Akrawi. 1949. *Education in Arab Countries of the Near East*, Washington: American Council on Education, 422; and J.K. Ragland. 1969. 'The Free Educational System of the Republic of Lebanon', Ph.D. thesis, University of Oklahoma, 3.
99. For an account of the content of these regulations see Ragland, 'The Free Educational System', 68–88.
100. See *Armenian Review*, 6 (2–22), 144.
101. Haigazian University. Ca. 1995. 'Celebrating the Fortieth Anniversary of Haigazian University College', pamphlet, 1–7.
102. Ibid., 9–10.
103. Ibid., 11–12.
104. *Travaux et Jours*, No. 39, April-June 1971, 77, note 2 : "L'existence d'une chaire a l'U.S.J. a été due exclusivement à l'initiative privée du P. Mécérian".
105. Based on Kaloustian, 'A Study of Armenian Schools', 28–29 and appendix B, 215–217.
106. For example the Collège Mechitariste; see A. Nasri Messarra. 1994. *Théorie Générale du Système Politique Libanais*, Paris: Cariscript, 118. Also see the observation on six Armenian elementary schools contained in M.G. Loussararian. 1960. 'A Study of the Armenian Elementary School System in Beirut', BA thesis, Beirut College for Women.
107. Interview with M. Vosguépéran Arzoumanian, member of the Educational Commission of the Armenian Apostolic community, in 'Note sur l'Enseignement Arménien au Liban', in *Travaux et Jours* No. 39, April-June 1971, 73.

108. Ibid., p. 76.
109. Khadduri, 'Constitutional Development in Syria', 156.
110. Constitution of Syria, 1950, Article 28, translated and quoted in Khadduri, 'Constitutional Development in Syria', 156–157.
111. W.L. Cleveland. 1971. *The Making of an Arab Nationalist: Ottomanism and Arabism in the Life and Thought of Sati' Al-Husri*, Princeton: Princeton University Press, 78–79; interestingly, Al-Husri had reached these position after having abandoned an early Ottomanism that he had envisaged as a 'broad-based system of loyalties in which there would be ample scope for the existence of a variety of languages, cultures, and individual responses', ibid., 63. On Al-Husri also see B. Tibi. 1997. *Arab Nationalism between Islam and the Nation-State*, 3rd edition, Houndmill, Basingstoke and London: MacMillan, part 3, 123–198.
112. Ibid., 157.
113. Seale, *The Struggle for Syria*, 121. Petran, *Syria*, 103.
114. Bedian, *A Study of Armenian Elementary Schools*, 47.
115. Ibid., 18–19.
116. Ibid., 21 and calculated on the basis of data contained in Appendix B, 119–123.
117. Ibid., calculated on the basis of Appendix B, 119–123.
118. Y. Suleiman. 2003. *The Arabic Language and National Identity*, Edinburgh: Edinburgh University Press, 124–125. 'Article 10 [of the 'Ba'th party constitution of 1962'] defines an Arab as one "whose language is Arabic, who has lived on Arab soil, or who, after having been assimilated to Arab life, has faith in this belonging to the Arab nation" '.
119. Ibid.
120. On the 6th National Congress of the Ba'th Party and the implementation of its directives see P. Guingamp. 1996. *Hafez El-Assad et le Parti Baath en Syrie*, Paris: l'Harmattan, 135–151; D. Roberts. 1987. *The Ba' th and the Creation of Modern Syria*, London and Sydney: Croom Helm, 65–76.
121. See, for instance the *Qarrar* No. 698 of 18 July 1965 by which the Miatsial school of Damascus changed its name into '*Nizam*'.
122. Guingamp, *Hafez El-Assad*, 178.
123. *Middle East Journal*, 22 (1), Winter 1968, 69, Chronology, Syrian Arab Republic.
124. Ibid.
125. Interview with Judge Krikor Eblighatian, Aleppo, 12 November 2003. Eblighatian's role as a mediator and representative of the Apostolic Church was endorsed by the three Armenian nationalist parties. Throughout the crisis Eblighatian remained in contact with the parties' leadership in Beirut (as their activities were restricted in Syria).
126. For example the Roman Catholic Church lost its school of Shaalan, Damascus. In May 1968, the government seized and nationalized fifty-four private schools; see Ragland, *The Free Educational System*, 3.

127. G.N. Atiyeh. 1995. 'The Book in the Modern Arab World: The Cases of Lebanon and Egypt', in G.N. Atiyeh (ed.), *The Book in the Islamic World. The Written Word and Communication in the Middle East*, New York: State University of New York Press, 242.

128. Haddad, *Fifty Years of Modern Syria and Lebanon*, 180–181.

129. F. Mermier. 2000. 'Beyrouth, Capitale du Livre Arabe?', *Monde Arabe Maghreb-Machrek*, 169 (numéro spécial), 100.

130. One of these exceptions was Simpat Panossian. Born in Iran, Genocide survivor and orphan, he received his education in Cyprus and spent most of his life between Latakia and the Kessab area.

131. K. Chahinian, 1988. *Œuvres Vives de la Littérature Arménienne*, Antélias: Catholicosat Arménien de Cilicie, 312.

132. A. Zaroukian. 1977. *Des Hommes sans Enfance*, translation from Armenian by S. Boghossian, Paris: Editeurs Français Réunis.

133. See K. Tölölyan, 'Elites and Institutions in the Armenian Transnation', paper given to the Conference on Transnational Migration: Comparative Perspectives, Princeton University, 30 June-1 July, 2001.

134. Based on information contained in M.A. Babloyan. 1986. *Hay Barperagan Mamoule: Madenakidagan Hamahavak Tzoutzag 1794–1980* [The Armenian Printed Press: Bibliographical List 1794–1980], Yerevan: The Armenian Soviet Socialist Republic Academy of Sciences, 353–354 and 362–364; and H. Bariguian and H. Varjabedian. 1973. *Badmoutioun Surio Hay Debaranneru* [The History of Syrian Armenian Printing Houses], Aleppo: AGBU Bibliographical Committee.

135. The newspaper somehow managed to continue publication until 1949. Bariguian and Varjabedian, *Badmoutioun Surio Hay Debaranneru*, 73–74.

136. Based on information contained in Babloyan, *Hay Barperagan Mamoule*, 353–354 and 362–364. The daily newspapers were *Aztag* (Dashnak), *Ararat* (Hunchak), *Zartonk* (Ramkavar) and the independent *Ayk*, owned by former MP Dickran Tospat.

137. For instance, by the end of the 1960s the Doniguian printing press had grown into one of the top Lebanese businesses in the sector, able to win lucrative contracts with government offices and agencies. Interview with Mr. Hagop Doniguian, publisher, Antelias, 23 Otctober 2003.

138. Interview with Berge Fazlian, Zalqa, 30 October 2003; interview with Zohrab Yacoubian, Bourj Hammoud, 20 October 2003.

139. *Vartanank* is the representation of a war between the Armenians and Persians which took place in the fifth century AD; the war, and one of its culminating moments, the battle of Avarair (451 AD), are taken as a symbol of the struggle of the Armenian people to defend their religion and identity.

140. Interview with Manuel Keshishian, Aleppo, 13 November 2003. Bariguian was one of the founders of the Nor Serount-affiliated theatrical group in 1919, together with Hagop Arakelian and Gulesser Demirjian. He was its director from 1921 to 1959; see the Nor Serount official website, http://www.norserount.org/en/theatre.php, page visited on April 13, 2004.

141. See N. Tomiche (ed.). 1969. *Le Théâtre Arabe*, Paris: UNESCO, 146–151. The public could watch these shows while smoking the water pipe or eating.

142. Varoujian Hadeshian founded the Theatre 67 group; Zohrab Yacoubian the Experimental Theatre group.

143. Interview with Berge Fazlian, Zalqa, 30 October 2003.

144. J. Tarrab. 1982. *Paul Guiragossian*, Beyrouth: Emmagoss; interview with Mr. Movses Herguelian, arts critic, Zalqa, 21 October 2003; interview with Ms. Maral Panossian, contemporary Armenian Lebanese artist, Beirut, 15 December 2003.

145. Interview with Mr. Movses Herguelian, arts critic, Zalqa, 21 October 2003.

146. On the basis of information provided by the Municipality of Bourj Hammoud there were still about 5,000 persons living in barracks at the end of the 1960s; see Social Action Committee of the Armenian Evangelical Union. 1970. *A Survey of Social Problems and Needs Within the Armenian Community in Lebanon*. Beirut, 33.

147. It was the case, for instance, of the Grtasirats association in Aleppo, representing the community of Aintab.

148. Based on Social Action Committee, *A Survey of Social Problems*; various pamphlets; interview with Mr. Hagop Pakradouni, Bourj Hammoud, 14 November 2002; interview with Mr. Sarkis Najarian, Beirut, 15 December 2003.

149. More than 40 patriotic unions were operating by the end of the 1960s; see Social Action Committee, *A Survey of Social Problems*, 91.

150. See A. Dagher. 1995. *L'Etat et l'Economie au Liban: Action Gouvernementale et Finances Publiques de l'Indépendance à 1975*, Beirut: CERMOC, Chapter 1, 37–52.

151. See K. Karam. 2002. 'Les Associations au Liban: Entre Caritatif et Politique', in S. Ben Néfissa (ed.), *Pouvoirs et Associations dans le Monde Arabe*, Paris: CNRS, 57–75.

152. Seale, *The Struggle for Syria*, 121.

153. Notes on the foundation of the Damascus chapter of Hamazkayin (in Armenian), handwritten by one of the original founding members, personal collection of the author.

154. See S. Boukhaima. 2002. 'Le Mouvement Associatif en Syrie', in S. Ben Néfissa (ed.), *Pouvoirs et Associations dans le Monde Arabe*, Paris: CNRS, 77–94.

155. Hinnebusch, *Syria, Revolution from Above*, 52–53.

156. A.A. Keuroghlian. 1970. 'Les Arméniens de l'Agglomération de Beyrouth, Etude Humaine et Economique', BA thesis, Beyrouth: Université Saint-Joseph, 53–54. On the basis of data provided by the Central Direction of Statistics of the Ministry of Planning, there were 61 Armenian businesses out of a total of 80. Shoe workshops in Bourj Hammoud would employ an average of 7–8 persons. A few of these were still visible in Bourj Hammoud in October 2005.

157. Ibid., 64. By the end of the 1960s the Armenians accounted for about 70% of the jewellers registered with the Lebanese Syndicate of Jewellers.

158. Ibid., 71.

158. Interview with Mr. Sarkis Demirdjian, Bourj Hammoud, 31 October 2003.

160. Interview with Mr. Paul Ayanian, Dora, 23 October 2003.

161. Keuroghlian, 'Les Arméniens de l'Agglomération de Beyrouth', 49. The source is the statistical data produced by the Ministry of Planning and refers to industrial businesses employing 5 or more people.

162. Interview with Mr. Garbis Dantziguian, Beirut-Mkelles, 29 October 2003; also see the published collection of memoirs of the founder, Kegham Dantziguian. 1985. *Yev Hatchoghetsa* [...and I succeded], Beirut.

163. Keuroghlian, 'Les Arméniens de l'Agglomération de Beyrouth', 55–57.

164. Ibid., 58.

165. C.L. Gates. 1998. *The Merchant Republic of Lebanon: Rise of an Open Economy*, Oxford: Centre for Lebanese Studies, 85. For an analysis of the nature and limits of the Lebanese *laissez-faire* capitalist model also see: F. Debié and D. Pieter. 2003. *La Paix et la Crise: Le Liban Reconstruit?*, Paris: Presses Universitaires de France, 27–48; R. Owen, 'The Political Economy of Grand Liban, 1920–1970'; R. Owen. 1988. 'The Economic History of Lebanon, 1943–1974', in H. Barakat (ed.), *Towards a Viable Lebanon*, London: Croom Helm, 27–41.

166. Gates, *The Merchant Republic*, 106.

167. Ibid., 128.

168. See Petran, *Syria, A Modern History*, 139–140.

169. Nationalizations affected a wide variety of industrial businesses, including tanneries (Tchatalbachian), shoemaking (Masarajian), chemical industries, carpet making, etc. See C. Babikian. Ca. 1983. 'L'Evolution du Rôle Politique des Arméniens au Liban de 1945 à 1975', BA thesis, Beirut: Université Saint-Joseph, 18.

170. The expressions are used in R. Hinnebusch. 1995. 'State, Civil Society, and Political Change in Syria', in A.R. Norton (ed.), *Civil Society in the Middle East*, Leiden, New York and Köln: E.J. Brill, 223.

# 4

# War, Migration, and Strategies of Survival: The Armenians between the Collapse of the Lebanese State and the Construction of Asad's Syria (1967–1989)

## Introduction

By the second half of the 1960s Lebanon and Syria represented two sharply contrasting paradigms of the accommodation of Armenian diversity in the countries of the Middle East. From an Armenian point of view, Lebanon could be undoubtedly regarded as a success story. The process of 'reconstruction of the Armenian world', as described earlier in this book, had proceeded to an extent and with a pace unparalleled in the region. Lebanon had become the new home for a fully developed system of communal institutions meant to organise and promote Armenian life, and Beirut had grown into a true capital of the Armenian diaspora, an unrivalled cultural hub serving Armenians across the region. The community had also been able to take part in – and enjoy the benefits of – the general economic success of the country. These achievements were mirrored in the spectacular demographic evolution of the community: the population growth of the original Lebanese Armenian refugees had been supplemented by the immigration of Armenians from other countries in the region, who were attracted by the opportunities that Lebanon seemed to offer, or encouraged to leave the unfavourable conditions which they found elsewhere. As a matter of fact, between independence and 1970 the Armenian population of Lebanon grew by an estimated 140 per cent, far more than the overall Lebanese population, which only doubled in the same period.[1] At the beginning of 1970, information provided by the Armenian Churches put the Armenian population in Lebanon at 180,000.[2]

Syria was, on the contrary, one of the countries from which migration to Lebanon originated. The Armenians, and the network of communal institutions that supported them, had been severely hit by political instability, by the emergence of authoritarian regimes and by the limits of Syria's economic development. In spite of the considerable size of the community, with the total number of Armenians remaining in the country reaching perhaps 150,000 at the end of the 1960s, the community's future as a culturally diverse group appeared seriously threatened, particularly after the crisis involving Armenian education in 1967.

The sharp differences in the situation of the Armenians in the two countries could be largely regarded as a consequence of the radically different turn that the evolution of the two states had taken since independence. The events at the end of the 1960s, a crucial, defining moment in the historical development of the Middle East, were going to shake once again the structure and functioning of the state in the two countries; in doing so, they also opened a new phase of redefinition of the spaces and conditions of co-existence of ethno-cultural groups. The key event marking this period, Israel's striking victory in the 1967 conflict, threw the entire Arab world into a deep political crisis. In Syria, the crisis helped trigger a struggle for power within the Ba'th leadership, resulting in Hafiz Al-Asad taking control of the government in November 1970 – a development that was to mark deeply the history of Syria, and establish one of the longest lasting regimes in the history of the contemporary Middle East. In Lebanon, the 1967 war and its aftermath lay at the origin of the formation of a strong, politicized and militarised Palestinian presence in the country; the presence of the Palestinians *de facto* dragged Lebanon into direct confrontation with Israel and introduced a highly destabilizing factor into the fragile Lebanese consociational system, a combination of elements that contributed to the breakout of the fifteen year-long civil war.

In the course of the 1970s and 1980s, these developments dramatically reopened the question of the position of the Armenian communities in Lebanon and Syria. In the span of a few years, the tragic turn of events in Lebanon significantly damaged the achievements of the Armenian community in the country, and profoundly shook the idea that the Lebanese consociational system was a durable, sustainable model for the presence of ethno-cultural and religious diversity in the Middle East. In Syria, on the contrary, the regime established by Hafiz Al-Asad offered some chances of recovery and showed that, within new limits fixed by the regime, and in spite of a state rhetoric that would sometimes suggest the opposite, Armenian diversity was not necessarily bound to disappear.

If the defeat of 1967 marked an epochal change in the history of the Arab world, the second half of the 1960s was no less crucial for the Armenians worldwide. The date of 1965, the 50th anniversary of the beginning of the Genocide, is often regarded as a symbolic turning point in the contemporary history of the Armenian people. In that year, for the first time, the authorities of the Soviet Republic of Armenia authorised the public commemoration of the Genocide on 24 April. The main event organised in Yerevan saw the participation of over one million people, and was later followed by the construction of a Genocide memorial and a monument commemorating the battle of Sardarabad of 1918.[3] The importance of these developments went far beyond signalling Moscow's change of approach regarding the Soviet Republic of Armenia,[4] and produced a far reaching echo in Armenian communities worldwide. The turn in Soviet Armenia seemed to open a new range of possibilities in relations between Armenia and the diasporas: the latter began to be regarded as parts of a permanent diasporic Armenian transnation, rather than splinters of a nation in exile.[5] More directly, the Armenian diasporas were affected by the new turn of events in at least two important aspects. On the one hand the 'Armenian spring' of 1965 facilitated the intra-Armenian *détente* which had started in the early 1960s, and contributed to the dropping of cold war divisions within the Armenian communities; on the other, it encouraged a phase of resurgence of Armenian nationalism in the form of renewed interest and activism *vis-à-vis* the question of the Genocide and Turkish responsibility for perpetrating it.

## Armenian Politics in the Levant from the Mid 1960s to the End of the Lebanese War

### The 'Time of Polarisation':[6] The Armenians and the Crisis that Led to the Lebanese War (1967–1975)

During the years following 1967, Lebanon was drawn into a profound political crisis largely centred on the issue of the presence of the Palestinian resistance in the country. As southern Lebanon became the main front of the Palestinian confrontation with Israel, the country became increasingly exposed to Israeli retaliations and attacks; at the same time, the impressive build-up of Palestinian military force grew into a serious challenge to the sovereignty of the Lebanese state in several parts of the country.

The tensions generated by the Palestinian presence mainly had the consequence of once again undermining the foundations of the national pact. The various confessional components of Lebanese society rapidly polarized on two fronts, for or against the Palestinian resistance. In general, the Muslim communities, including the Sunnis, the Shi'a and the Druze, sided with the Palestinians and blamed the Lebanese authorities (and notably the army) for not committing the country to the Arab front against Israel; on the opposite side of the spectrum, the Christian Maronite, right wing parties saw in the Palestinian presence, and its alliance with a left-leaning Muslim Lebanese leadership, a mortal threat to their position of leadership in the country and to the survival of Lebanese independence. Attempts at reaching negotiated solutions to the question were largely unsuccessful. An agreement signed in Cairo in 1969 between the Lebanese authorities and the Palestinian leadership failed to address the core of the problem, and the crisis reemerged in full virulence in 1973. Confessionally-based political parties formed militias: the country's confessional and clannish divisions became dangerously militarized.

The generalized polarization of Lebanese politics posed new problems to the Armenian community, particularly as the Maronite leadership began to put pressure on the Armenian parties to support them. Some of the marginal sectors of the Armenian political spectrum did in fact join the opposing fronts. It tended to be those individuals who belonged to the forces traditionally more integrated with non-Armenian Lebanese political organizations: the Armenians who had become members of the Kata'ib and – on the opposite front – a number of Armenian communists.[7]

The position of the Armenian nationalist parties, which represented the vast majority of the Armenian community, was more complex. The 'time of polarization' undermined the political strategy that had become a trademark of Armenian political participation, at least since the establishment of the Dashnak hegemony in the 1960s: a moderate conservatism *vis-à-vis* the preservation of the Lebanese consociational system and support for the political forces currently in government. As the Lebanese state institutions increasingly lost legitimacy and became perceived as part of the opposing fronts, the strategy of support for the status quo was not possible. The Armenian parties, however, resisted the pressures to take sides and adopted a position of neutrality which they maintained throughout the civil war.

The Armenian choice was in a sense the expression of a certain continuity in the parties' approach to Lebanon, a tribute to the Lebanese system and a statement against its demise; but also, in part, the consequence of the important transformations of Armenian politics sketched earlier in this work. The Dashnak party, for instance, was hardly the same political force that had co-operated with Camille Chamoun in 1958. By the early 1970s the party had largely completed the process of dropping its anti-Soviet, cold war tones and had switched to a neutralist, Third World-leaning position.[8] The Dashnak world leadership, increasingly under the control of its Middle Eastern wing, had put Armenian, anti-Turkish nationalism back at the centre of its discourse and agenda: in 1965 it had established a 'diplomatic arm', the Committee for the Defence of the Armenian Cause; in 1972, on the occasion of the 20th Congress, it engaged in the so-called 'Hay Tahd-ist[9] cultural revolution', a vast ideological program that radicalized the anti-Turkish strategy and called for the 'reinforcement of the struggle for the liberation of the Armenian lands of Turkey, by of all necessary means'.[10] In the context of these developments, it had become increasingly difficult for the Dashnak to join the Maronite front against the Palestinians. On the contrary, the Palestinians – like the Armenians, another people expelled from their land – were a powerful example to the nationalist Armenian youth of the early 1970s: left without conclusive support from the international community – or betrayed by it, according to different points of view – the Palestinians had arguably taken the pursuit of their national cause in their own hands and were fighting a guerrilla war for the liberation of their homeland. To use the terminology of the time, many Armenians found it difficult to consider the Palestinians as *ghuraba'*, 'foreigners', as they were described in the Maronite press.[11]

The political outcome of the evolution of Armenian politics, and of its position *vis-à-vis* the Palestinian question, was twofold: on the one hand, it resulted in the Dashnak party manoeuvring to distance itself from the Kata'ib; on the other, it encouraged a closer co-operation between the Armenian parties. Such developments became apparent in the early 1970s. The Dashnak co-operation with the Falangists, which had began in the 1960s, continued during the 1968 parliamentary elections and on the occasion of the election of President Suleiman Franjieh in 1970; in the 1972 polls, however, the Dashnak formed a strong Armenian front with the Hunchak and the Ramkavar and signalled its increasing uneasiness with the positions of the Kata'ib.

**Table 4.1. Armenian MPs elected in Lebanon, 1968–1972**

| Election year | Name of MPs | Place of election |
|---|---|---|
| 1968 | Movses Der Kaloustian | Beirut |
| 1968 | Khatchig Babikian | Beirut |
| 1968 | Souren Khanamirian | Beirut |
| 1968 | Joseph Chader* | Beirut |
| 1968 | André Tabourian | Metn |
| 1972 | Melkon Eblighatian | Beirut |
| 1972 | Khatchig Babikian | Beirut |
| 1972 | Souren Khanamirian | Beirut |
| 1972 | Joseph Chader* | Beirut |
| 1972 | Antranik Manoukian** | Beirut |
| 1972 | Ara Yerevanian | Metn |

\*   Armenian Catholic
\*\* Armenian Evangelical

The Armenians' determination to reject extremist positions and to work constructively for the preservation of Lebanese consociationalism was also reflected in their contribution to the cabinet, in which they maintained a fairly regular presence form 1969 to the beginning of the war. The most notable of the Armenian representatives in the cabinet, Khatchig Babikian, a lawyer and a highly respected figure within and outside the Armenian community, supported the view that 'working for general social improvements' best served the interests of the community and that 'the Armenian community could be badly hurt by prolonged civil disorders'.[12]

**Table 4.2. Armenian members of the Lebanese cabinet, 1969–1975**

| Name | President of the Council | Portfolio | Terms |
|------|--------------------------|-----------|-------|
| **Khatchig Babikian** | Rashid Karame | Health | 15/01/69 – 25/11/69 |
| **Khatchig Babikian** | Rashid Karame | Tourism | 25/11/69 – 13/10/70 |
| **Khatchig Babikian** | Saeb Salam | Information | 27/05/72 – 25/04/73 |
| **Khatchig Babikian** | Amine Al-Hafez | Planning | 25/4/73 – 08/07/73 |
| **Joseph Chader** | Takieddine El-Solh | Minister of State | 08/07/73 – 31/10/74 |
| **Souren Khanamirian** | Takieddine El-Solh | Tourism | 08/07/73 – 31/10/74 |

## The Lebanese War and Armenian 'Positive Neutrality' (1975–1989)

The deterioration of the crisis and the break out of a full-scale civil war in the spring of 1975 resulted in the rapid collapse of the Lebanese political and social system. The country's territory was broken up into a number of areas controlled by military forces on the ground. The constitutional system was *de facto* paralysed: no parliamentary elections were held until 1992; presidential elections and the formation of (highly ineffective) cabinets became the expression of the evolution of the conflict and of a complex alchemy of communal, regional and international factors.

The war presented the Armenian leadership with two types of problems. The first regarded the definition of the Armenian political position *vis-à-vis* the conflict itself and the forces participating in it; the second concerned the impact that the war was having on Armenian life in the country and the measures that should be taken in order to protect the community. When the fighting broke out in April 1975, the pressure on the Armenians to take sides grew stronger. Both the Dashnak and the Hunchak formed and trained their own militias and maintained contacts with the forces in conflict; they managed, however, to stay out of the fight and eventually reached a common position on the war. In a meeting held in Kantari, Beirut, the representatives of the Dashnak, Hunchak, Ramkavar and of the Armenian communists agreed that the Armenian community should remain neutral and engage in efforts to facilitate a solution to the crisis – a formula that became known as 'positive neutrality' and that would be maintained until the end of the war in 1990.

Armenian neutrality was of little avail in sheltering the community from the fighting. During the early phases of the war, the Armenians of Bourj Hammoud found themselves dangerously close to the Palestinian-controlled areas of Karantina, on one side, and Naba'a on the other; furious battles took place between Christian forces and the Palestinians in both locations. But, more importantly, the 'positive neutrality' stand taken by the Armenian leadership created the basis for a clash between the Armenians and the Maronite militias, and in particular with the Kata'ib. At best, the Armenian position was perceived by the Kata'ib leadership as yet another example of their limited devotion to Lebanon. At worse, it was called a betrayal, particularly in a phase in which the Maronite militias were conducting a campaign aimed at eliminating all differences within the East Beirut, Christian camp.[13] The Kata'ib would later declare in clear terms that '*l'on ne peut pas être libanais et chrétien et ne pas être contre Khadafi, contre les Palestiniens et contre la complot qui vise à chasser les chrétiens de ce pays*'.[14] In retrospect, it seems that 'positive neutrality' merely revealed that the Armenians of Lebanon had a different understanding of the crisis, and a different vision of the country and of the role that they wanted to play in it: arguably, they wanted to be citizens in a peaceful, confessionally-balanced Lebanon that allowed them to live as an Armenian community and participate to the transnational activities of the Armenian diaspora. The crisis between the Christian right and the Armenians exploded in full in October 1978, when the Falangists and the Chamounists attacked Bourj Hammoud: mortar shells, launched from the hill of Ashrafieh, fell on the densely populated residential and commercial Armenian district causing a large number of civilian casualties and extensive damage.[15] The Hunchaks were also targeted: the premises of the newspaper *Ararat* were destroyed by a bomb allegedly planted by the Lebanese Forces. A second, major attack against the Armenians took place in September 1979: Bourj Hammoud, once again, did not fall, in spite of three days of heavy fighting. The Armenian 'positive neutrality' was of little help for the Armenian residents of West Beirut too. Even if they were not specifically targeted, the security situation deteriorated over time, to the point that many Armenian families migrated to the eastern part of the city, where the majority of Armenians resided.

Occasional attacks by the Christian Lebanese Forces, and exchanges of fire with the Armenian militias continued in the 1980s: the premises of the Hunchak sports club Homenmen, for instance, were destroyed by a bomb in August 1984. However, the position taken by the Armenians became gradually accepted. The reasons for this are still not fully clear, and only a few hypotheses can be made at this stage. On one count, acceptance of Armenian 'positive neutrality' could be connected with successful Armenian 'diplomacy': the Armenian leadership became available to take part in co-ordination meetings with the rest of the Christian leadership and sometimes, to ensure political support to specific initiatives.[16] Other reasons might be found in the complex, continuously shifting system of relations that each force, militia, and organisation developed and maintained during the war. In the case of the Armenians, at some stage the community appeared to receive some political support from the USSR and began to play a role within the Syrian strategy in Lebanon.[17]

## The Lebanese Crisis and Armenian Terrorism

The resurgence of Armenian anti-Turkish nationalism, the inspiration and support of the Palestinian resistance, and the context of generalised violence and anarchy that characterised Lebanon in the 1970s, were all factors that contributed to the establishment and development in the country of Armenian terrorist organisations.[18]

The first of these to emerge, the Armenian Secret Army for the Liberation of Armenia (ASALA), was formed by a group of dissident Dashnak and Hunchak activists frustrated by the ineffectiveness of the political struggle against Turkey and violently critical of their party leaderships. The early nucleus of ASALA, which was perhaps formed as early as 1971, found protection and training with the Popular Front for the Liberation of Palestine led by George Habash.[19] The agenda of the group focused on the planning and carrying out of attacks against the Turkish government but also, more broadly, against any institution perceived as hostile to the Armenian cause. As a matter of fact, ASALA's first operation, in January 1975, was the bombing of the World Council of Churches in Beirut, accused of promoting the dispersion of the Armenian people. ASALA's first manifesto strongly attacked the Armenian nationalist parties for failing to obtain 'any result in sixty years' and declared that 'the time of the [Dashnak was] long gone'.[20] In the second half of the 1970s, from its base in West Beirut, ASALA directed a number of terrorist attacks and assassinations in Lebanon, France, Belgium, Greece, Switzerland, and the United States. The organisation's activities peaked between the end of the 1970s and the beginning of the 1980s: a training camp was allegedly set up in the Beka'a valley, recruitment increased, and so did the scope of operations.[21] ASALA even began the publication of a newsletter, and – in 1981 – a daily radio broadcast was started in Beirut. The Israeli invasion of Lebanon in 1982 marked a turn in the evolution of ASALA: the headquarters had to be moved to Damascus, and the organization radicalized its positions against the Dashnak. In 1983 internal rifts emerged and the organization, increasingly perceived as a 'gun for hire' often at the service of Syria, began to decline.

The formation – in 1975 – of a Dashnak-sponsored[22] (but never formally acknowledged by the Dashnak) terrorist organization, the Justice Commandos of the Armenian Genocide (JCAG), has been described as a reaction to the initial popularity of ASALA among the Armenian youth. The Dashnak leadership reportedly realized that 'the flow of young, male recruits to ASALA's ranks would increase in response to ASALA's more militant actions',[23] and could hardly accept being surpassed on the nationalist ideological terrain. Although the challenge represented by ASALA might well have played the role of a triggering factor, the development of the JCAG had deeper roots. To some extent it appears to have been the 'logical' expression of the evolution of the party's ideology and discourse between the end of the 1960s and the early 1970s, particularly in the light of the '*Hay Tahd*-ist cultural revolution' and the failure of diplomatic efforts aimed at the recognition of the Armenian Genocide by the United Nations.[24]

The JCAG's first operations, tragically notable for their effectiveness, took place in October 1975, when two commandos assassinated the Turkish ambassadors to Austria and France. In the following years, until the decline of the organization in the second half of the 1980s, the JCAG (later renamed Armenian Revolutionary Army – ARA) carried out dozens of similar attacks, resulting in the death of about 20 Turkish diplomats and members of their families.[25] As in the case of ASALA, the Beka'a valley allegedly provided the JCAG with a base for training and for the planning of operations.

## *Armenian Politics and the Construction of Asad's Syria*

The Arab defeat in the Six Day War marked a crucial turning point in the history of Syria, and lay at the origin of a deep crisis for the Ba'th regime that had emerged through the coups of 1963 and 1966. As in Lebanon, the crisis had been essentially triggered by the Palestinian question, but had then developed to the point of touching issues regarding the very nature of the regime, its strategies and priorities.

The painful loss of parts of Syrian national territory forced the leadership to make choices, and two distinct positions appeared to

emerge. On one side was Salah Jadid, the informal leader of the regime. His priority, and that of the radical intellectuals that supported them, remained the continuation of the 'revolution from above', the class struggle aimed at eliminating what remained of the power of the traditional bourgeoisie. Regionally, and *vis-à-vis* the question of the Golan Heights, they remained hostile to negotiated solutions and to a policy of co-operation with conservative Arab states; they supported the option of a 'revolutionary' war of liberation that would involve the Palestinian resistance. On the other side was the Minister of Defence, Hafiz Al-Asad, the emerging strong man of the regime. Asad intended to place Syrian nationalism, and the recovery of the captured territory, at top of the country's priorities. In order to achieve that – mainly through the reinforcing of the nation's military forces – he was pragmatically ready to soften the revolutionary character of the regime, to seek the co-operation of Egypt and the Arab monarchies of the Gulf, and to break the isolation of the regime from the country's bourgeoisie.[26]

In the years following 1967 the balance of power shifted gradually in favour of Asad, and, in November 1970, he took control of the country in a bloodless coup. In coming to power, Asad's priority was the consolidation of the regime. Asad was aware that, besides the army, over which he had full control, the bases of the Ba'th state were dangerously weak in many parts of Syrian society. His strategy of broadening the regime's bases of support was based on a combination of elements: the creation of a strong, centralized state able to dispense benefits of various kinds to key sectors of the society; the relaxation of some of the radical policies that the Ba'th regime had adopted in the mid 1960s; and the promotion of the concept of a distinct Syrian national identity integrated in a wider Pan-Arab nation.[27]

Within the framework of these efforts to consolidate power the Armenian community was offered the opportunity of a substantially transformed relationship with the Syrian state. At the official, formal level the state continued to disregard confessional or communal identities: Asad, the member of a minority himself, was well aware that the regime needed to play down the minority identity of many of its key figures if it wanted to obtain a certain level of legitimacy with the public at large.[28] However, at the informal level, the communal solidarity characterizing minorities like the Armenians represented an important asset, and could play an important role in providing the new leadership with support. It was at this informal level that, from the early 1970s, indications were given to the Armenian community of Syria that a new, more favourable *modus vivendi* could be built. While it would be inappropriate to speak of a proper 'pact' between the regime and the Armenian leadership, the terms of the new relation soon became clear: the practice of state control over the communal activities of the Armenians would be relaxed in return for the Armenians' support, or acquiescence. It also remained clear that control of the relation remained firmly in the hands of the regime: the informality of any concession being made meant that the state was able at any time to 'take back' what had been given.

The best example of the new *modus vivendi* between the Syrian state and the Armenians is perhaps to be found in the case of schools, as will be shown later in this chapter. As far as the political life of the Armenians was concerned, the new course was perhaps less evident: any activity of the Armenian nationalist parties remained formally non-existent and strictly unauthorised. At the 'visible' level, however, the institutional reforms introduced by Asad marked the return of Armenian representatives to formal participation in Syrian political life. In 1971 the veteran Judge Krikor Eblighatian was nominated, together with the Hunchak-leaning Roupen Dirarian, to the constituent assembly in charge of drafting the new constitution; and from 1973, the year of the first elections for the People's Assembly, the Armenians maintained a continuous presence in the Syrian parliament.[29]

There is no doubt that the choice of the Armenian candidates who ran successfully in the parliamentary elections primarily represented the preferences of the regime, and that these candidates were by no means freely selected by the community or by the Armenian parties. The design of the electoral districts contributed to making sure that the candidates of the government were indeed elected. In Aleppo, the impact of the Armenian vote, no matter how the Armenian parties might want to direct it, was dispersed in a large electoral district covering the whole city; Armenians would never be a majority in a single electoral district. In addition to that, the government could mobilize peasants and members of co-operatives and bring them to vote wherever it was necessary. Also, given the nature of the regime, it may be argued that the election of representatives to the parliament did not bring the community significantly closer to where 'real' power lay: the presidency, the Ba'th, the army and the security services. What is noticeable, on the other hand, is that the new regime appeared to be willing to ensure that the community was somehow represented.

In 1973 the support of the Ba'th party was instrumental in the election of Leon Wahid Ghazal, a trade unionist from an *Arman qadim* family, who was elected in Aleppo within the quota that the constitution reserved for workers and peasants.[30] The following elections, in 1977, marked the return to parliament of Judge Krikor Eblighatian, who was then re-elected in 1981 and 1986. As in 1953, when he had first become a member of parliament under Shishakli, Eblighatian was 'called to duty' by the regime's leadership: whenever elections were approaching, and electoral lists were being prepared, Eblighatian would be contacted by one of Asad's close associates, and asked to present his candidacy.[31] As had happened on previous occasions, the choice of Eblighatian appeared to originate from the fact that he combined political and diplomatic skills with a position of independence from the Armenian parties.

By the mid 1970s the political position of the Armenians within Hafiz Al-Asad's regime had been already defined by its main traits in a way that would remain consistent throughout the rule of the president, and beyond. A marginal Christian minority, with a minimal, negligible representation within the Ba'th party, the Armenians were becoming nevertheless one of the communities most trusted by the government: the Armenians had no ambitions in Syria and were not creating trouble. Their position in the country was given a formal recognition through the 'nomination' of a representative in the parliament; the political activities of the Armenian parties were restricted as far as they could become visible outside the closed, private spaces of the Armenian community.

The Lebanese war offered the opportunity to take the political relation between Syria and the Armenians a step forward, at least at the informal, 'under the surface' level. The Syrian perception of the Armenians as a loyal, trusted community was confirmed when the Syrian army first intervened in Lebanon in April 1976: the Syrian command's headquarters were established in 'Anjar, the Armenian village in the Beka'a. The presence of the Syrians in 'Anjar, combined with the Armenian need for protection from the right wing Maronite militias, prompted the Armenians, and most notably the Dashnak party, to pursue a strategy of cautious pro-Syrian orientation.[32] The Syrians, for their part, were interested in winning the co-operation, or at least the neutrality of one of the players in the Lebanese scene; but also, they arguably saw the potential benefits that Armenian co-operation could bring on other fronts: that of relations between Syria and Turkey, often strained, and that of relations with the USSR. The co-operation between the Dashnak and Syria was, however, characterized by ambiguities: on the one hand the recent memory of the Dashnak crisis in Syria in the course of the 1960s prompted the party's leadership to maintain a cautious attitude; on the other, the Syrians appeared to co-operate with ASALA, the Dashnak's most dangerous foe in the Armenian camp.

Table 4.3. Armenian members of Syrian parliamentary assemblies, 1971–1990

| Year of election or nomination | Name of MP | Place of election |
|---|---|---|
| 1971 | Krikor Eblighatian | – |
| 1971 | Roupen Dirarian | – |
| 1973 | Levon Wahid Ghazal | Aleppo |
| 1977 | Krikor Eblighatian | Aleppo |
| 1981 | Krikor Eblighatian | Aleppo |
| 1986 | Krikor Eblighatian | Aleppo |

## The Armenian Churches in Lebanon and Syria in the 1970s and 1980s

### *The Armenian Churches and the Lebanese War*

Similar to the position of the Armenian political parties, the Armenian Churches supported a position of 'positive neutrality' in the Lebanese war. The Catholicos of Cilicia, Karekin II, relentlessly called for an end to the hostilities. His comments and messages bore witness to the profound attachment he had to Lebanon, the pain he felt for the tragedy that was ravaging it, and his encouragement to the finding of a solution.[33]

Although not specifically targeted, many Armenian churches suffered damages during the war. In one episode, the Catholicosate of Cilicia came under fire on the eve of the 24th of April while people were commemorating the anniversary of the Genocide. Hundreds of churchgoers had just left the courtyard of the Catholicosate when, around midnight, shells fell within the precinct.[34]

### *The Armenian Churches in Syria under Asad*

The question of the relation between state and religion has traditionally been the subject of heated dispute – if not of violent confrontation – in Syrian politics since the time of the French Mandate. The regime inaugurated by Hafiz Al-Asad in 1970 was no exception. Asad was aware that the secularist approach promoted by the Ba'th represented a major obstacle to the legitimisation of the regime within important sectors of the Sunni community; in the framework of his efforts to expand the bases of his power, Asad appeared willing to soften the party's position and to seek a compromise. On a personal level, he made efforts to appear publicly as a pious Muslim and obtained a *fatwa* backing up the Islamic credentials of the Alawis.[35]

However, the first major test of Asad's policy on religion, though, the unveiling of the constitution in 1973, showed the limits of his opening to the Islamic opposition and caused a protest that he put down with the use of force.[36] Although the final text conceded that the president had to be a Muslim, the constitution failed to declare Islam the religion of the state and left the secular structure of the state substantially unaltered. The main provision regulating the position of religion in the state, Article 35, established that 'freedom of belief is guaranteed and the state respects all faiths. The state guarantees the free exercise of religion as long as this does not jeopardize public order'.[37] From the point of view of the Armenians, the new constitution came as a reassurance that their religious rights would continue to receive protection. The recognition of the autonomy of the communities in all matters regarding personal status remained also virtually unaltered.

Besides their religious role, the Armenian Churches played a key role in the mechanism of the relation between the new Syrian regime and the Armenian community. During the difficult moments caused by the radical turn of events under Nasser and under the Ba'th in the 1960s, the Churches had been important in providing shelter for Armenian diversity. Churches, less exposed to closures and expropriations than parties and associations, had become, for instance, the custodians of communal property. Under Asad the Armenian Churches maintained, and arguably expanded, their pivotal role in the relation between the community and the state. As the Churches were nominally in charge of a large part of communal activities, selective concessions from the government to the advantage of the Armenian community – from the establishment of a summer camp for Armenian boy scouts, to the construction of a community centre, or the authorization of a publication – could be quietly and conveniently presented as facts that concerned the religious sphere of a group of citizens and allow the Syrian leadership to preserve the façade of a state that was colour-blind with regard to the ethnic identity of its citizens.

## Armenian Education in Lebanon and Syria: The 1970s and 1980s

### The Lebanese War and the Disruption of Armenian Education

Armenian education suffered enormously during the Lebanese war. The fifteen year-long conflict seriously jeopardized the networks of institutions so laboriously created since the arrival and settlement of the refugees. Ironically, on the eve of the conflict, the Armenian educational system in Lebanon had perhaps reached the full completion of its growth and was engaged in a process of rationalization and consolidation. By the end of the 1960s Armenians could rely on well-organised networks of schools, covering kindergartens, primary and secondary education. Many of the schools had grown in capacity in order to accommodate a population of pupils which was expanding in proportion to the community's demographic development. The number of students enrolled in Armenian schools rose from to 13,398 in 1964–1965 to 18,526 in 1972–1973, and to a peak of about 21,000 in the academic year 1974–1975.[38]

In the early 1970s the Armenian community's educational leadership was increasingly shifting its concern from the problem of being able to provide a basic Armenian education for all to the question of raising the quality of teaching and the performance of students, particularly with regard to the non-Armenian part of the curriculum. The general level of preparation of the Armenian teachers had risen significantly throughout the 1960s: as far as the Armenian Apostolic schools were concerned, the percentage of teachers who only held a title of primary education – or post-primary education – had dropped from 77.3 per cent to 28.5 per cent between the years 1962–1963 and 1970–1971.[39] Performance, however, was not always satisfactory: in 1970, only 10 per cent of the students of the Armenian Apostolic schools passed the Lebanese Baccalaureate.[40] The teaching of Arabic, which was co-ordinated with the Lebanese Ministry of Education and performed by instructors paid by the state, was an area of particular concern for the principals of the Armenian schools.[41]

Concerns about the quality of Armenian education and discussion of how to integrate it within the Lebanese national education system were abruptly swept aside by more pressing problems arising from the outbreak of the war. The position of 'positive neutrality' adopted by the Armenian political leadership was of little avail for the protection of the community's institutions from the fighting: initially, the fate of Armenian schools depended largely on their location in the territory. In Beirut itself Armenian schools were present both in the area to the west of the *centre-ville* and in the eastern Christian district of Ashrafieh. Schools were also located in Bourj Hammoud, the densely populated Armenian quarter, and further along the coast, in the Christian-controlled districts. During the first phases of the war the schools in West Beirut were caught in the middle of the fighting. The deteriorating security situation made it impossible for students and staff to travel safely from home to the schools, forcing the school boards to suspend all activities. In Kantari, the Armenian Evangelical College was repeatedly taken over by different militias and used as a military outpost.[42] Re-opening, during periods of truce, took place amongst great difficulties due to the damage suffered by buildings and equipment.

In the longer run, when it became evident that the war was not going to be resolved over a short period of time, school boards had to take the difficult decision of relocating activities in a way that could make regular school attendance possible. This often took place through the initial step of opening branches in East Beirut in order to avoid daily, dangerous crossings of the green line. As the Armenian population gradually moved out of West Beirut, the branches in that part of the city were closed, and the schools effectively 'migrated' along with their pupils. The AGBU's Hovaghimian Manoukian, for instance, left its premises in the proximity of the Sérail and re-opened in Sinn El-Fil; the 'national' (Apostolic) Khanamirian school, moved to Fanar. Relocations were sometimes particularly troubled, as in the case of the Jemaran-Palandjian: the school, located in the Zoqaq El-Blatt district of West Beirut, saw the number of its students drop from about 1,200 to a mere 200 during the first phases of the war. The school was briefly hosted at the Catholicosate of Cilicia in Antelias, then temporarily relocated to Dbayeh and to Bourj Hammoud, until the completion of the construction of its current premises in Mzher.[43]

As the war continued in the second half of the 1980s, the relocations were no longer a sufficient measure to tackle the challenges that the Lebanese crisis posed to Armenian education. In particular, the migration of a large proportion of Armenian families – as mentioned earlier in this chapter – resulted in a dramatic fall in the enrolment at Armenian schools. By the end of the 1980s, the system of Armenian schools suffered from overcapacity; as a consequence, a number of schools were closed, reversing a trend of growth that had been continuous since the 1920s. Moreover, during the last part of the war, the security situation in some of the sectors inhabited by the Armenians dramatically deteriorated, and schools were affected once again: in one episode, a school bus driving pupils home was hijacked by a militia commando; the children were kept hostage for several hours.[44] The following table indicates that between the last pre-war school year and the first post-war school year the Armenian community lost about twenty per cent of its schools and a striking forty-three per cent of its students.

**Table 4.4. Armenian schools and students in Armenian schools, Lebanon, 1974/ to 1991/2[45]**

| Academic year | No. of schools | No. of students |
|---------------|----------------|-----------------|
| 1974–75 | 56 | 21,000 |
| 1987–88 | 47 | 12,924 |
| 1991–92 | 45 | 11,939 |

The impact of the two decades of war on the strictly educational dimension of the Armenian schools, and in particular on their effectiveness in preparing new generations of Armenian Lebanese, are harder to assess. Without any doubt the war resulted, at times, in the disruption of school attendance and teaching. However, in spite of all the problems, the solid and structured educational leadership of the community and the links with the traditional sponsor institutions of the diaspora remained in place throughout the period, providing the organization and support necessary to keep the Armenian school system together. As far as the curricula were concerned, the crisis of the state and of national unity did not result in the reversal of the Armenian effort to seek a deeper integration of their schools within the Arab context in which they were located. On the contrary, the efforts of the Armenian schools to improve the Arab part of their curriculum continued throughout the 1970s and 1980s.[46]

## Armenian Education in Syria under Asad

After the take-over of power by Hafiz Al-Asad in 1970, Armenian education in Syria was able to make a partial recovery from the deep crisis of the late 1960s. In general terms, while the regulatory framework relevant to private schools remained substantially unchanged, relations between Armenian schools and the state improved: Armenian education found an informal *modus vivendi* with the state authorities and – within that – it was able to recover some spaces of autonomy.

The legal framework in which Armenian schools operated did not significantly depart from the philosophy adopted in the second half of the 1960s. The national educational policy continued to be characterized on the one hand by a strong emphasis placed on the nation-building and Arabizing mission of education, and, on the other, on close state control over private educational establishments. The Syrian constitution of 1973, Chapter 3, Article 21 stated that the national system of instruction had to 'create an Arab, national, socialist generation with scientific training and one attached to its land, proud of its legacy, animated by a spirit of struggle for the realization of the goals of the nation in unity, liberty, socialism'.[47] Article 23 (1) further added that 'Socialist national education underlies the building of a united Arab socialist society. It tends to consolidate moral values and to realize the higher ideals of the Arab nation, to develop society, and to serve humanity. The state promotes and protects this system of education'.[48] Finally, for Art. 37 (4), '[the state]controls the educational system and directs it in such a way as to make it relevant to the needs of society and production'.[49]

The nation-building and Arabizing mission assigned by the state to education reflected heavily on the curriculum and on extra-curricular activities (national and pseudo-military celebrations, exhibitions of flags, portraits of the President, etc.) which Armenian schools, as any other school in the country, were required to follow. Armenian schools also continued to be bound by the unfavourable conditions of the compromise reached in 1967, including the limitations that it imposed on the freedom of the curriculum and the imposition of government-appointed school principals.

However, in daily practice, the interpretation of the conditions of the agreement became increasingly relaxed. As far as the curriculum was concerned, the distinction between the four weekly periods dedicated to the teaching of Armenian language and the three periods reserved for the teaching of religion became blurred: since the time officially allocated to the teaching of Armenian was highly insufficient, teachers could informally use the periods dedicated to religion for the teaching of language, according to need. A similar relaxation in relations between the Armenian private schools and the state could be observed with regard to the selection and role of the government-appointed school principals. The practice tended to develop in the sense of the selection by the government of Arab school principals who would be eager to minimise interference with the Armenian ownership of the school. In addition to that, the role of the Ministry-appointed principals became limited, in practice, to the formal rather than substantial aspects of running the schools, the latter remaining in the hands of the Armenian 'representative of the owner' and of the school board.

## Armenian Associations and the State in Lebanon and Syria: The 1970s and 1980s

The Armenian network of associations which had been gradually developed through the decades provided the community with crucial support during the years of the Lebanese war. In the context of the general collapse of the Lebanese state, of frequent gaps in the provision of basic services, and of reduced personal mobility, Armenian associations were called to play an important part in catering for the needs of the community.

Since the early phases of the war, the Armenian quarters, including the traditionally Hunchak areas on the Beirut side of the river and the Dashnak-controlled Bourj Hammoud, became semi-autonomous enclaves within a wider region controlled by the Lebanese Forces. Within the Armenian areas, whose borders were guarded and defended by the Dashnak and Hunchak militias, the community developed a form of self-government, filling the gap left by the collapse of the Lebanese central government. In Bourj Hammoud, a comprehensive, fully structured self-administration emerged, effectively co-ordinating the efforts of the political leadership with those of the associations, of the patriotic unions, and of the Churches. The National Council (*Hazkayine Khorhourt*), as it was termed, was formed at the end of April 1976 to arrange for the provision of those services that had been disrupted by the war: the care of the sick and wounded, electricity supply, telephone and postal communication, etc. It developed to the point of covering an impressively wide variety of issues, from the provision of medical services to the administration of justice, the collection of taxes, and the promotion of economic activities. The associations that participated in the efforts of the National Council included some of the international organisations that had traditionally supported the community: AGBU, the Jinishian Memorial Program, the Howard Karagheusian Commemorative Corporation, and the Swiss Friends of the Armenians.[50]

The experience of self-administration and the widespread involvement of Armenian civil society in the activities of self-help during the difficult times of war acted as a powerful reinforcement of the Armenian communal self-consciousness and provided effective support to the population. However, as the war continued during the 1980s an increasing number of Armenian families decided to leave the country and settle abroad. The phenomenon of migration during the war was by no means limited to the Armenians. It is almost certain, on the other hand, that the migration ratio was higher within the Christian communities, and that the Armenians contributed significantly to the phenomenon.[51] Precise data is unfortunately unavailable; however, it is a common opinion, within the community itself, that about half the Armenian population left the country, reducing the overall figure from perhaps 200,000 in 1975 to 100,000 in 1990. Armenian migration was mainly directed to the countries of the Western world where the Armenian diaspora was well established; these included, in particular, the United States, where immigration from the Middle East had been facilitated by legislation introduced in 1965.[52]

In Syria, the approach of the regime of Hafiz Al-Asad in defining relations between state and associations was characterized by a substantial continuity with the past: the state maintained a direct involvement in the establishment and running of quasi-governmental mass organizations entrusted with the task of mustering political support and promoting the regime's ideology; independent associations continued to be regarded as potential threats to central power and remained subject to intense governmental control, particularly during the 1980s. Armenian associations were, in general, no exception. As in the case of the schools, Armenian associations had to adopt elements of the Syrian national rhetoric and drop – or conceal – the most visible or 'political' aspects of their programs. Certain activities and groups, like the Boy Scouts, were often restricted. On the other hand, Armenian charities, cultural, and sports associations were never specifically targeted by state censorship, and – as the reputation of the Armenians as a 'trusted' community grew over the years – were increasingly allowed to quietly maintain their identity and role. Enrollment and participation in Armenian associations remained a common fact among the Armenians of Syria, sometimes in parallel with quasi-compulsory participation in state-directed organizations.

## Armenian Culture and Media in Lebanon and Syria during the 1970s and 1980s

The civil war inflicted a severe blow on the production and diffusion of Armenian culture in Lebanon. By the time the war ended, in 1990, Beirut was no longer the flourishing centre of Armenian culture that it had been before 1975: the variety and quality of Armenian cultural production available had declined sharply.

The crisis of Armenian culture in Lebanon had two main dimensions. The first involved the protagonists of the cultural scene: since the first phases of the war, in 1975–6, many of the best artists and intellectuals of the community decided to leave the country and migrate to other Armenian diasporas, in large part those in the Western world. The second, whose consequences were felt at a later stage, involved the public: the mass migration of the Armenians of Lebanon to the United States, to France, Australia, and so on, resulted in a general decline of the demand for Armenian 'cultural products' in the country. For those who remained, the world of Armenian culture was badly hit in terms of its physical assets, organisation and diffusion; cultural spaces were sometimes lost, while programs were disrupted by the lack of security and by the restrictions in movement that it imposed.

The decline of Armenian cultural production in Lebanon had severe repercussions for Armenian culture in the whole Levant. The Armenian cultural circles of Syria and Palestine, crippled by a haemorrhage of talent caused by three decades of outward migration, looked to Beirut as a focus for inspiration and centre of excellence; the war resulted in their increased isolation. In Syria, Armenian cultural activities survived in the schools, in the Armenian associations, and under the patronage of the Churches, but they hardly attained a level of quality that could make them relevant nationally and internationally.

### Literature, Theatre, and Music

In the span of a few years, the Armenian literary world in Lebanon lost many of its best authors and circles. Particularly damaging was the crisis of the most important literary magazines published in Beirut, the spaces of expression *par excellence* where literary debate took place. Antranik Zaroukian's weekly, *Nairi*, was directly affected by the fighting, and was repeatedly forced to halt publication. After a first interruption, between October 1975 and the end of August 1977, the production of the magazine was again suspended for almost a year between the summer of 1978 and May 1979. Other breaks affected publication in 1981 and 1982; eventually, in March 1983, Zaroukian moved to Paris and publication stopped altogether.[53] A similar fate, marked by sudden closures, hopeful re-openings, and erratic publication characterised the other two main literary and artistic weeklies: Simon Simonian's *Spurk*, and Sarkis Guiragossian's *Pakin*.[54] The literary scene was also impoverished by the death of important authors, including Simonian himself, and Karnig Attarian.

The war severely damaged Armenian theatre too. A number of the best authors and interpreters decided to leave the country and to look for opportunities in other Armenian diasporas. Among those who left was the founder of the Varant Papazian group, Berge Fazlian, who moved to north America in 1975. Others did the same and, one by one, most of the approximately fifteen Armenian groups present in the scene at the beginning of the 1970s interrupted their activity. The migration of the best professionals, associated with that of the Armenian population in general, precipitated a rapid decline of Armenian theatre in Lebanon. The movement did not disappear altogether, but became more amateur and provincial. Paradoxically, the few groups that remained often managed to sell out their shows in the two theatres of Bourj Hammoud, staging comedies that represented the life of the community in those difficult times: the breakup of Lebanon into self-contained areas under the control of different militias limited the movement of the public and theatre became again one of the few available forms of entertainment for those living in the main Armenian enclaves.[55]

The migration of artists, and the declining quality of performance characterized the Armenian Lebanese musical scene too. A number of talented classical musicians left Lebanon, including soprano singer Arpiné Pehlivanian. The flourishing Armenian pop music scene of the early 1970s was also heavily hit: most of its interpreters, including the star singer Adiss Harmandian, moved to the United States. Some, like Manuel Menenghetchian, sang about Armenian 'positive neutrality', voicing the melancholy of many Armenian Lebanese for lost peace and hope for a solution to the crisis.

'The black clouds have spread over you, Lebanon/ Hail started falling and stabbed your soul/ Storms and thunder shocked your soul, Lebanon/ Earthquakes have shaken you, Lebanon/ Destroyed your life, Lebanon/ Brothers turned into lions against each other/ Tearing up your heart, Lebanon/ Sisters turned into eagles against each other / Pricking your eyes, Lebanon / Your clear waters were all painted with blood, Lebanon / [...] Why, why, Lebanon? / [...] Your cedars will bloom again / And the bells will chime / With new songs of peace / And from the domes of the mosques / Songs will be heard wishing you love and unity / Two brotherly rows will stand like Mount Sannine / And singing loudly will worship you, Lebanon'.[56]

## Armenian Media during the Lebanese War

As in the case of many other establishments and businesses, Arab or Armenian alike, the fate of Armenian newspapers, periodicals, printing presses, and publishing houses depended in large part on their location during the various phases of the conflict. Most of them were – in one way or the other – affected, and had to take up new strategies to continue their activity. The Armenian daily papers suffered greatly, and struggled to continue regular activity. The Dashnak daily *Aztag*, which was originally produced and printed in West Beirut, found itself increasingly separated from its public, mostly living in the eastern part of the city. In 1982, following the Israeli invasion, the paper was transferred to Bourj Hammoud.[57] *Zartonk*, the Ramkavar daily, was also located in a critical area, close to the green line and the port of Beirut. The building hosting *Zartonk*, the Ramkavar-owned Tekeyan Centre in Gemmayzeh, was frequently shot at, and publication became erratic, particularly in 1976.[58] *Ararat*, the Hunchak daily, became the target of politically motivated attacks, allegedly by the Lebanese Forces: the headquarters of the paper were destroyed by an explosion on 9 May 1979 and publication had to stop until November of that year. In 1983 *Ararat* moved its printing house to the Sahagian-Levon Megerditchian college.[59] The only formally independent Armenian daily, Dickran Tospat's *Ayk*, suffered more than the others. Located in close proximity to the green line, the paper struggled to continue publication and, at the end of June 1975, closed down.[60]

In the context of a highly deteriorated security situation, in which the movement of people and the distribution of newspapers and magazines had become dangerous, an increasing role in the diffusion of Armenian information, culture, and entertainment was played by the radio. The appearance, during the 1980s, of a number of low-budget Armenian radio stations in Lebanon was made possible by technological advances (which reduced costs), and by the climate of general deregulation determined by the collapse of state. The first of these were Radio Paradise, and the Dashnak party's radio station, Vana Tzain (Voice of Van); other stations followed, including Radio Libano-Hay, Voice of Love, and Nairi, the Hunchak party's radio station.[61]

# The Armenian Communities and the Lebanese and Syrian Economy in the 1970s and 1980s

## *The Lebanese Crisis, the War, and the Economy of the Armenian Community*

Scholars have often pointed to the importance of economic factors in explaining the civil and political crisis that led to the Lebanese war. Many have underlined the limits of the Lebanese path of economic development and shown that the model of the 'merchant republic' contributed to the generation of inequality and fuelled social tension; a 'dark side' of the 'Lebanese miracle' that was only partially counterbalanced by the efforts of the *chehabist* state to ensure a better distribution of wealth and a more balanced regional development of the country.[62] In particular, as the government struggled to resist constant inflationary pressures, the purchasing power of workers and peasants was eroded: Nasr, writing in 1978, estimated that in the decade between 1964 and 1974, 'while workers' wages increased by 47 per cent, the official cost of living index increased by at least 110 per cent', resulting in an 'important decrease, in real terms, of the already low standard of living of the workers'.[63] It has also been argued that, although by the early 1970s the economic and social gap between the different communities in the country appeared to be closing, some of the inequalities mentioned tended to follow lines of confessional division, with the leading Christian communities maintaining a position of relative advantage.[64] In other words, in a general economic scenario – still in the early 1970s – characterised by growth and increased affluence, some categories of workers and some confessional groups in the country appeared to be the 'losers' of the Lebanese economic miracle.

This was not the case with the Armenians. On the eve of the war they generally appeared to be among those who had been able to reap benefits from the period of sustained growth that characterised the country from the 1950s, an outcome which was arguably related to the successful economic emancipation of the Armenian working class (from unskilled to skilled, from salaried to self-employed), to the general success of Armenian entrepreneurship, and to the efficiency of the Armenian network of social self-help institutions. It is perhaps possible to affirm that the Armenians in the early 1970s were living in a phase of economic prosperity and development.

The war disrupted the Lebanese 'economic miracle' and deeply affected the economy of Armenian firms and households. The Lebanese economic system of the 'merchant republic' was shattered and gradually replaced by a militia-dominated 'war system'.[65] The first and most immediate effect of the war on the economy was the destruction of capital. As the fighting largely took place in urban and peri-urban areas (particularly in Beirut), buildings and machinery were damaged or destroyed, stocks and banks looted, and industrial and commercial facilities occupied by militias. According to UN estimates, the damage to infrastructures and physical assets alone, over the 1975–1990 period, amounted to $25 billion.[66] Secondly, the national labour market, that had gradually developed – particularly under *chehabism* – was broken down: the war effectively compartmentalised Lebanese territory making personal movements from one sector to the other dangerous or – at times – impossible. The conventional national market and system for the distribution of goods was also broken up: militias took up the functions of the commercial brokers and exploited positions of rent (ports, checkpoints), extracting fees on imports, exports and on the national distribution of goods. The fifteen years of civil war reduced the per capita GNP to one-third of its value in 1975.[67]

The fate of Armenian firms, in large part small and medium-size commercial and industrial enterprises, chiefly depended on the location of their activities and on the changing conditions of access to local and international markets. Some businesses, caught in battle zones, were badly hit;[68] others were only marginally affected or even prospered thanks to the fact that competition had been reduced. Many entrepreneurs closed down their businesses and migrated, causing the overall size of the Armenian sector of the economy to shrink; however, the nature of the conflict, fought on an intermittent basis, and characterized by shifting alliances and fronts, also allowed phases of recovery. In general, the fact that the ownership or the workers of a business were Armenians – and thus strictly speaking 'neutral' – was of little or no consequence in avoiding material damage, looting, disruption of activities and closures. However, Armenian identities appeared – at times and in certain areas – to offer advantages in terms of freedom of movement of persons and goods across sectors, and thus promoted a certain role for the Armenians as economic mediators.[69] In the absence of comprehensive and detailed information, anecdotal evidence may help in sketching a rough picture of the effects of the war on Armenian firms and offer examples of their strategies of adaptation and survival.

The Dantziguian factory in Mkelles, located in a critical area of confrontation between Christian militias and the Palestinians, was damaged by a major fire in the early stages of the war; for some time workers and management could not reach the facilities and activity stopped. As the war continued, the demand for the firm's products, metal fittings for the construction industry, shrank considerably, and activities were almost completely re-located abroad: an office was opened in Sharjah in the United Arab Emirates, a branch was registered in France, and substantial contracts were won in Egypt and Thailand.[70] Ayanian, which was trading in electrical equipment, also suffered fires and damages to its stores and facilities; but, more importantly, the firm lost its capacity to trade with the Middle Eastern markets it used to serve.[71] Vivaro, a small enterprise producing and distributing shoes, was able to take advantage of a certain, relative security enjoyed in the Armenian quarter of Bourj Hammoud. The firm did good business during most of the war: the war damaged the import of shoes from the Far East, creating some form of protection for the Lebanese industry; at the same time, competing firms located in the industrial district of Beirut (the Madinat Sin'aiyah) were badly affected by the war, a fact that strengthened the position of the producers located in Bourj Hammoud. As a consequence, the small Vivaro workshop worked at full capacity, cramming up to twenty-seven workers into a small building, using generators to remedy the frequent shortages of electricity. The distribution of the product out of the Armenian quarters was also fairly successful. Boxes of shoes would be sent to the port of Jounieh, loaded on small fishing boats and shipped to other parts of Lebanon, including West Beirut; militias controlling the ports would be paid a fee.[72]

The overall effects of the 'war system' and of the collapse of the 'merchant republic' on the economic conditions of Armenians households are hard to assess. The lack of data on the evolution of income within the community, the problem of how to consider Armenians who migrated (temporarily or permanently), and conflicting evidence emerging from interviews, all tend to leave the picture cloudy. It may appear paradoxical that many Armenians today remember the years of the war as a period of relative affluence – at least until the dramatic devaluation of the Lebanese pound during the second half of the 1980s. Sure enough, however, many Armenian families' possessions were hit, as they had properties and belongings damaged, occupied or destroyed by the war.

## The Armenians and the Political Economy of Syria under Asad

The rise to power of Hafiz Al-Asad in 1970 marked an important turn in the evolution of the Syrian political economy.[73] Under the new regime the state considerably reinforced its leading role in the economy, both in its capacity as regulator and planner, and in that of entrepreneur and employer, particularly as Asad committed the country to a vast program of import-substituting industrialization. At the same time, and *de facto* reversing the approach of the Ba'th in the 1960s, the development of the private sector was encouraged: private investors were called to play their part in strengthening the national economy, acting 'in the shadow of state-led growth' and focusing on 'less capital-intensive ventures […] such as trade and services, light manufacturing industries, and construction'.[74] As part of measures meant to encourage the private sector, foreign trade was partially liberalized, in the framework of what became later described as

Syria's first *infitah*, or 'open door policy'. Meanwhile, Asad's policy of *détente* with the oil-rich monarchies of the Gulf increased the possibilities of Arab economic co-operation and made large amounts of financing available to the state.

Scholars have observed that the new course of the Syrian political economy in the 1970s was largely driven by the need of the new leadership to enlarge its basis of support and consolidate its power. Extended control over the economy and the availability of rents (from Arab aid and the incipient Syrian oil industry) could be and were used by the state to win the support of key components of the society. For Hinnebusch the state was transformed into a 'font of patronage'; under the new system 'individuals and small groups' would compete 'for access to state patronage – whether jobs, contracts, or other privileges'.[75] Access to state contracts and privileges meant, for the clientele that managed to obtain them, concrete possibilities of enrichment and social advancement.

Competition for access to patronage often made use of connections based on regional, confessional and communal identities; however, evidence suggests that it would be wrong to assume that only certain communities –most notably the President's Alawi community – reaped the benefits.[76] Indeed, the case of the Armenians confirms that other communities had chances too, and that personal connections to the leadership were more important than other allegiances. A few Armenian entrepreneurs, particularly in Damascus, managed to develop those connections and obtained substantial benefits, rising to the status of the so called *tabaqa jadida*, the new commercial, bourgeois Syrian upper class. The most relevant example is perhaps that of the Yacoubian family, whose construction firm is said to have significantly benefited from the personal connections it managed to establish with President Hafiz Al-Asad and his family entourage.[77] The Boghossian family of Damascus, involved in a number of joint ventures with the Yacoubians and holding several agencies for imported industrial products, seem to offer another example.[78]

Besides the small elite, most of the Armenian community, including the large middle class and lower-middle class of Aleppo, appears to have generally benefited from the period of economic growth that characterized the country in the course of the 1970s. The increased well-being enjoyed by the Armenians can perhaps be measured by their investments in real estate. In the course of the 1970s the Armenian residential quarters of Aleppo were renewed, and the brick houses built in the 1930s were replaced by tall concrete buildings. It was only in the second half of the 1980s, when Syria went through a severe balance of payments crisis and the *infitah*, liberalising economic policy, was temporary shelved, that the community suffered the effects of crisis. The fall in the price of oil and the consequent reduction of the flow of Arab aid to the country exposed the limitations and weaknesses of the national political economy and triggered a severe financial crisis. Armenian commercial and industrial entrepreneurs were damaged by the restrictions imposed on imports, while soaring inflation hit the purchasing power of families.[79]

# Notes

1. Estimate based on a comparison of data contained in A.H. Hourani. 1946. *Syria and Lebanon: A Political Essay*, London, New York and Toronto: Oxford University Press, appendix B, table II, 386; Social Action Committee of the Armenian Evangelical Union. 1970. *A Survey of Social Problems and Needs Within the Armenian Community in Lebanon*. Beirut, 30; VV.AA. 1972. *The Middle East and North Africa*, 19 (1972–73), London: Europa Publications, 499. Population data concerning the different communities of Lebanon are easily the object of disagreement. Although rather precise information is in general available to the religious and political authorities, official statements on population are made with extreme caution, due to their potential effect on the legitimacy of the current confessional balance within the consociational political system (one of the reasons why official, national censuses were not held since 1932). The Armenian communities are no exception: the official data presented by the Churches are often criticized for being exaggerated but also, even if rarely, for being too conservative.

2. Social Action Committee, *A Survey of Social Problems*, 30. The break up of the three denominations is as follows: Apostolics 150,000; Catholics 22,500; Evangelicals 7,500.

3. In the battle of Sardarabad, fought on May 22–24, 1918, an Armenian volunteer army defeated and repelled the advance of the Turkish army into Armenia, saving its independence. See C.J. Walker. 1990. *Armenia: the Survival of a Nation*, second edition, London: Routledge, 254–255.

4. It has been noted that this change of approach was not without ambiguities; Moscow balanced a policy of toleration of Armenian nationalism with a close control over it, so that it could defuse potential nationalist explosions internally and avoid any embarrassment in international relations with Turkey. See G. Minassian. 2002. *Guerre et Terrorisme Arméniens*, Paris: Presses Universitaires de France, 19.

5. On the shift between 'exilic nationalism' and 'diasporic trasnationalism' in the Armenian diasporas see K. Tölölyan. 2001. 'Elites and Institutions in the Armenian Transnation', paper presented at the conference Transnational Migration: Comparative Perspectives, Princeton University, 30 June-1 July.

6.  The expression is used, in French, by S. Kassir. 1994. *La Guerre du Liban: De la Dissension Nationale au Conflit Régional*, second edition, Paris and Beirut: Karthala and CERMOC, Chapter 3, 69–92.

7.  It is hard to assess the number of Armenians who engaged in each of the fronts. There is little doubt that the figure put forward by Schahgaldian for the Armenians who had become members of the Kata'ib – 'no less than 5,000' – is highly exaggerated; see N.B. Schahgaldian. 1979. 'The Political Integration of an Immigrant Community into a Composite Society: the Armenians in Lebanon, 1920–1974', Ph.D. dissertation. New York: Columbia University, 254. According to Karim Pakradouni, a member of the party since the late 1950s and, by 1975, a prominent figure in the organisation, Armenian membership was between 1,000 and 1,500. These were prevailingly Armenians of the 'third generation', for most part residents of non-Armenian areas and predominantly Armenian Catholics. Interview with Mr. Karim Pakradouni, president of the Kata'ib party, Beirut, 18 October 2005.

8.  Minassian, *Guerre et Terrorisme Arméniens*, 8.

9.  The Armenian expression *Hay Tahd* translates as 'the Armenian case' and it defines the post-Genocide Armenian effort to place the issues of the Genocide and the lost lands 'on the agendas of Western states and media'. See a note by Prof. K. Tölölyan on the difference between '*Haigagan Hartz*' [The Armenian question] and '*Hay Tahd*' [The Armenian case] published on the webpage http://groong.usc.edu/ro/ro-19980921.html, visited on March 22, 2007.

10. Minassian, *Guerre et Terrorisme Arméniens*, 28, translation by the author.

11. Kassir, *La Guerre du Liban*, 71.

12. See M.C. Hudson. 1968. *The Precarious Republic: Modernisation in Lebanon*, New York: Random House, 141.

13. See Kassir, *La Guerre du Liban*, 119; Kassir describes a 'witch hunt' conducted by the Maronite leadership and aimed at eliminating Christian leftist elements residing in East Beirut.

14. Minassian, *Guerre et Terrorisme Arméniens*, 55, quoting from *Le Réveil*, 14 September 1979.

15. Ibid., 54.

16. The most notable of these was, of course, the election of President Bashir Gemayel in 1982. Interview with Mr. Karim Pakradouni, President of the Kata'ib party, Beirut, 18 October 2005.

17. Largely, the role of a neutral, stabilizing factor within the Christian sector. See Minassian, *Guerre et Terrorisme Arméniens*, 54–55.

18. Given the secrecy that surrounded the establishment and activity of these organisations, it is no wonder that information on the issue is scarce and not always reliable. See A. Kurtz and A. Merari. 1985. *ASALA, Irrational Terror or Political Tool*, Jerusalem: The Jerusalem Post and Westview Press; M.M. Gunter. 1990. *Transnational Armenian Activism*, London: Research Institute for the Study of Conflict and Terrorism; F.P. Hyland. 1991. *The Armenian*

*Terrorism: The Past, the Present, the Prospects*, Boulder, San Francisco and Oxford: Westview Press; Y.I. Al-Jahmani. 2001. *Turkiya wa al-Arman* [Turkey and the Armenians], Damascus: Dar al-Hawran; Minassian, *Guerre et Terrorisme Arméniens*.

19. Minassian, *Guerre et Terrorisme Arméniens*, 29.
20. Hyland, *The Armenian Terrorism*, 27.
21. Kurtz and Merari, *ASALA*, 24–27.
22. There has been some controversy regarding the link between the Dashnak and the JCGA: the Dashnak leadership has traditionally denied that the JCGA was ever structurally linked to the party. The existing literature, however, seems to leave little space for doubt. For Minassian '*Même s'il reste encore quelques irréductibles qui refusent d'associer le CJGA à la FRA* [Fédération Révolutionnaire Arménienne, Dashnak], *il n'y a aujourd'hui aucun doute sur l'identité des membres du CJGA et leur appartenance au réseau* dachnak' (Minassian, *Guerre et Terrorisme Arméniens*, 32). On the link between the Dashnak and the JCAG also see Hyland, *The Armenian Terrorism*, 61–62.
23. Hyland, *The Armenian Terrorism*, 62.
24. Minassian, *Guerre et Terrorisme Arméniens*, 35.
25. Hyland, *The Armenian Terrorism*, 68.
26. See P. Seale. 1988. *Asad of Syria: The Struggle for the Middle East*, London: I.B. Tauris, 142–153.
27. R. Hinnebusch. 2001. *Syria: Revolution from Above*, London and New York: Routledge, 65–88.
28. On the promotion of a national Syrian identity as a means to legitimize the Alawi leadership see S. Valter. 2002. *La Construction Nationale Syrienne: Légitimation de la Nature Communautaire du Pouvoir par le Discours Historique*, Paris: CNRS.
29. With the exception of the period 1990–1992, as will be shown in the next chapter.
30. That is, half of the People's Assembly. Permanent Syrian Constitution of 13 March 1973, Article 53.
31. Usually the Minister and then Vice President Abd El-Halim Khaddam.
32. Minassian, *Guerre et Terrorisme Arméniens*, 63–64.
33. See H.H. Karekin II, Catholicos of Cilicia. 1989. *The Cross Made of the Cedars of Lebanon*, Antelias: Catholicosate of the Great House of Cilicia.
34. Interview with Ms. Manoushag Boyadjian, eyewitness, Dbayeh, 27 November 2002.
35. Hinnebusch, *Syria, Revolution from Above*, 66; Seale, *Asad of Syria*, 173.
36. Hinnebusch, *Syria, Revolution from Above*, 66.
37. Permanent Syrian Constitution of March 13, 1973.
38. J. Tanielian. 2002. *Lipananahay Tebrotze: Tiver yev Mdoroumner* [The Armenian Schools in Lebanon, Some Data and Some Ideas], Beyrouth, 50; the same study also appeared in *Zartonk* on August 17, 24, 31 and September 7 and 14, 2002.

39. 'Note sur l'enseignement Arménien au Liban', in *Travaux et Jours*, 39 (April-June 1971), 77.
40. Ibid.
41. Ibid., 75.
42. Interview with Mr. Zaven Messerlian, principal of the Armenian Evangelical College, Beirut, 4 July 2002.
43. Interview with Ms. Manoushag Boyadjian, former teacher at Jemaran and principal at the Yeghishe Manoukian college, Dbayeh, 27 November 2002. Haigazian University also suffered enormously, caught in the disputed neighbourhood of Kantari. Teaching was relocated to East Beirut in the second half of the 1980s.
44. Ibid.
45. Tanielian, *Lipananahay Tebrotze*, 50.
46. The Mechitarist college, for instance, only started teaching subjects in Arabic in 1976; the Nazarian college introduced courses of civics, history and geography in Arabic in 1977–78. See A. Nasri Messarra. 1994. *Théorie Générale du Système Politique Libanais*, Paris: Cariscript, 118–119.
47. Constitution of the Syrian Arab Republic, 1973, translation by P.B. Heller.
48. Ibid.
49. Ibid.
50. Presentation brochure, 'Hazkayine Khorhourt 1976–1977'.
51. See R. Assaf and L. Barakat (ed.). 2003. *Atlas du Liban*, Beirut: Presses de l'Université Saint-Joseph, 80. It is estimated that the overall number of migrants during the period 1975–1990 was close to 900,000.
52. Tölölyan, 'Elites and Institutions in the Armenian Transnation', referring to the Hart-Celler Act of 1965, which altered the immigration quotas for a number of countries, including Lebanon, Syria, Iran, Egypt and Turkey.
53. J. Tanielian. 1986. *Lipananahay Debakroutioune Baderazmi Darineroun 1976–1984* [Armenian Lebanese printing during the war years 1976–1984], Beirut, 79–80.
54. Ibid., 80–82.
55. Interview with Zohrab Yacoubian, Bourj Hammoud, 20 October 2003. An example of this wartime Armenian theatre is Yacoubian's series of bitter comedies on Bourj Hammoud.
56. 'Manuel', *Lipanan* [Lebanon], song from the album *Yerevan, Lipanan* [Yerevan, Lebanon], ca. second half of the 1970s; translation from Armenian by Ms. Talar Khatchigian.
57. Tanielian, *Lipananahay Debakroutioune*, 75.
58. Ibid., 76.
59. Ibid.
60. Ibid., 74. See the chief editor's farewell note in *Ayk*'s last issue, published on June 30, 1975.
61. Interview with Armen Abdalian, director of Dashnak Radio station *Vana Tzain*, Bourj Hammoud, 30 October 2003.

62. See, for instance, Hudson, *The Precarious Republic*, 63–70; S. Nasr. 1978. 'Backdrop to Civil War: the Crisis of Lebanese Capitalism', *MERIP Reports*, 73, 3–13; A. Dagher. 1995. *L'Etat et l'Economie au Liban*, Beirut: CERMOC, 103 ff.; E. Picard, 1996. *Lebanon, a Shattered Country*, New York and London: Holmes & Meier, 92–95; F. Debié and D. Pieter. 2003. *La Paix et la Crise: le Liban Reconstruit?*, Paris: Presses Universitaires de France, 27–48.

63. Nasr, 'Backdrop to Civil War', 11.

64. Kassir, *La Guerre du Liban*, 43.

65. See Debié and Pieter, *La Paix et la Crise*, 49–76.

66. Republic of Lebanon, Ministry of Finance, Country Profile, www.finance.gov.lb/main/aboutus/CountryProfile/CountryOverview.pdf, 10, retrieved on July 25, 2004.

67. Ibid.

68. These included, for instance, the many Armenian shops in the central Beirut commercial district looted and destroyed in the first phase of the war.

69. See Debié and Pieter, *La Paix et la Crise*, 70 : '*les plus neutres des groupes communautaires, les Arméniens, les Grecs catholiques, par exemple, voient leur rôle d'intermédiation se développer*'.

70. Interview with Mr. Garbis Dantziguian, entrepreneur, Mkelles, 29 October 2003.

71. Interview with Mr. Paul Ayanian, entrepreneur, Dora, 23 October 2003.

72. Interview with Mr. Varoujian Khandjian, entrepreneur, Bourj Hammoud, 9 December 2003.

73. On the political economy of Syria under Asad see, among others, E. Longuenesse. 1979. 'The Class Nature of the State in Syria: Contribution to an Analysis', *MERIP Reports*, 77, 3–11; V. Perthes. 1995. *The Political Economy of Syria under Asad*, London and New York: I.B. Tauris; Hinnebusch, *Syria, Revolution from Above*, 87–88.

74. Perthes, *The Political Economy of Syria*, 50–51.

75. Hinnebusch, *Syria, Revolution from Above*, 87.

76. See, on this, Perthes, *The Political Economy of Syria*, 181–187.

77. Besides the core business of construction, the Yacoubians are agents for Kodak, Nokia, and of other imported industrial goods. Raffi and Nazo Yacoubian are said to be personal friends of President Bashar Al-Asad. Various interviews.

78. Author's interviews.

79. See Hinnebusch, *Syria, Revolution from Above*, 128–129.

# 5

# Difficult Recovery and Uncertain Future: The Armenians in Lebanon and Syria in the 1990s and Beyond

## Introduction

The 1990s and the first half of the 2000s have appeared to be a period of uncertainty about the fate of Armenian cultural diversity in the Levant. Uncertainty has been in part fuelled by the conditions of the Lebanese and Syrian economies: the difficult economic recovery of post-war Lebanon and the economic crisis that has variably affected Syria since the second half of the 1980s have taken their toll on the Armenian communities of the two countries, contributed to the phenomenon of migration, and raised questions about the financial sustainability of the system of Armenian communal institutions.

In Lebanon, uncertainty has also emerged with the opening – among the community – of a phase of reflection on the very meaning of the presence of Armenian cultural diversity in the country. The reflection has been, first of all, connected to the experience of the war, and to the profound, often contradictory changes that it has produced in the way Armenians regard Lebanon. On the one hand, the war has eroded the sense of 'trust' in Lebanon of many Armenians, the idea that Lebanon can be a 'permanent' home, an environment that is hospitable socially, politically, and economically. This has of course encouraged migration, but also – in the case of families who did not migrate – generated widespread disillusionment about the prospect of living in Lebanon, particularly among the younger generations.[1] On the other hand, in a striking contradiction, the experience of the war seems to have reinforced the sense of belonging to Lebanon for many of those who remained or returned. In other words, the war, the shared endurance, and even the communal self-help and self-governance efforts appear to have been significant 'Lebanonizing'[2] experiences, common as they were with those of most fellow Lebanese. The trend toward the further 'Lebanonization' of part of the community has encouraged some marginal elements to adopt openly assimilationist approaches; for the majority, however, it seems to have revived and given momentum to the already mentioned shift from the feeling of being a 'nation in exile' to that of being a 'permanent transnational diaspora', based in Lebanon and attached to both its Armenian *and* Lebanese identity.

The reflections on the meaning of Armenian identity in post-war Lebanon have also been deeply influenced by a crucial event in the history of the Armenian people: the independence of the Republic of Armenia in September 1991, seventy-one years after the fall of the first Armenian Republic in 1920. Independence, and the crisis in Karabagh between 1988 and 1994, have become important foci and symbols of traditional, 'exilic' Armenian nationalism, reinforcing the predominance of Armenian concerns over Lebanese ones. However, by facilitating a dramatic increase in the interaction between Armenia and the diasporas, independence has helped dispel myths about Armenian nationalism and helped to identify, or encouraged to search for alternative ways to understand Armenian identities.

In the light of the varied and highly contradictory positions that have emerged, the community's reflection on the meaning and role of Armenian cultural diversity in Lebanon appears, early in the 2000s, far from resolved. What shape, and what content contemporary Armenian Lebanese identities should aspire to remain largely unclear. The debate is also, in part, about power and leadership within the community; in particular, between political parties, *within* political parties, and between political parties and the community at large.

In Lebanon, the opening of some form of debate over Armenian identity has taken place in the context of the process of reconstruction of the Lebanese state that started in 1989–1990. Reconstruction posed once again the question of how to organize relations between the state and the diverse ethno-cultural groups forming Lebanese society. Given the existing local, regional, and international constraints, the path followed was that of continuity with the past, and with the consociational formula that – as this book has shown – has in the past offered the Armenians a chance to preserve their cultural diversity in Lebanon. The key question in the relation between the Armenians and the Lebanese state today is whether the new version of the consociational agreement – and, more generally, the re-establishment of the 'Lebanese model' – will again fully serve the Armenian community's needs and aspirations. In the light of the tragic failures of consociationalism in Lebanon it would be irresponsible not to imagine alternatives that both overcome confessionalism and safeguard the cultural needs and rights of diverse cultures. As for the Armenians, it appears that uncertainties about how the Armenian community envisages the space and role of its cultural diversity in Lebanon have affected its position toward post-war reconstruction: so far, the Armenian leadership appears to have lacked unity and a clear long-term strategy, while it has – for the time being – fully accepted and supported to the new 'temporary' restoration of the Lebanese consociational agreement. This sort of conservative 'default approach' might appear to some as the safest available path; to others it is the only one available. There is no clear indication, however, that it will stop the cultural decline which began with the war.

In Syria, a certain reflection on the meaning and role of Armenian cultural diversity has also been present within the community; however, the debate has not matched the one in Lebanon, neither in extent nor depth. For the Armenians of Syria too, the independence of Armenia and the question of Karabagh were important events contributing to re-shape their contemporary Syrian-Armenian identity. The increase of personal visits to Armenia (for tourism, or to participate in Armenian events of various kind), the availability of TV broadcasts from Armenia, and – for a few – even direct participation in fighting in Karabakh, have provided new strong connections with an Armenian world outside Syria. However, these connections seem to have been interpreted mostly through the lens of traditional 'exilic nationalism', rather than within the logic of a 'permanent' Syrian diaspora. In other words, they seem to have reinforced the notion of Armenian separateness, the model of an Armenian 'parallel' life in Syria, rather than promoting new approaches to integration.

The reasons for this are complex, but – once again – appear to depend largely on the nature of the Syrian Ba'thist-Asadist state. The political formula that has dominated Syria since 1970, and that was substantially extended after the death of president Hafiz Al-Asad, seems to leave little space for approaches to 'Armenianness' that are alternative to the unspoken-unwritten existing agreement between the community and the state described in the previous chapter. On the one hand, any deeper involvement of the Armenians in the Syrian state can hardly be imagined in a form that does not compromise their cultural diversity; on the other, the Syrian state can hardly accept greater involvement of the Armenians in 'diaspora activities' without undermining the regime's main, formal, legitimizing political discourse.

## Armenian Political Participation in Contemporary Lebanon and Syria

*The Re-establishment of the Lebanese Consociational System: The Ta'if Agreement and the Armenians*

The first steps of the political reconstruction of Lebanon were taken in October 1989 with the signing of the Ta'if agreement. The agreement, reached while hostilities were still raging and ratified by what remained of the Lebanese parliament elected in 1972,[3] provided the political formula to end the war. At its core, it consisted in the re-establishment of the national pact, of which it reproduced the twin, main propositions: the independent identity of Lebanon, and its belonging to the wider Arab family.[4] The agreement, and the unofficial political understandings that accompanied it, also provided for the re-establishment of the consociational political system based on confessional affiliations. In a sort of ritual evocation of the spirit of the national pact of 1943, confessionalism was declared once again a temporary arrangement, and its abolishment identified as an 'essential national objective'; however, as an observer has pointed out, 'the most salient feature of Lebanons's postwar political system [was] the solidification of political communitarianism'.[5] The post-war version of consociationalism adjusted the confessional balance to give Christians and Muslims equal representation in the parliament and reinforced the executive powers of the cabinet at the expense of those of the President of the Republic.[6]

Not surprisingly, the role played by the Armenians in the negotiations that led to the Ta'if agreement was marginal. Historically outsiders in Lebanon, the Armenians had also voluntarily steered clear from participation in the war and lacked the political weight necessary to be admitted to the informal, inner circles where key decisions were made. Nevertheless, the community played its part: it was represented in Ta'if by a delegation of three, jointly supported by the main Armenian political forces.[7] The Armenians co-signed the agreement, contributed to its ratification, and supported it politically.

Using the meter of traditional Lebanese confessional politics, the new version of the consociational scheme which emerged from Ta'if could be regarded as positive for the community: within the readjusted confessional balance, the Armenians did not lose out. Ta'if had, first of all, provided yet another confirmation that the Armenians represented one of the permanent members of the Lebanese family: working papers produced during the negotiations allegedly indicated them formally as the 'seventh main community' of the country.[8] It should be observed that, as far as parliamentary representation was concerned, in the new, 108–member chamber the overall ratio of parliamentary seats reserved for the Armenians decreased from about 5 per cent to 4.6 per cent. However, the community managed to maintain the number of deputies that it had in 1972 (four Apostolic, and one Catholic), and when the number of members of parliament was raised to 128, the Armenians were granted a sixth seat (five Apostolic and one Catholic). Armenian representation in the Lebanese parliament had never been larger, particularly when considering that the Armenians formed a substantial part of Lebanon's Protestant community and that there was a realistic chance that an Armenian would be chosen to occupy the Protestant seat too.

Parliamentary representation was not the only area in which the Ta'if scheme granted the Armenians a fair share of political participation. For what concerned the government, the new political arrangement regulated in detail – although only at the informal level – the confessional composition of the cabinet, assigning to Muslims and Christians an equal number of ministerial posts. Armenians would be assigned one ministerial post in any cabinet formed by at least fourteen members, and at least two posts in the case of cabinets of twenty-eight members or more.

**Table 5.1. Scheme of the confessional composition of 14–members cabinets in post-Ta'if Lebanon**

| Confession | | Ministerial positions |
| --- | --- | --- |
| **Muslim** | Sunni | 3 Ministers (including the Prime Minister) |
| **Muslim** | Shi'a | 3 Ministers |
| **Muslim** | Druze | 1 Minister |
| **Christian** | Maronite | 3 Ministers |
| **Christian** | Greek Orthodox | 2 Ministers |
| **Christian** | Greek Catholic | 1 Minister |
| **Christian** | Armenian | 1 Minister |

The principle of the confessional distribution of governmental posts was maintained for the public administration too, albeit – formally – only for the upper echelon[9] of the civil service and without pre-assigning specific posts to any community. The text of Ta'if specified that '[d]urant la période transitoire [...] la règle de la représentation confessionnelle est abolie et le critère de la qualification et de la spécialisation sera retenu [...] à l'exception des fonctions de première catégorie et leur équivalents, qui seront repartis par égalité entre chrétiens et musulmans, sans spécification d'aucune fonction à aucune communauté en particulier'.[10]

The so-called 'first category', included 256 positions, to be divided equally between Christians and Muslims; the Armenian quota, calculated out of the Christian half on the basis of a political agreement, amounted to six or seven appointments.[11]

## The 'Practice' of Ta'if: Armenian Public Participation in Lebanon in the 1990s and Early 2000s

If the theory of Ta'if could be regarded as positive from the point of view of the Armenian leadership – as it restored guaranteed spaces for the community's public participation in Lebanon – its practice, during the 1990s and early 2000s, has been less generous. In the confessional perspective that continues to dominate post-war Lebanon there is a widespread perception among the Armenians that the representation 'rights' of the community are not fully respected; that is, the Armenians do not hold as many public positions as they should under Ta'if. As far as appointments in the public administration are concerned, in November 2002 only four 'first category' civil servants were Armenians (out of the six or seven that the community could expect to have): one of the Vice-Presidents of the Central Bank, the head of the General Inspectorate, the Director General of the Ministry of the Environment, and the Director General of the Central Statistical Office.[12] At the second category and lower levels Armenians were comparatively even less represented, with only a handful of civil servants. If, for the lower levels, this could be ascribed to a matter of choice – that is, to the traditional propensity of the Armenians to favour self-employment and private sector careers – the same cannot be said for the upper echelons: in this case the under-representation seems to be the result of the substantial political weakness of the community when it comes to negotiations for appointments.

Recently, the gap between the theory and the practice of the confessional system has appeared even more evident with regard to the composition of cabinets. Amidst the protests of the Armenian community, the cabinet formed in October 2000 and led by Prime Minister Rafiq Hariri included only one Armenian minister instead of two, in spite of the fact that it consisted of thirty members.[13] The government reshuffle of April 2003 failed to address the substance of the problem: on the contrary, the question took an ironic turn when the leader of the Kata'ib party, Karim Pakradouni, was appointed to the position of Minister for Administrative Reforms. Pakradouni, an Armenian Orthodox by birth, can hardly be regarded as a figure that represents the Armenians: a long-term militant of the Christian right, and a close collaborator of the late president Bashir Gemayel, he has virtually no political connections with the Armenian community.[14] Protests against the appointment of Pakradouni as one of the Armenian ministers were expressed at the highest level, but achieved no result. The Catholicos of Cilicia, Aram I, noted that

> *Malheureusement, nous avons constaté à notre grand regret que les droits de notre communauté ont été négligés ces derniers temps. [...] L'état libanais repose sur le respect des droits des communautés et leur*

*participation à la chose publique, et nous insistons sur la relation qui existe entre le respect des droits et la participation. Par conséquent, il faut établir* une différence entre l'appartenance d'office à une communauté donnée par le biais d'une carte d'identité et une appartenance effective *qui confère une réelle représentativité.*[15]

In the new political phase that began with the assassination of former PM Rafiq Hariri, the Armenian community's representation in the cabinet has grown weaker and its political marginalization more evident. In the twenty-four ministers strong cabinet formed by PM Fouad Siniora at the end of June 2005, the Armenians failed to secure a key post or to obtain a second representative. They were solely represented by Jean Oghassabian, a Hariri-supported relative newcomer who can count on a limited following within the Armenian community itself.[16]

Identifying the reasons for the community's political weakness in obtaining the observance of the confessional quotas set by Ta'if is not a straightforward exercise. Weakness appears to be the result of a combination of factors. Among these, the decline of the demographic presence of Armenians in the country does play a role. It is true that the Armenian community was not alone in suffering from migration during the war; it is, however, the case that a larger Armenian population, and the number of votes that it could carry, would be more important for the Armenians than for others, as it could make up for the comparative lack of other sources of power which have been important in post-war Lebanon (traditional legitimacy, control of militias or of similar strategic resources, the backing of regional or international powers, and so on).

A measure of the demographic crisis of the community, and of its effect on the political 'weight' of the community, is given by the analysis of data regarding Armenian participation in parliamentary elections. For 1996 and 2000 the figures for Armenian participation in the vote are remarkably low, at around 24 per cent of the eligible electors, against a national average that has ranged between 40 and 44 per cent.[17] On the occasion of the elections of 2000, Armenian votes amounted to a mere 28,000, out of a total number of eligible electors of more than 116,000. Although these low figures stem, in part, from an actual lack of interest of the Armenian public in electoral participation, there is reason to believe that they also indicate that a high percentage of Armenian electors are simply not living in the country. An important Armenian party official, who has access to detailed information on the Armenian electoral districts, confidently told this author that, in the 2000 elections, Armenian participation had actually been satisfactory, and that only about 3,000 of the eligible Armenian electors did not make it to the polling stations. Projections based on this figure would suggest that the current, overall Armenian population living in Lebanon and holding Lebanese citizenship hardly reaches 53,000.[18]

Besides the issue of demographic decline, the community's political weakness seems the result of a crisis that, since the end of the civil war, has affected the Armenian political leadership and relations with the society it represents. Symptoms of this crisis are not hard to find. Party officials often complain about the lack of participation in the political activities of the community, particularly where youth are concerned. In an interview, a prominent Hunchak figure complained that the party's youth is increasingly able to forget their party affiliation and side with the highest bidder, regardless of the party's position.[19] While the parties have so far been able to substantially maintain the loyalty of the vote of Armenian families in general elections, this cannot be taken for granted in the future.

The Lebanese-Armenian nationalist parties appear, first of all, to be suffering from a crisis of ideology. In the case of the Dashnak, the second half of the 1980s saw the beginning of a process of revision and partial demise of the *'Hay Tahd*-ist cultural revolution' and the rapid abandoning of the terrorist strategy that it upheld. However, the new phase has so far failed to produce a clear, consistent and credible vision of what the party's aims and strategies should be in the twenty-first century, particularly after the independence of Armenia. The party has found it uneasy getting past its historical 'revolutionary' character and finding forms of sustainable institutionalization both in Armenia and the diaspora.[20] Locally, the Lebanese Dashnak is perceived by many as a party whose ideology has been eroded over the years and that is today increasingly unable to understand and address the demands of the contemporary Armenian Lebanese diaspora. The party, which maintains secretive traits in its organization and membership, has decided so far to operate without obtaining a formal registration from the Lebanese authorities, a fact that seems to confirm that it is not ready to become, locally, a fully Lebanese institution.[21] The central theme of Dashnak discourse, the Armenian cause, remains a primary concern for virtually all Armenians in Lebanon; however, the community is, more than ever, willingly or not, coming out of the 'Armenian ghettos' and discovering itself as Lebanese. More than ever, Armenian cultural diversity in Lebanon appears under pressure (as witnessed, for instance, by the continuing crisis of the Armenian schools), and in search of new formulas of co-existence. In front of a changing Armenian community the party tends to appear on the defensive, rather than being pro-active. Similar observations could be made for the Lebanese Hunchak: while the party remains formally committed to its nationalist and socialist agenda, it appears hardly able to formulate a long term, sustainable strategy for the preservation of Armenian diversity in Lebanon.[22]

Dissatisfaction with the Armenian parties also appears to be a reaction against their monopolization of the communal institutions and overall dominance of Armenian life, increasingly perceived by many as undemocratic and intrusive. The Dashnak, still the hegemonic force within the Armenian community, is criticized for the control that it seeks to maintain over the Armenian Apostolic Church, in Armenian economic life, and in the running of Armenian communal institutions (school boards, charities, etc.). In Bourj Hammoud, its traditional stronghold, the party arguably maintains traits of quasi territorial control, exploiting in full the opportunities granted by the weakness of Lebanese state institutions.[23] Anything, from planning permission to the settlement of a dispute between neighbours, or the sale of a shop or an apartment, might be subject to some form of intervention by the party, either directly or through the local administration that it controls. A Dashnak official, who declared himself to be in charge of the 'liaison' between the party and the Lebanese Police, revealed that incidents involving Armenians in Bourj Hammoud, and reported to the Police, are sometimes referred by the latter to the party for an informal settlement.[24] The party also appears to maintain its own informal means of enforcement and has been accused of resorting to violence and intimidation.

The first Lebanese parliamentary elections after the end of the war were characterized, in the Armenian political camp, by a continuing Dashnak dominance. In 1992 and 1996, in the context of elections heavily influenced by the political intervention of Syria in Lebanese affairs,[25] the Dashnak managed to maintain its pivotal position within the Armenian sector and to lead winning Armenian lists including Dashnak, Hunchak and Ramkavar/AGBU figures.[26] On both occasions the Armenian coalitions sided with the strong, Syrian-supported lists of the government in charge.

The political scene became more complex following the election of President Emile Lahoud in 1998. In 2000 the antagonism between Lahoud and Hariri forced the Armenian parties to make a choice between supporting the governmental list of Prime Minister Salim Hoss, or siding with Rafiq Hariri in his attempted political comeback. In the political jockeying that preceded the elections, the unity of the Armenian camp – and indeed any illusion about its political consistency – was shattered by Hariri's determination to create a base of support within the community. As a part of a campaign to boost his image among the Armenians, Hariri opened offices in the Armenian neighbourhoods, dispensed aid to needy families, and introduced a fifteen minutes news service in Armenian on his own television network, *Al-Mustaqbal*. As the elections approached, Hariri disregarded the traditional leading role of the Dashnak in forging the electoral alliances in the Armenian sector and proceeded to autonomously pick his own candidates; in the process, internal splits within the Hunchak and Ramkavar parties also came to play a role.[27] As far as the Dashnaks were concerned, negotiations to join the Hariri list failed when it became evident that the party could only join on Hariri's conditions: notably, renouncing the candidacy of an Armenian for the Protestant seat and renouncing a long-standing tradition of maintaining an 'Armenian bloc' of deputies in parliament. The vote marked a political revolution for the Armenians: the Dashnak party managed to obtain the vast majority of the Armenian vote, but the Hoss list in which it ran lost the elections. As a result, for the first time in decades, Dashnak hegemony was defeated: the Dashnak only scored a modest victory in the Metn where the Minister and incumbent MP Sebouh Hovnanian was re-elected.

The defeat of the Dashnaks, and Hariri's successful 'raid' into the Armenian community, were far from being the final demise of the party's hegemony within the Armenian Lebanese diaspora. At the same time, the extremely poor ballot score of the 'Haririan'[28] winners within the community does not allow one to conclude that Armenian political opinion has effectively chosen an alternative: the new MPs obtained their seats with only a handful of Armenian votes. The elections of 2000 underlined, more generally, the collective political weakness of the Armenian position in Lebanon and stood as an example of the potential limitations of the Lebanese system in producing a fair representation of the community.

These limitations were strikingly confirmed in the course of the 2005 elections, which followed the assassination of Rafiq Hariri. The coalition led by Hariri's son, Sa'ad, disregarded calls for a more solidly supported Armenian representation: the Dashnak party was once again left out, on grounds that it was not part of the coalition that had participated in the anti-Syrian, anti-Lahoud popular demonstration of 14 March 2005.[29] In the Beirut constituencies, with no chance of winning against the all-powerful Hariri electoral machine, the Dashnaks decided to boycott the elections, and the four incumbent pro-Hariri Armenian MPs won uncontested the seats reserved for the community in an uncontested vote. The Armenian participation touched an all time-low, revealing the wide gap that exists between the community and its elected representatives. The Dashnaks managed to avoid complete exclusion from the new parliament thanks to a successful political alliance with Michel 'Aoun in the Metn: their candidate, Hagop Pakradouni, benefited from the Aounist success and won with a substantial margin. Incumbent MP George Kassardji was also re-elected with Dashnak support in the Zahleh district of the Beka'a.

**Table 5.2. Armenian MPs elected in Lebanon, 1992–2005**

| Election year | Name of MPs | Place of election |
|---|---|---|
| 1992 | Khatchig Babikian | Beirut |
| 1992 | Souren Khanamirian | Beirut |
| 1992 | Yeghia Jeredjian | Beirut |
| 1992 | Hagop Tchukhadarian (Cath.) | Beirut |

| 1992 | Nourijean Demirdjian (Evang.) | Beirut |
| 1992 | Chahe Barsoumian | North Metn |
| | | |
| 1996 | Sebouh Hovnanian | North Metn |
| 1996 | Khatchig Babikian[30] | Beirut |
| 1996 | Hagop Demirdjian | Beirut |
| 1996 | Hagop Tchoukhadarian (Cath.) | Beirut |
| 1996 | Apraham Dedeian (Evang.) | Beirut |
| 1996 | Yeghia Jeredjian | Beirut |
| 1996 | George Kassardji | Zahleh |
| | | |
| 2000 | Sebouh Hovnanian | North Metn |
| 2000 | Hagop Kassardjian | Beirut III |
| 2000 | Jean Oghassabian | Beirut III |
| 2000 | Serge Toursarkissian (Cath.) | Beirut III |
| 2000 | Yeghia Jeredjian | Beirut III |
| 2000 | George Kassardji | Zahleh (Beka'a II) |
| | | |
| 2005 | Hagop Pakradouni | North Metn |
| 2005 | Hagop Kassardjian | Beirut III |
| 2005 | Jean Oghassabian | Beirut III |
| 2005 | Serge Toursarkissian (Cath.) | Beirut III |
| 2005 | Yeghia Jeredjian | Beirut III |
| 2005 | George Kassardji | Zahleh (Beka'a II) |

**Table 5.3. Armenian representation in the post-Ta'if Lebanese cabinets (1989 to date)**

| Cabinet | Members | Armenian Minister(s) | Portfolio | Terms |
|---|---|---|---|---|
| **Salim Hoss** | 14 | Souren Khanamirian | Industry and Oil | Nov. '89 – Dec. '90 |
| **Omar Karame** | 30 | Khatchig Babikian Jack Choukadarian | Justice Environment | Dec. '90 – May '92 |
| **Rashid El-Solh** | 24 | Chahe Barsoumian | Industry and Oil | May '92 – Oct. '92 |
| **Rafiq Hariri** | 30 | Chahe Barsoumian Hagop Demirdjian | State, then Social Affairs Economy and Commerce | Oct. '92 – May '95 |
| **Rafiq Hariri** | 30 | Chahe Barsoumian Hagop Demirdjian | Industry and Oil Municipalities | May '95 – Nov. '96 |
| **Rafiq Hariri** | 30 | Chahe Barsoumian Hagop Demirdjian | Industry and Oil Municipalities | Nov. '96 – Nov. '98 |

| | | | | |
|---|---|---|---|---|
| **Salim Hoss** | 18 | Arthur Nazarian | Environment | Dec. '98 –<br>Oct. '00 |
| **Rafiq Hariri** | 30 | Sebouh Hovnanian | Sports and Youth | Oct. '00 –<br>Apr. '03 |
| **Rafiq Hariri** | 30 | Sebouh Hovnanian<br>(Karim Pakradouni) | Sports and Youth<br>Administrative<br>Reforms | Apr. '03 –<br>Oct. '04 |
| **Omar Karame** | 19 | Alain Tabourian | Minister of State | Oct. '04 –<br>Apr. '05 |
| **Najib Mikati** | 14 | Alain Tabourian | Telecommunications,<br>Youth and Sports | Apr. '05 –<br>Jun. '05 |
| **Fouad Seniora** | 24 | Jean Oghassabian | Minister of State for<br>Administrative<br>Development | Jun. '05 –<br>present |

## Armenian Public Participation in Syria: The 1990s and Early 2000s

During the last decade of the presidency of Hafiz Al-Asad, and under his son and successor Bashar Al-Asad, Armenian participation in public life in Syria has been characterized by a substantial continuity with the past. The question of ethnicity remains one of the most persistent taboos in Syrian official discourse. The regime grants forms of recognition to the country's traditionally rich religious diversity, but continues to systematically play down the existence of allegiances to distinct communal or ethno-cultural identities; most crucially, it severely obstructs their autonomous political mobilization. The extent to which the rule of Asad has been successful in creating an overarching Arab-Syrian identity is open to debate. Clearly, a gap between public discourse and social reality continues to be perceivable in today's Syria: Syrians are generally well aware of the diverse ethnic, cultural, and religious make-up of their towns and villages, and of the role that ethnicity plays in Syrian politics, but so are they about the regime-imposed red lines concerning discussion on the issue in public spaces. Both the regime and the society at large appear to be aware of the gap, and often find it convenient to resort to a neutral and still not untrue formula: *kulna suriyyin*, 'we are all Syrians'. What exactly this neutral formula hides is hard to tell. What happens within the diverse communal spheres that exist in contemporary Syria, far from the spotlights pointed at an authoritarian, highly centralized government, is not easy to study or describe. If it is easy to see that the diverse ethno-cultural identities of Syria have not been erased by the project of construction of a national

Arab-Syrian identity, it is much harder to tell in what sense and in what respect they were maintained.

Research on contemporary Syria has emphasized the continuing role of Alawi sectarian allegiances in consolidating the regime; but, also, research on the Druze community of the Hawran has shown that forms of confessional and communal solidarity and representation not only still exist, but are also informally recognized as politically relevant.[31] The Armenian community is no exception: besides a façade which denies it, the community continues to exist as a political subject and to be informally recognized as such by the regime. Of course, Armenians participate individually, as any other Syrians, in a set of experiences of 'national' socialization (in schools, in universities, in the army, and so on); however, these experiences have not eroded the strong communal solidarity that binds them. Cases of deeper integration with the Syrian Ba'thist regime have remained rare: at the beginning of the 2000s only about 400 Armenians were members of the Ba'th party.[32] Armenian communal solidarity continues to produce a small but valuable political capital. The informal political 'agreement' between the state and the community described in the previous chapter still holds, and has been reiterated under the presidency of Bashar Al-Asad. Throughout the 1990s, and during the critical phase of the succession of President Hafiz Al-Asad, the regime was able to maintain a solid sense of trust in the community. In the tradition of the Asad regime, the dividends for Armenian loyalty and acquiescence were made available to the community mostly outside the strictly political sphere: they took the form of informal concessions in the running of Armenian affairs within the network of Armenian communal institutions (Churches, schools, clubs, cultural associations, etc.). Strictly political activities, including open Armenian party activism, remain banned.

In fact it is not hard to see that the parties' role has not evaporated. This is suggested, for instance, by the continuing sense of party 'affiliation' that many families preserve, where the term 'affiliation' does not stand for formal adherence to an ideology and formal participation to an organization, but rather for the feeling of belonging to an Armenian cultural sub-world, whose symbols and boundaries are connected – directly or indirectly – to a party. Manifestations of these 'feelings of affiliation' may include regular attendance at a particular recreational or cultural club, a particular church, or the choice of the Armenian elementary school that the children will attend, or the discreet display – inside the family house – of party symbols, the playing of national songs, etc.

This indicates that the parties – and particularly the largely dominant Dashnak party – are allowed to survive, and not only as mere ideas: they are present as partly-virtual, partly-material networks that connect the community internally and with the external, transnational Armenian world, providing for some of its needs. Paradoxically, one could argue that the regime-imposed restrictions on Armenian political activism have actually contributed to shield the parties from the phenomenon of erosion of their symbolic capital that has characterized other Armenian diasporas, including Lebanon.

In terms of participation in Syrian public life, Armenians continued to be granted – with the exception of a two-year interval between 1990 and 1992 – a symbolic representation in the Syrian parliament. In 1994, after more than fourty years since his first appointment under Shishakli, Judge Eblighatian stepped down. There is little doubt that the regime's leadership has continued to play the key role in the process of selection of the Armenian representative. However, it appears that lately the community's institutions have been allowed a greater involvement. In the case of the 2003 elections, the successful candidate, lawyer Sounboul Sounboulian, has received a sort of pre-electoral blessing from the representatives of the three Armenian Churches, and from a 'convention' of representatives of Armenian associations.[33] Armenians are also represented in the local administration of Aleppo: in November 2003 one Armenian was sitting in the fifty-members *Majlis Al-Madina* (Aleppo City Council), and another in the ninety-nine-member *Majlis Al-Muhafaza* (Aleppo Governatorate Council).

**Table 5.4. Armenian MPs elected in Syria, 1992–2003**

| Election year | Name of MPs | Place of election |
|---|---|---|
| 1992[34] | Krikor Eblighatian | Aleppo |
| 1994 | Simon Libarian[35] | Aleppo |
| 1998 | Simon Libarian | Aleppo |
| 2003 | Sounboul Sounboulian | Aleppo |

## Armenian Churches and the State in Contemporary Lebanon and Syria

The core logic of the Ta'if agreement – that is, the revival of the national pact – implied the confirmation of the traditional approach of the Lebanese state toward religion. Not surprisingly, the key source of legislation on the issue has remained Article 9 of the Constitution, which affirms the principle of freedom of conscience, the position of neutral 'respect' of the state toward all confessions, and recognises the right of the communities to regulate their religious affairs and questions of personal status. Little if any progress has been made in the efforts to develop a corpus of secular personal status law: the religious institutions of the various components of Lebanese society maintain vast autonomy and quasi-exclusive authority in important areas of the daily life of their respective communities. In Syria too, the 1990s and early 2000s have marked no departure from the past, and the religious policy of the state has remained consistent with the lines which emerged during the 1970s: the state guarantees freedom of belief and continues to grant to religious communities a set of autonomies on questions of personal status (Article 35 of the Constitution of 1973).[36]

From the perspective of the Armenian communities, the continuing, substantial freedoms granted by these approaches – essentially rooted in the Ottoman and Mandate policies – play a positive role in the preservation of Armenian diversity in the two countries. For the Armenians of Lebanon and Syria, the Churches remain important spaces of communal interaction; they maintain their function as pivotal identity-markers and identity-custodians, able to offer accessible ways of reconnecting with the communities' spiritual and historical origins, with some of the deepest traits of their distinct identity. Besides the strictly religious dimension, the Armenian Churches remain the quasi-exclusive authority in charge of issues regarding family law (marriage, divorce, fosterage, alimony, etc.), and important centres of organisation of social life: they manage schools, charities, promote Armenian cultural activities, and so on. In the case of the Armenian Apostolic community, the role of the Church as a social actor continues to be expressed through a set of elected institutions based on the Armenian National Constitution of 1863. These institutions, in which both laymen and clergy are represented, include a 'national' assembly, a religious committee, a tribunal (mostly in charge of family law disputes), an executive committee (in charge of all non-strictly religious issues), and several sub-committees. Although actual participation has been lacking recently, elections take place regularly both in Lebanon and Syria.[37]

In Lebanon, the re-establishment of the consociational agreement has also restored the basis for a certain political role that religious authorities have traditionally played in the Lebanese system. As indicated earlier in this book, this role is in part merely symbolic: it has to do with the fact that access to political careers, positions within the public administrations and so on, strictly depends on the individuals' belonging to a recognised confessional community.[38] But also, religious authorities in Lebanon tend to maintain a certain role as political actors by intervening in political debates.[39] As far as the Armenians are concerned, this is particularly the case with the Apostolic Church, and – specifically – with the figure of the Catholicos of Cilicia. The addresses of the Catholicos, most notably on Christmas day and on the 24th of April Genocide commemoration, usually contain political views and indications directed at both the Armenian community and, more in general, the Lebanese political system.

In the regulatory and – at least in Lebanon – political context in which the Armenian Churches are still able to function as important poles of preservation and promotion of Armenian diversity, elements of worry seem to come, as in the case of Armenian politics (or, as it will appear, of the schools), from within the community, rather than from without. In fact, the clergy is not always satisfied with the level of participation in the religious activities of the community: the Catholicos of Cilicia has, for instance, drawn attention the fact that 'a considerable proportion of the youth is gradually drifting away from active and responsible participation in the life of the Church'.[40] Churches are looking with concern at a certain, gradual decline of their flocks. This is in considerable part due to migration, but also to the growing phenomenon of intermarriage. Marriage with non-Armenians, or even marriage with Armenians of a different confession, used to be regarded as a taboo in the early days of the Armenian presence in Lebanon and Syria. Today, intermarriage with Arab Christians is on the increase. It is estimated that 5–10 per cent of the about 300 marriages celebrated every year at the Apostolic dioceses of Aleppo are between an Armenian and an Arab spouse.[41] Intermarriage with Arab Muslims is, on the other hand, nearly non existent.[42]

**Table 5.5 Armenian Apostolic churches in Lebanon, 2003**

| No. | Church | Location |
| --- | --- | --- |
| 1 | Cathedral of St. Gregory the Illuminator | Antelias |
| 2 | Church of St. Nichan | Beirut – downtown |
| 3 | Church of St. Agop | Beirut – Jeitaoui |
| 4 | Church of St. Kevork | Beirut – Rmeil |
| 5 | Church of the Resurrection | Beirut – Badawi |
| 6 | Church of St. John the Baptist | Beirut – Hayachene |
| 7 | Church of the Forty Martyrs | Bourj Hammoud |
| 8 | Church of St. Vartan | Bourj Hammoud |
| 9 | Church of St. Sarkis | Bourj Hammoud |
| 10 | Church of Our Lady | Bourj Hammoud |
| 11 | Church of St. Maryam | Bikfaya |
| 11 | Church of the Assumption | Jounieh |
| 12 | Church of Azounieh | Azounieh |
| 13 | Church of St. Boghos | Anjar |
| 14 | Church of the Pentecost | Taraboulus |

**Table 5.6. Armenian Apostolic churches in Syria, 2003**[43]

| N. | Church name | Location |
|---|---|---|
| 1 | St. Karasnits Mangantz, mother church | Aleppo |
| 2 | St. Mother of God | Aleppo |
| 3 | St. Gregory the Illuminator | Aleppo |
| 4 | St. St. George | Aleppo |
| 5 | St. Hagop | Aleppo |
| 6 | St. Hagop | Qamishli |
| 7 | St. Hovannes Garabed | Hasakeh |
| 8 | St. Hagop | Ras el 'Ain |
| 9 | St. Astvadzazin | Derik |
| 10 | St. Astvadzazin | Raqqa |
| 11 | St. Cross | Tell Abiad |
| 12 | St. Anna | Yacoubieh |
| 13 | St. Hripsime | Yacoubieh |
| 14 | St. Kevork | Genemieh |
| 15 | St. Stepanos | Aramo |
| 16 | St. Kevork | Aramo |
| 17 | St. Holy Martyrs | Deir Ez-Zor |
| 18 | St. Haroutioun (chapel and monument) | Margada |
| 19 | St. Astvadzazin | Kessab |
| 20 | St. Astvadzazin | Kaladouran |
| 21 | St. Astvadzazin | Latakia |

**Table 5.7. Armenian Catholic churches in Lebanon, 2003**

| N. | Church | Location |
|---|---|---|
| 1 | Church of the Assumption | Bzoummar |
| 2 | Church of Notre Dame | Bzoummar |
| 3 | Church of the seminar | Bzoummar |
| 4 | Cathedral of St. Gregory and St. Elias | Beirut – Place Debbas |
| 5 | Church of the Annunciation | Beirut – Jeitaoui |
| 6 | Church of the school of the Mechitarists of Venice | |
| 7 | Church of St. Saviour | Bourj Hammoud |
| 8 | Church of the Holy Cross | Zalka |
| 9 | Church of Our Lady of Fatima | Zahleh |
| 10 | Church of Our Lady of the Rosary | Anjar |

## Table 5.8. Armenian Catholic churches in Syria, 2003[44]

| N. | Church | Location |
|----|--------|----------|
| 1 | St. Mary Cathedral (Om Al-Mou'awanat) | Aleppo |
| 2 | Church of the Holy Cross | Aleppo – Hay 'Ouroube |
| 3 | Church of Saint Barbara | Aleppo – Suleymanieh |
| 4 | Church of the Holy Trinity | Aleppo – Midan |
| 5 | Church of St. Mary of the Assumption | Aleppo |
| 6 | Church of the Resurrection | Aleppo cemetery |
| 7 | Church of the Martyrs | Raqqa |
| 8 | Church of St. Joseph | Qamishli |
| 9 | Church of the Sacred Family | Hasakeh |
| 10 | Church of St. Gregory the Illuminator | Deir Ez-Zor |
| 11 | Church of St. Mary of the World | Damascus Bab Touma |
| 12 | Armenian Catholic Church[45] | Damascus Bab Touma |
| 13 | Church of St. Michael | Kessab |

## Table 5.9. Armenian Evangelical churches in Lebanon, 2003

| N. | Church | Location |
|----|--------|----------|
| 1 | The First Evangelical Church | Beirut – Kantari |
| 2 | Armenian Evangelical Church | Beirut – Ashrafieh |
| 3 | Armenian Evangelical Church | Beirut – Rmeil |
| 4 | Armenian Evangelical Church | Bourj Hammoud – Adana |
| 5 | Armenian Evangelical Church | Bourj Hammoud – Marash |
| 6 | Armenian Evangelical Church | Bourj Hammoud – Gomidas |
| 7 | Armenian Evangelical Church | Zahleh |
| 8 | Armenian Evangelical Church | Anjar |

## Table 5.10. Armenian Evangelical churches in Syria, 2003[46]

| N. | Church | Location |
|----|--------|----------|
| 1 | Armenian Evangelical Emmanuel Church | Aleppo |
| 2 | Armenian Evangelical Bethel Church | Aleppo |
| 3 | Armenian Evangelical Martyrs Church | Aleppo |
| 4 | Armenian Evangelical Christ Church | Aleppo |

| 5 | Evangelical Syriac Church[47] | Aleppo |
| 6 | Armenian Evangelical Kessab Church | Kessab |
| 7 | Armenian Evangelical Kaladouran Church | Kessab area |
| 8 | Armenian Evangelical Ekizolouk Church | Kessab area |
| 9 | Armenian Evangelical Korkune Church | Kessab area |
| 10 | Armenian Evangelical Church | Homs |
| 11 | Armenian Evangelical Church | Damascus |

## Coping with Economic Crisis: The Socio-Economic Position of the Armenians in Contemporary Lebanon and Syria

The 1990s and the early 2000s have been a time of change, uncertainty and crisis for the Lebanese and Syrian economies. In Lebanon, post-war governments had to face up to the legacy of fifteen years of conflict: the widespread destruction of the country's infrastructures and physical assets, rampant inflation, a shortage of human resources (due to the collapse of national education, migration of skilled manpower, brain drain), and the segmentation of national territory and the labour market. These severe problems also combined with some of the traditional social and regional imbalances that have affected the Lebanese economy since independence.[48]

More than a decade after the process of reconstruction began, and in spite of the fact that central Beirut today projects the image of a restored, glittering wealth, a true recovery is still largely lacking and Lebanon struggles with a severe economic and social crisis. One of the most spectacular indicators of the crisis is the explosion of public debt. Mostly a consequence of the ambitious reconstruction plans, debt grew from about $150 million in 1992, to nearly $30 billion ten years later, and over $35 billion by May 2005.[49] The servicing of debt absorbs, by far, the largest part of government revenues and contributes to tying the government's hands when it comes to intervening on the national economic agenda. Lebanon's GDP growth rate was high in the early 1990s (38.6 per cent in average between 1991 and 1993),[50] but it gradually slowed down and stopped in 2000. The country maintains an economy in deficit: it exports little and imports most of what it consumes. The labour market remains largely stagnant, the cost of living high, and the gap between rich and poor grows wider.[51]

In Syria, the severe financial crisis suffered in the second half of the 1980s prompted a critical revision of the national political economy. Between the end of the decade and the early 1990s the regime carefully turned away from its traditional statist approach and embarked on a strategy of controlled liberalization of the economy.[52] The new phase, epitomized by the introduction of a new law liberalizing investments, Law 10 of 1991, was initially encouraged by post-Gulf war aid from oil-rich Arab countries and by an increased domestic production of oil. However, changing external conditions, the limitations of the liberalization process, and persisting political and bureaucratic constraints slowed down the economy. In the decade between 1991 and 2001 per capita GDP growth failed to gain momentum;[53] in June 2000 the country maintained a trade deficit, had an unemployment rate estimated at 20%, and a public debt standing at more than $21 billion.[54]

In the early 2000s, with inflation rates substantially under control in both Lebanon and Syria, the main economic worries for households come from the question of employment. In Lebanon the labour market has been described as segmented in three, disconnected sub-markets: an expanding market of low-pay unskilled labour, increasingly filled by (mostly Syrian) foreign workers; a market for highly skilled, highly educated *cadres*, who also compete in Western labour markets; and a market for intermediate positions, squeezed by the expanding first segment and culturally attracted by the second.[55] In Syria, the young, fast growing population keeps a high pressure on the labour market: it is estimated that the market should currently accommodate about 200,000 new entrants every year, and the national agency for unemployment has recently indicated that disguised unemployment within the public sector could range between 30 and 40 per cent.[56]

The main problem, when trying to assess the socio-economic position of the Armenians within this context, is the lack of comprehensive information regarding the community, since economic data is not collected on an ethnic or confessional basis. Resorting to impressionistic and anecdotal material collected through interviews and personal visits appears here inevitable. What can be confidently affirmed is that the high inflation rates and the difficulties related to the labour markets experienced in Lebanon and Syria between the late 1980s and the 1990s have particularly damaged the position of the middle classes of both countries. The Armenians, largely represented in that social group since – roughly – the 1960s, have therefore suffered.

The Lebanese-Armenian and Syrian-Armenian upper class consists today of a mere handful of families of the most successful entrepreneurs who were able to survive the war and to position themselves strategically in the Lebanese market for reconstruction, or to master the rules of the relation between the regime and the private sector in Syria. For the rest, Armenians tend to belong to the strained, under-pressure middle class. Manufacturers and traders who used to do business with several countries in the Middle East, or to play an important role in national markets, are now confronted with stiff competition from cheaper imports from the Far East, or with problems of rising costs and declining net margins. In Lebanon, the production of shoes, once an Armenian-dominated sector, is in decline, and increasingly taken over by Shi'a entrepreneurs; only a few of the once-numerous small and medium-size firms producing shoes in Bourj Hammoud are still active. Many artisans and shopkeepers in Damascus and Aleppo have simply closed and sold up. So have tailors, who have seen their middle-class market shrink. Some niches do resist, however: particularly in the case of jewelry, where Armenians seem to maintain a competitive position.

The declining economic and social position of the middle classes is a key element to understand the current uncertainty regarding the future of Armenian diversity in the Levant, particularly for the impact that it has on the educational choices of families, and on migration. As far as education is concerned, Armenian middle-class families appear to be keen to invest in better education for the younger generations, particularly when they realize that they do not have profitable economic opportunities, or sufficient assets to 'pass on', when, for example, the 'family business' (be it a small manufacturing firm, or a retail outlet, a restaurant, etc.) is not as profitable as it used to be, or not sufficient to support two or three families.[57] The educational options that offer more chances of success – that is, of placing young Armenians competitively in the labour market – tend to have two characteristics: first, they are expensive, thus limiting the options of the lower middle class; second, they tend to involve a deeper integration with the non-Armenian environment, or – conversely – to sacrifice some aspects of Armenian socialization, particularly in the case of non-Armenian secondary schools.[58]

Whether investments in education are affordable or not, the erosion of the economic position of the Armenian middle class encourages migration and weakens the Armenian presence in the Levant. The awareness of migration as an option is dramatically widespread in contemporary Lebanon and Syria – and more generally in the Arab world – regardless of ethnic or confessional affiliation.[59] In the case of Lebanon the national migratory balance has been negative throughout the 1990s and reached a peak in 1996, when the net losses reached 185,000.[60]

Unfortunately, it is hard to provide accurate estimates of Armenian migration. It is generally accepted that the Christian communities constitute a higher proportion of the departures – and this of course includes Armenians; however, official, disaggregated data on the migration of Armenians are not available, neither for Lebanon, nor for Syria. The Armenian Churches and the political parties, for their part, tend not to publicize details on the issue, as this, at least in the case of Lebanon, could affect the political position of the community. The general impression, gathered through interviews with clergy of the three Churches, party officials, and families is that migration is not uncommon, but neither has it the character of a mass exodus. As far as the destinations are concerned, most Armenians from Lebanon and Syria tend to migrate to the Western world, particularly the United States, Canada, France, but also Australia, where they tend to join local, existing diasporas.

## Armenian Associations and the State in Contemporary Lebanon and Syria

In the context of the economic and social crisis described in the previous paragraph, the role of the Armenian associations in Lebanon and Syria has become particularly important.

Firstly, associations have acted as a safety net providing crucial support to the community's economic and financial conditions. Both in Lebanon and Syria, where the provision of social and medical services by the state is often limited or inadequate, and where private sector provision is generally expensive, the most vulnerable sectors of the Armenian population have relied heavily on the communal structures of self-help. As far as medical needs are concerned, the Howard Karagheusian Commemorative Corporation (HKCC), the Armenian Relief Cross (ARC), and the Armenian Educational and Benevolent Union (AEBU), have run reliable networks of medical centres and dispensaries and have provided no-cost, or low-cost, services to thousands of families. The HKCC's health centre in Bourj Hammoud alone, for instance, has been able to ensure free medical supervision for most of the Armenian schools in Lebanon, to run a vast vaccination program, and to serve the needs of attendants ranging yearly between 10,000 and 13,000.[61] Housing, support to the disabled, the elderly and the poor, and vocational training are some of the areas in which Armenian associations have also been active, effectively contributing to absorb the impact of the economic crisis.[62]

Secondly, associations have, both directly and indirectly, contributed to the preservation of Armenian ethno-cultural diversity in a period in which this has been threatened by the effects of economic crisis. On the one hand, by relieving pressure on family budgets, they have arguably contributed to limit the propensity to migration and freed resources that could be invested in Armenian private education or other Armenian cultural activities. On the other hand, associations have played a direct role as centers of promotion of Armenian culture. They have provided spaces for Armenian socialization, and offered structural, constant connections with the resources of the Armenian diaspora outside Lebanon and Syria. In this sense, cultural associations like Hamazkayin, the numerous Armenian students' associations, sports and recreational associations, like the scouts, the Dashnak's Homenetmen, the Hunchak's Homenmen, and the AGBU's Antranik continue to be important, in particular for their appeal to the youth.

The fact that associations have so far been able to continue their role of economic and cultural support to the community should not overshadow the fact that this has been for some increasingly difficult, and that the Armenian self-help network itself appears under a certain stress. As local fundraising is inevitably in crisis and largely insufficient, the resort to voluntary work and to financial support from the richer Armenian diasporas worldwide has become increasingly important: two of the most notable social actors among the Armenian non-profit sector – the HKCC and the Jinishian Memorial Program – operate almost solely with funds received from their respective foundations in the United States.

As far as relations with the state are concerned, the regulatory framework in which associations have operated in the 1990s and in the early 2000s has remained largely unchanged, both in Lebanon and Syria; at the same time, however, the actual *modus vivendi* between associations and state has been often developed – or contested – outside the formality of the law.

In Lebanon, the right of association continues to be grounded in Article 13 of the Constitution, and regulated by the old Ottoman law of 1909. The post-Ta'if practice, however, has often revealed the inadequacy and ambiguity of the current legal framework, particularly with regard to the official registration of associations, the issuing of licenses, and the nature and scope of the governmental control involved. Many associations, including a number of Armenian institutions, continue to operate without formal registration. Episodes of restrictive interpretation of the law by the government have exposed the fragility of the position of the associations under the current regulatory framework.[63]

In Syria, the right of association continues to be based on Article 39 of the Constitution, while the main law regulating associations dates back to the time of the United Arab Republic. The law continues to provide the state with powerful tools with which exercise control over the associations. In the case of the Armenian community, the practice has been in the sense of a continuation of the 'tacit pact' between the community and the state described earlier in this book.[64]

## Armenian Education in Lebanon and Syria during the 1990s and Early 2000s

*Ta'if and the Reform of Educational Policy in Lebanon: The Continuing Crisis of the Armenian Schools*

The post-war period in Lebanon has been marked by efforts to reform the national educational system. Guidelines regarding education were, first of all, included in the Ta'if agreement. Part I, 3, section E, of the agreement confirmed the principle of freedom of teaching contained in the Constitution, and the state 'protection' of private schools, but also called for 'the reinforcement of the control of the state over private schools and on textbooks'.[65] The reform of national education envisaged in Ta'if would include '[l]a révision et le développement des programmes dans le but de renforcer l'appartenance et l'intégration nationales, et l'ouverture spirituelle et culturelle, ainsi que l'unification du livre scolaire dans les matières d'histoire et d'éducation nationale'.[66]

The affirmation of these principles reflected the view that the failure to use education as a tool of national integration (as in Syria, for instance) had been an important cause for the divisiveness of national politics and, ultimately, of the social disruption that led to the civil war.[67] The propositions of the Ta'if agreement on education, criticized by some for being 'vague' and 'subject to various interpretations',[68] could potentially mark a turning point in the relation between state and private education in Lebanon; however, the announced 'reinforcement of the control over private schools' hardly materialized. The regulatory follow-up of Ta 'if, consisting of a 'New framework for education in Lebanon' (*Haykaliya jadida li al-ta'lim fi lubnan*, 1995) and a revision of the national curriculum (completed in 1997), did restructure and update national educational programs, but carefully avoided challenging private schools' autonomy.[69]

In spite of conditions of freedom and autonomy that many Armenian school boards and school principals continue to describe as ideal for Armenian education, the system of Armenian schools in Lebanon never made a full recovery after the war. On the contrary, the number of Armenian schools and students has continued to drop since 1990. In the ten academic years between 1991/2 and 2001/2 the number of schools has fallen from 45 to 33 and the number of students is currently just above 8,000 – a substantial loss compared to the nearly 12,000 of 1991/2.[70]

**Table 5.11. Armenian schools and students in Armenian schools 1964/5 to 2001/2** [71]

| School year | No. of schools | No. of students |
| --- | --- | --- |
| 1964–5 | 44 | 13,398 |
| 1972–3 | 56 | 18,526 |
| 1974–5 | 57 | 21,000 |
| 1987–8 | 47 | 12,924 |
| 1990–1 | 45 | 11,939 |
| 2001–2 | 33[72] | 8,418 |

The continuing crisis of Armenian schools is explained by a combination of factors. The first one has to consider is the already mentioned overcapacity of the Armenian educational system.[73] The population decrease caused by the war had a partially delayed effect on the schools: some of these, already suffering from a lack of students at the end of the war have managed to continue activity for a few years into the 1990s. Besides that, further migration after the war, has contributed to exacerbate the problem.

A second factor concerns the effects of the post-war economic crisis on school enrollment. As Lebanese average incomes have been put under stress by the economic slump, families have found it increasingly difficult to pay for private education and so enrollment in Armenian schools has dropped. While the income crisis affects most components of the Lebanese society and not the Armenians alone, its consequences could become particularly disruptive for Armenian culture in the country, since the teaching of Armenian language and culture is virtually only available in private Armenian schools.[74]

Other explanations for the falling enrollment in Armenian schools are to be found in the changing attitudes of some Armenian Lebanese families toward the importance of Armenian education. Some of the higher-income families prefer non-Armenian, prestigious private colleges to Armenian schools, believing that this choice would offer a better education and better opportunities. Other families, from all social backgrounds, believe that Armenian schools place an excessive burden on students. In fact, as Armenian schools prepare students to stand in national examinations (*Licence* and *Baccalauréat*), they adopt an extended curriculum, combining the subjects prescribed by the national curriculum with Armenian subjects. As a result, weekly time tables in Armenian schools include up to 40 periods a week, compared with a mere 32 in standard Arab schools. Students, for their part, are said to take Armenian subjects less seriously, as they are not crucial for the purpose of succeeding in national examinations.[75] The following table presents an example of the weekly composition of courses in an Armenian private school in Lebanon during the school year 2002/3.

**Table 5.12. Weekly periods at Yeghishe Manoukian College, Dbayeh, 2002–3, I to IX grade[76]**

| Subjects | I | II | III | IV | V | VI | VII | VIII | IX |
|---|---|---|---|---|---|---|---|---|---|
| Armenian | 7 | 7 | 7 | 7 | 6 | 6 | 6 | 6 | 4 |
| Arabic | 8 | 8 | 8 | 7 | 7 | 7 | 7 | 7 | 6 |
| English | 8 | 8 | 7 | 7 | 6 | 6 | 6 | 6 | 6 |
| French | – | – | – | – | 2 | 2 | 2 | 2 | 2 |

| | | | | | | | | | |
|---|---|---|---|---|---|---|---|---|---|
| Mathematics | 5 | 5 | 5 | 5 | 5 | 6 | 5 | 6 | 6 |
| Science (Armenian) | 2 | 2 | 2 | – | – | – | – | – | – |
| Science | – | – | – | 2 | 3 | 3 | 3 | 3 | – |
| Biology | – | – | – | – | – | – | – | – | 4 |
| Religion (Armenian) | 1 | 1 | 1 | 1 | 1 | 1 | 1 | 1 | - |
| Armenian history (Armenian) | 2 | 2 | 2 | 2 | 2 | 2 | 2 | 2 | 2 |
| Geography (Armenian) | – | – | – | 1 | – | – | – | – | – |
| Civics (Armenian) | 1 | 1 | – | – | – | – | – | – | – |
| Geography (Arabic) | – | – | – | 1 | 1 | 1 | 1 | 1 | 2 |
| History (Arabic) | – | – | – | – | – | – | – | 1 | 2 |
| Education (Arabic) | – | – | 1 | 1 | 1 | 1 | 1 | 1 | 1 |
| Sports | 1 | 1 | 1 | 1 | 1 | 1 | 1 | 1 | 1 |
| Singing | 1 | 1 | 1 | 1 | 1 | 1 | – | – | – |
| Music | 1 | 1 | 1 | 1 | 1 | – | – | – | – |
| Talent showing | 1 | 1 | 1 | 1 | 1 | 1 | 1 | – | – |
| Handicraft | 1 | 1 | 2 | 1 | 1 | 1 | – | – | – |
| Drawing | 1 | 1 | 1 | 1 | 1 | 1 | 1 | – | – |
| Other | – | – | – | – | – | – | 3 | 3 | 4 |
| *Total periods* | *40* | *40* | *40* | *40* | *40* | *40* | *40* | *40* | *40* |

As tuition fees often cover the largest part of school budgets, falling enrollment has resulted in financial crisis for many schools. Boards have responded to financial crisis in several ways. In the most severe cases schools were merged with other institutions or closed down. In general, schools called for an increased support from the traditional self-help structures within the local communities and the diaspora, a strategy that seems to have produced only partial results on account of the widespread economic crisis in Lebanon and – according to some – the decreasing support of the transnational diaspora to the Lebanese Armenian community. As for local attitudes towards Armenian culture and the importance of its preservation, the Armenian leadership, including the Churches, has openly encouraged the community to remain attached to Armenian education.

In the early 2000s, the future of Armenian schools in Lebanon remains uncertain. Some observers identify the key to the solution of the crisis in a process of rationalization of the system of schools, including strategic closures, relocations and the improvement of quality. Indeed, some Armenian schools which are conveniently located and which have focused on the quality of the education they offer have managed to perform comparatively well, if not to record a certain success.[77] However, rationalization is rarely painless. In the case of the Armenian community, it tends to raise questions concerning the preservation of the cultural and political diversity that the schools express. Armenian schools in Lebanon are mainly affiliated to seven distinct organisational centres: the three Armenian Churches (Apostolic, Catholic and Evangelical), the three political parties (Dashnak, Hunchak, Ramkavar) and the Armenian General Benevolent Union (AGBU). Mergers or closures of schools would easily take the significance of political events and would probably alter delicate balances within the community. In a sense, the current struggle is not to preserve *one* network of Armenian schools, but to preserve *several* of them. In the struggle, schools are to some extent competing with each other.[78]

Table 5.13. Affiliation of Armenian schools, per grade and general, 2001/2[79]

| School ownership | Elementary | Elementary to intermed. | Elementary to secondary | Only intermed. & secondary | Total |
|---|---|---|---|---|---|
| Apostolic Church | 6 | 2 | 2 | 1 | 11 |
| Catholic Church | 1 | 1 | 4 | – | 6 |
| Evangelical Church | 2 | 1 | 4 | – | 7 |
| AGBU | 1 | 1 | – | 1 | 3 |
| Dashnak | – | – | 1 | – | 1 |
| Hunchak | – | 1 | – | – | 1 |
| Ramkavar | – | 1 | – | – | 1 |
| Total | 10 | 7 | 11 | 2 | 30 |

An important form of support for Armenian education recently came from the state, when Lebanese law recognized the Armenian language as one of the accepted, optional second 'foreign' languages in the national Baccalaureate examinations, a fact that may contribute to reduce the burden of the curriculum in Armenian schools. The provision also carries a remarkable symbolic importance: it constitutes an example of 'internalization' of Armenian culture within Lebanese national culture, a case of how Armenian culture may be recognized as a component of Lebanese national culture, and – perhaps – an indication of how the state could play a role in preserving Armenian cultural diversity in the country. Given the nature of the Lebanese political system, most Armenians live under no illusion about the possibility the state could intervene financially in support of Armenian schools. The issue, however, has become part of the Armenian Lebanese debate on the schools: a proposal was advanced regarding the establishment of a governmental 'special' school catering for the Armenians of Bourj Hammoud.[80]

In the framework of the current difficulties of the Armenian system of educational institutions, higher education is not an exception. Early in the

1990s the AGBU decided to discontinue the activities of the Hussissian College. Against this trend, Haigazian University has successfully managed to market its courses outside the Armenian community and enrolls a substantial number of non-Armenian students. However, enrollment for courses in Armenian Studies remains poor.

## Armenian Education in Syria in the 1990s and Beyond

During the 1990s and in the early 2000s, the relation between the Syrian state and the Armenian educational system has largely followed the lines which had been defined in the course of the 1970s. The ownership of schools has remained private and Armenian, in large part under the Armenian Churches' names; the Ministry of Education has maintained a system of institutional structures and procedures for the supervision of private schools, including the governmental appointment of school principals. The curriculum has continued to be determined by the Ministry: until today, Armenian schools must adopt in full the standard state curriculum, in Arabic, and are allowed to add three periods per week of 'Armenian religion' and four periods of 'language of the religion'.

Within and besides the formal regulatory framework, the practice of the relation between the state and Armenian schools has evolved without significant turns, and has been characterized by a general atmosphere of relaxation and mutual co-operation. On the one hand, the government has required – and obtained – the participation of Armenian schools in national educational programs and in the promotion of Syrian identity and of the Ba'th regime: Armenian institutions, as do other Syrian schools, closely follow the curriculum, display national and party flags, portraits of the president, actively celebrate Syrian national festivities (Independence day, anniversary of the Correctionist Movement, etc.), and participate to the activities of the Ba'th juvenile organisation, the *Tala'i'a al-Ba'th* (Vanguard of the Ba'th).

On the other hand, the government has consistently sought to minimize interference in Armenian schools and has appeared to regard benignly a certain liberal interpretation of rules. The distinction between the weekly periods dedicated to religion and to Armenian language often remains blurred, the teaching of language being privileged; periods dedicated to music are also used to extend the pupils' exposure to Armenian culture and heritage. The administrative practice of appointing tolerant, non-intrusive principals has continued: in a recent case, in Raqqa, one of the Directorates of Education has appointed an Armenian to the post of principal of one of the Armenian schools.[81] The exhibition – alongside Syrian, Arab, and Ba'thist symbols – of Armenian symbols, is tolerated: in an Armenian school in Damascus visited in November 2003, portraits of Hafiz and Bashar Al-Asad were displayed along with those of

Avicenna, Tigrane the Great, a number of Armenian literary figures, and a poster dedicated to the 'martyrs of Nagorno-Karabagh'. A similar combination of Syrian and Armenian symbolism could be observed during the celebration of the end of the school year 2001/02 of the Miatzial/Al-Nizam School of Damascus: in front of a large audience of parents and relatives, Armenian pupils performed an elaborate show which included the singing of the Armenian and Syrian national anthems, traditional dances, the reading of Armenian and Syrian poetry, and a drama representing Syria's mission as a guide of the Arab nation.[82]

The atmosphere of relaxation and co-operation in relations between the state and Armenian schools, however helpful, cannot fully undo the effect of the restrictions that have affected Armenian education since the crisis of the second half of the 1960s. In the case of the teaching of Armenian, the four periods per week reserved for the 'language of the religion' remain hardly sufficient to acquire a perfect knowledge of the language. Flexibility allows teachers to bridge the gap in part, but not in full: an experienced teacher, interviewed in November 2003, stated that 'the level of knowledge of Armenian started to be poor from 1967', and that 'the old generation used to *think* in Armenian; the new generations think in Arabic and write in Armenian'.[83] The teaching of Armenian national history, for its part, remains formally a taboo. Further problems regard the funding of schools. Tuition fees and other charges for private schools are formally set by the government; the rate is usually insufficient to cover costs, and schools have to systematically turn to the financial help of local donors or of Armenian institutions of the diaspora.[84]

In spite of a certain decrease in population due to migration, Armenian schools in Syria appear less affected by the crisis of enrollment that characterizes schools in Lebanon.[85] This seems to stem from three main factors. Firstly, Armenian schools are often perceived as a better-quality educational option compared to governmental schools: as a matter of fact, many schools attract a certain number of non-Armenian students from (mostly Christian) middle-class backgrounds. Secondly, the community seems to be more attached to its cultural tradition or more concerned about losing it: Armenian families rarely consider alternative options, with the possible exception of the very upper class. And, finally, the cost of Armenian education has remained, in spite of the economic crisis, generally affordable.

## Armenian Cultural Production and the State in Contemporary Lebanon and Syria

Armenian publications and media, music, and arts in general – together with Armenian schools – continue to be an important and visible dimension of the life of the Armenians of Lebanon and Syria. In both countries, to different degrees, Armenian culture, news and entertainment are produced, or imported and circulated, catering almost exclusively for the Armenian communities. Selections of Armenian newspapers, fiction and essays, films, music, folkloric dance, and theatrical performances are normally available in cities and places where the Armenian presence is substantial. Armenian cultural associations, among which the Dashnak's cultural arm, Hamazkayin, stands out, manage networks of clubs and offer an impressive variety of cultural events and opportunities.[86]

In spite of all this, it is not hard to form the picture of a general situation of crisis of Armenian culture in Lebanon and Syria, particularly when making comparisons with the pre-civil war era. The continuing decline of Armenian theatre, of the Armenian literary scene, the sclerosis of the Armenian press, the poverty of Armenian-Lebanese or Armenian-Syrian popular music, and, in general, the lack of internationally recognized cultural talents are facts that can be easily detected by any non-superficial observer.

When analysing the causes of the problem, two elements obviously come to the fore: the Lebanese war, and the economic and social crisis suffered by the Lebanese and Syrian societies. Both have contributed, on the one hand, to encourage the best Armenian artists and intellectuals to leave the region, depriving the local scene of its cultural avant-garde; on the other, to determine a general decline of the Armenian 'critical mass' that constituted at once, the public, the source of inspiration, and the provider of new young talent. Besides this is perhaps a third, more controversial, and still largely unexplored issue: the question of the changing approach of the young, more Arab-integrated generations towards Armenian culture and Armenian identities in general; a further element that, if confirmed, is bound to have an impact on the decline of the demand for Armenian culture in Lebanon and Syria.

In the context of this situation of crisis, the approach of the Lebanese and Syrian states toward culture, and Armenian culture in particular, is not of much help. In Lebanon, the resumption of the confessional, consociational 'normality' after the civil war has restored the traditional, substantial freedom for Armenians (as for any Lebanese) to plan and organise their cultural world as they wish; however, as Armenian culture in Lebanon is caught in a crisis, the state cannot, by its very nature, offer any support to its preservation. One could hardly imagine, to take a hypothetical example, that part of the budget of the Ministry of Culture could be spent, say, to support Armenian theatre; the move would be arguably perceived as an undue 'bonus' to one of the confessional families of Lebanon.

In Syria, where the cultural policy of the state is still largely hostage to the Arab-Syrian Ba'ath nationalist discourse and to the perceived needs of national security, the regime maintains a set of rules and practices that make the production, the distribution, and access – in general – to culture more difficult than it could be: these include, in particular, a severe censorship on printed materials and the requirement of authorization or security clearance for public meetings. As far as the Armenians are concerned, the effects of these rules and practices are significantly reduced by the informal, 'tacit pact' often mentioned within this research: the sense of trust the regime has developed for the Armenians has contributed to remarkably expand the area of 'cultural freedom' enjoyed by the community, particularly when the 'consumption' of Armenian culture takes place within Armenian spaces: the family, the cultural association, the club. However, the fact that the range of Armenian culture in Syria is significantly less varied than in Lebanon can hardly go unnoticed, and, as this research has shown earlier, this is – at least in part – a consequence of the state's cultural policy.

## The Continuing Decline of Armenian Theatre

Drama continues to be a widespread expression of Armenian cultural life in both Lebanon and Syria. Participating in a play in Armenian, preparing scenes and costumes, memorizing parts, are common experiences for most pupils of Armenian schools. Hamazkayin and AGBU maintain their theatre groups and a number of other Armenian institutions stage shows in Armenian. As for venues, the community in Beirut can count on the two theatres of Bourj Hammoud, the Mesropian and Der Melkonian, while in Aleppo at least four large halls belong to Armenian institutions.[87]

In spite of this, it is not hard to understand that the movement is going through a serious crisis. The crisis concerns, firstly, the artistic quality of the shows: the authors and artists who had made the success of pre-war Armenian Lebanese theatre seldom returned when the war ended; new generations could not be formed, all resulting in a lack of professionalism that is hard to shake off. The general lack of funding is reflected in the quality: direction, acting and, in general, the standards of production tend to remain amateurish. Secondly, war and economic crisis have severely hit the public of Armenian theatre: on the one hand families have migrated, on the other the middle class, the traditional public of theatre, has seen its budget for entertainment shrinking. Caught in a downward bound spiral, Armenian theatre finds itself trying to compete with more popular, alternative forms of entertainment such as television, movies, discos, or shopping and tends to turn to a light-comedy genre in order to fill the halls and earn the much-needed cash to survive.[88]

Similar to other forms of Armenian cultural production in the Levant, Armenian theatre is not simply struggling with a crisis of quality and audience but also, and most importantly, with a crisis of ideas about its role as a communal (Armenian) institution. If the role of Armenian theatre had been that of helping the first and second generation of refugees to find and cultivate their Armenian, collective identity, contemporary Armenian theatre must find the ideas and language to speak to a new generation that has greatly developed its network of social and cultural relations with the Arab environment in which it lives. According to Berge Fazlian, who moved back to Lebanon in 1996 after 20 years spent in Canada, these ideas and language have not been found yet and Armenian theatre in Lebanon survives 'without a goal'.[89] Under these conditions theatre is reduced to the role of yet another space of Armenian cultural socialization which the Armenian leadership (Churches, political parties) employs with decreasing effectiveness.

## Armenian Publishing in Contemporary Lebanon and Syria

The case of Armenian publishing in Lebanon is perhaps useful to illustrate another dimension of the crisis of Armenian culture in the Levant. First of all, as in the case of theatre, the publishing sector suffers from a lack of authors. Many left during the Lebanese civil war, and did not return, impoverishing the literary scene.[90] Secondly, publishers have to cope with the effects of the decline of the Armenian population and, thus, the decline of the market for Armenian books. In the case of Doniguian, Armenian titles in the catalogue can now be counted on the fingers of one hand, and are mostly reprints (including dictionaries and a popular cookbook).[91] Another once important commercial publisher, Edition Sevan, has closed following the death of the founder, novelist Simon Simonian.

Not that Armenian publications are disappearing from Lebanon. In fact, a fairly impressive number of titles is still printed and distributed in the country. One of the reference bookshops for the Armenian community of Lebanon, the bookstore of the Catholicosate of Cilicia in Antelias, currently stocks around 1,000 titles, in large part printed in Lebanon; the yearly Armenian book fair held in Antelias in autumn 2002, gathering together the catalogues of all the Armenian publishers of Lebanon, sold around 7,500 items.[92] However, it is interesting to note that the two main publishers of the Armenian sector are the Catholicosate of Cilicia, and the Dashnak's Hamazkayin, both non-commercial – or not primarily commercial – actors, a fact that suggests that Armenian publishing in Lebanon is now essentially institution-led, rather than being market-led. In the case of the printing house of the Catholicosate of Cilicia, for instance, the commercial nature of the enterprise is secondary to the role it plays within the Church, and as provider of a high cultural service for the Armenian diaspora worldwide.[93]

In Syria, Armenian publishing has still not made a recovery from the crisis it suffered during the 1960s. Although Armenian publishers are not specifically targeted, and can benefit from the mentioned relaxed relations between the regime and the Armenian community, state control over publications remains in general severe: publishing is subject to the approval of the Directorate of the Censorship (*Mudiriat al-Raqabah*) of the Ministry of Information. By the end of 2003 only two main Armenian publishers appeared to be regularly active: the Apostolic Church's printing house, Arevelk, and Guiliguia, a private enterprise founded in 1993.[94]

## Armenian Newspapers, Radio, and Television

As far as Armenian media are concerned, television emerged during the 1990s as a major provider of news and entertainment. Since the independence of the Republic of Armenia, and thanks to satellite technology, Armenian families in Lebanon and Syria have become accustomed to watch the two channels broadcasted from Armenia, Hayastan 1 (the official state television) and Armenia TV. Parallel to this, there has a series of attempts to produce and broadcast Armenian television programs in Lebanon.[95] The first regular program in Armenian was broadcasted in 1996 – for eight months – on the private network ICN: fifteen minutes of news in Armenian, from Monday to Saturday. In 2000, in view of the parliamentary elections, Rafiq Al-Hariri also started an Armenian program of news on his Future television network.[96] Finally, in April 2003, a new program produced by the Armenian Catholic Patriarchate started broadcasting from Lebanon on Nour Sat, the satellite channel controlled by the Christian television network Télé-Lumière.[97]

The popularity of television programs broadcast from Armenia raises interesting questions about the potential impact that they may have on Armenian identities and life in the Levant. Television from Armenia provides the public in Lebanon and Syria with direct access to alternative views on the motherland, on the Republic of Armenia and its role, on Armenian nationalism, and on the diaspora, views that may be different from those mediated by the communal leadership in the Levant (parties, Churches). Also, Armenian television gives a visual meaning to names and places that would otherwise remain abstract items of Armenian diaspora socialization (Sardarabad, Karabakh, etc.); it emphasizes cultural (for example linguistic) differences between the Republic of Armenia and the Lebanese and Syrian diaspora; it may help in placing the Armenian Lebanese and Syrian diaspora in the wider perspective of the world diaspora (for instance covering issues regarding Armenian communities in other parts of the world).

Regardless of its quality, criticized by some, Armenian satellite television is today part of the world of Armenian media in Lebanon and Syria, and competes with other, locally produced, media products. In Lebanon, as far as newspapers are concerned, only the party-sponsored press have managed to survive the civil war. The Dashnak's *Aztag*, the Hunchak's *Ararat*, and the Ramkavar's *Zartonk*, continue daily publication, but they appear under pressure for two main reasons: first, the economic crisis in Lebanon has hit the revenues from advertising, affecting the economics of publishing; second, there seems to be a certain disaffection on the part of the younger generations with regard to Armenian political newspapers, perceived by some as 'sclerotised', 'boring', or useless.[98] The circulation of the papers is limited: in 2002 Aztag only printed 3,000 copies per day, and Ararat 2,500–3,000.[99] The Armenian newspapers published in Lebanon maintain a limited distribution in Syria: a modest number of copies are shipped daily from Beirut to Damascus for security clearance and then delivered countrywide, mostly to subscribers.[100] As for the publishing of newspapers in Syria itself, only one weekly is currently available: *Kantsasar*, printed by the Armenian Apostolic Prelacy in Aleppo.

Over the 1990s, a popular role among Armenian media was played by FM radio stations. The regulatory reform of 1998, however, has determined an increase in costs and driven most of them out of the market.[101] At the end of 2003 only the Dashnak radio station, Vana Tzain (Voice of Van), held a valid broadcasting licence.

## Armenian Music in Contemporary Lebanon and Syria

Armenians remain prominent within the musical scene of Lebanon and Syria. An Armenian, Harout Fazlian, is the co-director of the Lebanese national orchestra, and so are many of the players in the orchestra and teachers in the national *conservatoire*. Folkloric concerts and choirs are frequently organized by Armenian groups and cultural associations in Lebanon and Syria alike.

On the other hand, the lively Armenian pop music scene that once characterized Lebanon has not survived, and a number of observers point out that the local production of Armenian music has seen its quality eroded. Cultural influences have always played a role in Armenian music (Western, Greek, Turkish); however, contemporary Armenian popular music produced in Lebanon is criticized for having lost its traditional roots. On the shelves of music stores specializing in Armenian music, the traditional popular successes of the 1960s and 1970s compete with a contemporary, commercial genre largely influenced by Arab and Western disco music. When looking for quality, some turn to the musical scene of the Armenian Republic. The *Vana Tzain* radio station, which is openly committed to broadcast what its staff portrays as 'pure' and 'genuine' Armenian music, resorts largely to contemporary music produced in Armenia.[102] It has been pointed out, however, that this rather confusing 'search for purity' or 'roots' might be one of the most deceiving frontiers of Armenian cultural preservation. Reflecting on the role of Armenia in preserving and developing the Armenian national musical heritage, Khatchig Tölölyan has recently observed that much of the contemporary musical production of Armenia should not be considered as a model, and that the idea that Armenia is a sanctuary of Armenian musical purity is largely mythical. Indeed, the challenges that globalization poses to Armenian music worldwide require resources that the small Republic can hardly provide alone.[103]

# Notes

1. The declining sense of trust and increasing disillusionment about living in Lebanon are by no means trends limited to the Armenian community; in the case of the Armenians, however, these trends interplay with – and are perhaps reinforced by – the Armenians' diverse identity and their connections with non-Lebanese, Armenian diaspora networks.
2. The term has been recently used by Armenian Catholic MP Serge Toursarkissian, one of the outspoken supporters of a further integration of the Armenians into Lebanese society and culture. Interview with MP Serge Toursarkissian, Beirut, 22 October 2003.
3. Only 72 of the 99 MPs elected in May 1972 still survived by the end of 1989.
4. See the Ta'if Agreement, I, 1 (General Principles), A and B: '*Le Liban est une patrie souveraine, libre, indépendante, patrie définitive de tous ses fils* [...]. *Le Liban est Arabe d'identité et d'appartenance*'. Translation by Béchara Ménassa.
5. E. Picard, 1996. *Lebanon, a Shattered Country*, New York and London: Holmes & Meier, 156.
6. There is a vast literature analysing Ta'if and the post-war, political reconstruction of Lebanon. See, among others D. Collings (ed.). 1994. *Peace for Lebanon? From War to Reconstruction*, London: Lynne Rienner; F. Debié and D. Pieter. 2003. *La Paix et la Crise: le Liban Reconstruit?*, Paris: Presses Universitaires de France; M.C. Hudson. 1999. 'Lebanon after Ta'if: Another Reform Opportunity Lost?', *Arab Studies Quarterly*, 21 (1), 27–40; S.A. Ofeish. 1999. 'Lebanon's Second Republic: Secular Talk, Sectarian Application', *Arab Studies Quarterly*, 21 (1), 97–116; S. Kassir. 2000. 'Dix Ans après, Comment ne pas Réconcilier une Société Divisée?', *Monde Arabe Maghreb-Machrek*, 169, 6–22.
7. The delegation included MPs Melkon Eblighatian (head of the delegation), Katchig Babikian, and Antranik Manoukian.
8. Interview with Mr. Hagop Pakradouni, Dashnak party official, Bourj Hammoud, 14 November 2002. Documents of such kind have not been made publicly available so far.

9. Positions in the civil service in Lebanon are divided into four categories (I, II, III, IV).

10. Ta'if agreement, I, 2, G (1).

11. Interview with a prominent Dashnak official who does not wish to be named, Bourj Hammoud, 13 November 2002. The first category includes, for instance, so called *cadres*, members of special councils, diplomatic corps, judges, the head of the Lebanese University, etc. Appointments are said to follow confessional-consociational rules at all levels of the public administration, 'down to the last of the street sweepers'.

12. Interview with Mr. Benjamin Vousakjian, Dashnak official, Beirut, 13 November 2002.

13. The second 'Armenian' seat in the cabinet went to the Evangelical Basil Fulayhan, a close advisor of Prime Minister Rafiq Hariri.

14. On the occasion of the congress of the Kata'ib held in Beirut in November 2003, Pakradouni sought to enhance the Arab identity of the party and openly stated that 'we [Kata'ib] are Arabs, and proud of being it'; a slogan that could hardly come from any other political leader of Armenian extraction.

15. Emphasis added. Excerpt from the Christmas sermon pronounced on 6 January 2003, at a time when the government reshuffle was being politically prepared. See *L'Orient-Le Jour*, 7 January 2003. Also see the communiqué of the Ramkavar party on the question, in *L'Orient-Le Jour*, 30 January 2003 : an '*appel pressant* [...] *refusant toute proposition visant à confier au chef des Kataëb, Karim Pakradouni, un quelconque portefeuille ministériel, censé être dévolu à la communauté arménienne, dans un éventuel prochain gouvernement. Étant donné qu'il ne représente pas les Arméniens, qu'il n'a pas mûri dans un environnement arménien, et que sa nomination serait une injustice faite à l'encontre de la communauté*'.

16. Oghassapian became Minister of State for Administrative Development.

17. For the national average, see N. Nassif. 2000. 'Les Elections Législatives de l'Eté 2000', *Monde Arabe Maghreb-Machrek*, 169, 116–127. For the Armenian percentage A. Sanjian. 2000. 'Armenians and the 2000 Parliamentary Elections in Lebanon', *Armenian News Network/Groong*, http://groong.usc.edu/ro/ro-20000907.html, retrieved on May 20, 2007. Armenian participation in the elections of 2005 was also low, but considerations on it are made more complicated by the Dashnak party's decision to boycott of the vote in Beirut – see further in the chapter.

18. Interview with a senior Dashnak party official who does not wish to be named. The 53,000 figure is an approximation obtained by multiplying the estimate of the total of the Armenian electors present in Lebanon (28,000 + 3,000) by a 1.7% coefficient often used within contemporary Lebanese politics in this type of calculations. When Armenian residents holding non-Lebanese citizenship are added-in, the overall Armenian population of Lebanon would reach 60,000–70,000.

19. 'People sell themselves for 100 US dollars. I can give the example of the last elections, we know of some youths who accepted to campaign for Gabriel Al-Murr for 100 US dollars'. Interview with a senior Hunchak party official who does not wish to be named, Beirut, July 2002. The problem of the lack of participation in political and party life is on the agenda of the three Armenian parties. See *L'Orient-Le Jour*, 30 January 2003.

20. For a perspective on the ideological wanderings of the Dashnak in the 1990s and beyond, see G. Minassian. 2002. *Guerre et Terrorisme Arméniens*, Paris : Presses Universitaires de France, Chapter 4.

21. Dashnak officials explain that the party's statute, pleading allegiance to the Armenian nation, lacks the commitment to Lebanon required to obtain registration.

22. Interview with Mr. Sebouh Kalpakian, Secretary General of the Hunchak party, Beirut, 4 July 2002.

23. On the role of the Dashnak party in Bourj Hammoud see T. Khayat. 2001. '*La Route de la Discorde : Construction du Territoire Municipal et Aménagement Métropolitain a Borj Hammoud*', in A. Favier (ed.), *Municipalités et Pouvoirs Locaux au Liban*, Beirut: CERMOC, 207–225.

24. Interview with a mid-low rank Dashnak official who wishes not to be named, Beirut, 2002.

25. On the role of Syria in post-Ta'if Lebanese politics, see F. Nasrallah. 1994. 'Syria after Ta'if: Lebanon and the Lebanese in Syrian Politics', in E. Kienle (ed.), *Contemporary Syria: Liberalization between Cold War and Cold Peace*, London: British Academic Press, 132–138.

26. In 1992 the Ramkavars boycotted the elections, like most non-Armenian Christian groups. The Dashnaks, informally recognized by the Syrians as the representative force within the Armenian camp, were left free to negotiate the composition of the lists to make sure that no troubles would emerge for Syria on the Armenian track. In 1996, political negotiation between the parties produced a scheme by which the joint list would include a representative each for the Dashnak and Hunchak, three seats for independents of Dashnak inclination, and one Ramkavar/AGBU figure.

27. The splits were not a direct consequence of Hariri's intervention, but were exploited in the bargaining and in the electoral campaign.

28. In political satire, 'Haririān? sounds as the Armenianized version of Hariri's name.

29. It may be pointed out, however, that Sa'ad Hariri included in one of his lists a Hizbullah candidate, in spite of the fact that Hizbullah was not part of the anti-Syrian, anti-Lahoud field, and did not participate in the 14 March demonstration.

30. Deceased in November 1999 and substituted by André Tabourian.

31. See B. Schaebler. 2001. 'Identity, Power, and Piety: the Druzes in Syria', *ISIM Newsletter*, 7/01, 25.

32. A. Sanjian. 2001. 'The Armenian Minority Experience in the Modern Arab World', *Bulletin of the Royal Institute for Inter-Faith Studies*, 3 (1), 149–179. Not

much is known about the nature of these memberships, and on how these are reconciled with the Armenian identities of their bearers. But it appears that Ba'th affiliations would hardly improve an individual's credentials within the community; on the contrary, 'opportunistic' enrollments in the Ba'th, as opposed to those instrumental to benefit the community at large, might contribute to marginalize an individual

33. The 'convention' took place in an Armenian theatre in Aleppo and was attended by about 500 persons. Sounboulian ran in the *Qa'imeh Halab Watanieh Mustaqil* [Indipendent National List of Aleppo] and was elected with nearly 86,000 votes. Interview with MP Sounboul Sounboulian, Aleppo, 14 November 2003.

34. Following by-elections. No Armenian was elected in the general elections of 1990.

35. Libarian, an employee of a tractor factory, was elected for the quota reserved to the 'workers and peasants'.

36. See the previous chapter, section on religion. The legislation officially recognizing religious communities dates back to the Mandate (1936).

37. Interview with Mr. Krikor Dounkian, Apostolic Prelacy, Aleppo, 26 November 2003.

38. It is of course true that this belonging may well be merely formal, and that actual individual beliefs or relations with the religious authorities are, in principle, irrelevant. In other words, it is true that, as the registration of individuals as members of one community comes 'automatically' (at birth, or following a conversion, etc.), the religious authorities have no power over their civil rights. On the other hand, it is also true that full political legitimacy within a community can hardly be found without some form of blessing from the religious authority in question. The case of Karim Pakradouni, mentioned in the previous paragraph, offers a good example relevant to the Armenian community.

39. One of the most notable cases is, perhaps, that of the Maronite Patriarch: in the post-war political phase, characterized by a generally weak Christian leadership, Mgr. Nasrallah Sfeir has arguably emerged as one of the top players on the Lebanese political scene.

40. H.H. Aram I, Catholicos of Cilicia. 1997. *The Challenge to be a Church in a Changing World*, New York: The Armenian Prelacy, 36.

41. Interview with Mr. Krikor Dounkian, Apostolic Prelacy, Aleppo, 26 November 2003.

42. Ibid.; interview with Rev. Paul Haidostian, Beirut, 20 November 2002; interview with Father Agostino Kousa, Aleppo, 28 November 2003; interview with Rev. Serop G. Megerditchian, Aleppo, 27 November 2003.

43. Interview with Mr. Krikor Dounkian, Apostolic Prelacy, Aleppo, 26 November 2003.

44. Interview with Father Agostino Kousa, Aleppo, 28 November 2003.

45. Currently not in use. Ibid.

46. Interview with Rev. Serop G. Megerditchian, Aleppo, 27 November 2003.

47. Currently not used as an Armenian church, but owned by the Armenian community. Ibid.

48. There is a rather vast literature on the effects of the war on the Lebanese economy, and on post-war economic developments. See, among others, Debié and Pieter, *La Paix et la Crise*; C. Nahas. 2000. 'L'Economie Libanaise et ses Déséquilibres', *Monde Arabe Maghreb-Machrek*, 169, 55–69; A.A. Kubursi. 1999. 'Reconstructing the Economy of Lebanon', *Arab Studies Quarterly*, 21 (1), 69–95; N. Saïdi. 1998. *Growth, Destruction, and the Challenges of Reconstruction: Macroeconomic Essays on Lebanon*, Beirut: Lebanese Center for Policy Studies.

49. The figure for 1992 is reported in A.A. Kubursi, 'Reconstructing the Economy of Lebanon', 79; for 2002 see *Middle East Economic Digest*, 45 (50), 16 December 2002. The official figure reported by the Lebanese Authorities in May 2005 is $35.604 bn. According to more than one specialist, a more accurate reading of the Lebanese public accounts would put the figure at around $50 bn. See *L'Orient-Le Jour*, 1 August 2005.

50. Calculated from Arab Monetary Fund data.

51. Debié and Pieter, *La Paix et la Crise*, 16–17 and 151–155.

52. See R. Hinnebusch. 2001. *Syria: Revolution from Above*, London and New York: Routledge, 131–135.

53. According to Arab Monetary Fund data, the figure averaged $1,092.

54. *L'Hebdo Magazine* (Beirut), 30 June 2000, 18.

55. Nahas, 'L'Economie Libanaise', 64–65.

56. *L'Orient-Le Jour*, 12 March 2004, reporting views of the Director of the agency, Mr. Hussein Al-Amash.

57. During an interview with the author, a young Syrian Armenian has suggested that, when a small-size family business is available and profitable, the family tends to 'save' the money necessary for a university degree; unless obtained in one of the top universities of Lebanon or in the Western world, degrees are considered near to useless as tools to improve employability.

58. It is the case of families renouncing Armenian secondary education for more prestigious private schools.

59. 'A poll conducted by the Arab HDR team in 2001 showed that more than half of young Arab people surveyed wanted to emigrate to other countries, mostly to industrialized countries outside the region', United Nations Development Programme, Regional Bureau for Arab States. 2002. *Arab Human Development Report 2002: Creating Opportunities for Future Generations*, New York: UNDP.

60. Debié and Pieter, *La Paix et la Crise*,155.

61. Howard Karagheusian Commemorative Corporation. 2002. *Director's Annual Report*, Beirut: HKCC; interview with Rev. Robert Sarkissian, director HKCC, Bourj Hammoud, 7 June 2002. The figure refers to the early 2000s. Medical services available include dental clinic, hearing tests, ophthalmic tests,

laboratory tests, gynaecological visits, etc. It is important to stress that the centre is open to the general public, regardless of confessional affiliation; it does, however, serve a vast majority of Armenians.

62. Ibid.; Jinishian Memorial Programme. 2001. *Serving the Least of These: the 35th Anniversary of the Jinishian Memorial Programme*. Louisville, Kentucky: The Presbiterian Church; various interviews.

63. In 1992, with a controversial decree, the government withdrew the certificate of registration of 138 associations, on grounds that they were engaging in political activities. The political nature of that provision, and the inconsistency of this type of approach, has encouraged the view that the law was sometimes arbitrarily interpreted to accommodate the agenda of Syrian dominance in the political life of Lebanon. See K. Karam. 2002. 'Les Associations au Liban: Entre Caritatif et Politique', in S. Ben Néfissa (ed.), *Pouvoirs et Associations dans le Monde Arabe*, Paris: CNRS, 71.

64. See S. Boukhaima. 2002. '*Le Mouvement Associatif en Syrie*', in S. Ben Néfissa (ed.), *Pouvoirs et Associations dans le Monde Arabe*, Paris: CNRS, 89, speaking of a '*pacte tacite entre le pouvoir politique et* [les] *associations, selon lequel les dirigeants associatifs garantiraient le respect de l'ordre public et politique en contrepartie d'une relative liberté dans les activités de l'association*'.

65. Ta'if agreement, Part I, 3 (Other Reforms), Section E (3); translation by Béchara Ménassa.

66. Ibid., Section E (5).

67. This view has been opposed by a number of scholars and observers. See, for instance, T. Hanf. 1980. 'Education and Consociational Conflict Regulation in Plural Societies', in F. Van Zyl Slabbert and J. Opland (eds.), *South Africa: Dilemmas of Evolutionary Change*, Grahamstown: Institute of Social and Economic Research, Rhodes University, 224–248; A. Nasri Messarra. 1994. *Théorie Générale du Système Politique Libanais*, Paris: Cariscript. For Nasri Messarra, '*s'il y a une certaine fragmentation culturelle, elle est le résultat non du système éducationnel, mais de sa non-légitimation dans la conscience collective*' (p. 121).

68. S.C. Inati. 1999. 'Transformation of Education: Will it Lead to Integration?', *Arab Studies Quarterly*, 21 (1), 60.

69. Ibid., 55–68. See, in particular, the case of the teaching of religion, absent from the new curricula.

70. On the contemporary crisis of Armenian schools see in particular J. Tanielian. 2002. *Lipananahay Tebrotze: Tiver yev Mdoroumner* [The Armenian Schools in Lebanon, Some Data and Some Ideas], Beyrouth.

71. Ibid.

72. Excluding 3 religious seminaries and 2 special schools for the disabled.

73. See Chapter 5, section on education.

74. Interview with Ms. Manoushag Boyadjian, school principal, Dbayeh, 6 November 2002. Also see Howard Karagheusian Commemorative Corporation, *Director's Annual Report*, 35: 'School fees are a nightmare for our families'.

75. Author's interviews with a number of Armenian school principals.
76. Yeghishe Manoukian College, Dbayeh, November 2002.
77. It is, for instance the case of the Mesropian Catholic school of Bourj Hammoud.
78. Competition between schools raises a number of questions about the changing attitudes of Armenian families to their religious, cultural, and political traditions; similar situations have been perhaps observed in the past, when 'regional' schools supported by patriotic unions were closed and Armenian regional, sub-ethnic cultures were gradually lost.
79. Adapted from Tanielian, *Lipananahay Tebrotze*, 49.
80. See *Ardziv* (Beirut), 9 (15–16/207–208), October 2002, 11. The proposal, by Vartan Tashjian, envisages the closure of a number of existing schools and the creation of a larger school catering for 2,000–2,500 students of all grades. For a review of a number of options in the co-operation between state and communal schools in the Lebanese context, see Nasri Messarra, *Théorie Générale*, 122–125.
81. Interview with Mr. Jirair Reisian, school principal, Aleppo, 19 June 2002.
82. Syria, represented by a young girl, would liberate herself from chains, and – with the help of stone-throwing boys – lead the other Arab nations to the rescue of the prisoner Palestine. The celebration took place at the Russian cultural institute of Damascus on 14 June 2002.
83. Interview with an Armenian teacher who wishes not to be identified, Damascus, 6 November 2003.
84. Donations from the Calouste Gulbenkian Foundation, the Armenian Relief Cross, the Jinishian Memorial Program, AGBU, and other institutions play a crucial role in ensuring the financial sustainability of the schools, and provide a significant number of scholarships to individual students.
85. According to Sanjian, 'The Armenian Minority Experience', in 1996 there were 27 schools and 11,000 students in the country.
86. Among the associations and clubs, two examples are particularly impressive: Hamazkayin's Levon Shant centre in Bourj Hammoud (a sort of 'house of Armenian culture', offering courses in painting, music, dance, etc.), and the Spidak Club in Aleppo.
87. The Nazarian (AGBU, ca. 500–600 seats), Kaprielian (Grtasirats Association, ca. 650–700 seats), Aharonian and Zavarian (Hamazkayin, ca. 450 and 370 seats respectively).
88. Interview with Mr. Berge Fazlian, Zalqa, 30 October 2003; interview with Mr. Manuel Keshishian, Aleppo, 13 November 2003.
89. Interview with Mr. Berge Fazlian, Zalqa, 30 October 2003.
90. Interview with Mr. Hagop Doniguian, publisher, Antelias, 23 October 2003; interview with Father Norayr Ashekian, director of the printing house of the Catholicosate of Cilicia, Antelias, 24 October 2003.
91. Interview with Mr. Hagop Doniguian, publisher, Antelias, 24 October 2003.
92. Interview with Ms. Suzy Ohannessian, Antelias, 24 October 2003.

93. This view is confirmed by the fact that the printing house of the Catholicosate receives support from donations from the Armenian diaspora. In particular, the Calouste Gulbenkian Foundation has provided new machinery. The Catholicosate exports and distributes its catalogue through the Armenian Apostolic Prelacies in the diaspora (notably to Syria, Iran, Greece, USA, Cyprus, Venezuela, Canada). Interview with Father Norayr Ashekian, director of the printing house of the Catholicosate of Cilicia, Antelias, 24 October 2003.

94. Guiliguia, owned and managed by the son of Judge Krikor Eblighatian, Matig, has published around 125 titles in Armenian since its foundation. Interview with Mr. Matig Eblightian, Aleppo, 11 November 2003.

95. For information on Armenian television in Lebanon I have relied on an interview with Vartan Tachjian, Bourj Hammoud, 15 October 2003. Tachjian has been involved as an editor in many of the TV news projects in Lebanon.

96. The program ran for 5 days a week, and it consisted of 30 minutes of local and Armenian news fully in Armenian, without subtitles.

97. The program, called *Lousamoud*, is a 30–minute weekly containing news, an interview with an Armenian-Lebanese personality, and coverage of religious and cultural themes. The program is fully subtitled in Arabic.

98. Various casual interviews, Lebanon, Autumn 2003.

99. Interview with Aharon Shekerdemian, editor in chief, *Ararat* newspaper, Beirut, 10 June 2002; interview with Mr. Shahan Kandaharian, editor in chief, *Aztag* newspaper, Bourj Hammoud, 3 May 2002.

100. The process of clearance is described as a mere formality and is yet another example of the sense of relaxed relationship between the Armenian community and the regime. Interview with Aharon Shekerdemian, editor in chief, *Ararat* newspaper, Beirut, 10 June 2002; interview with Mr. Shahan Kandaharian, editor in chief, *Aztag* newspaper, Bourj Hammoud, 3 May 2002.

101. The legal document that assigned licences was the Marsoum 13474, Official Gazette No. 52, 19 November 1998. Under the new regulatory framework, Vana Tzain had to pay 100 million Lebanese pounds for the license, and a further 25 million for each yearly renewal. Interview with Armen Abdalian, director of *Vana Tzain* radio station, Bourj Hammoud, 30 October 2003.

102. Interview with Armen Abdalian, director of Vana Tzain radio station, Bourj Hammoud, 30 October 2003.

103. K. Tololyan. 2002. *Redefining Diasporas: Old Approaches, New Identities*, London: Armenian Institute, 48: 'the homeland takes music brought back from Russia and the west, recasts it slightly, endows it with Armenian lyrics, and re-exports it. In other words, the homeland is the source of a music which is not in any cultural sense national, folkloric, or traditional, but enjoys the cachet of the homeland-national'.

# Conclusion

This book set out to examine the experience of the Armenian communities in Lebanon and Syria from the 1920s to the present. Its key interests of enquiry have stemmed from the observation that the Armenians appear to have successfully maintained, for more than eight decades since their mass-resettlement in the Levant, a distinct identity as an ethno-culturally diverse group, in spite of being a relatively small minority within a very different, mostly Arab environment. While not excluding other factors, this work has argued that the comparative success of the community in preserving its cultural distinctiveness must be understood in close relation with the process of formation and evolution of the Lebanese and Syrian states.

The book supports a number of conclusions, in part specific to the Armenians, and to Lebanon and Syria, in part more general. The first is that the evolution of the two states, and in particular of their approach towards ethno-cultural diversity, had a significant influence on the way the Armenian communities have evolved and, ultimately, on the comparative success of the preservation of their diverse identity. Chapter 2, in particular, has shown that the political system established by the Mandate authorities created remarkable opportunities for the (re)construction of a new, post-Genocide Armenian world in the Levant: on the one hand, it maintained the principle of official recognition of specific cultural autonomies that had characterized the Ottoman tradition; on the other, it created constitutional spaces and political conditions for the integration of the Armenians into the Lebanese and Syrian parliamentary systems. The Armenian refugees who resettled in Lebanon and Syria from the early 1920s were able to seize those opportunities and to gradually develop a vast system of Armenian institutions that became the backbone of the Armenian effort for cultural preservation and development. Chapter 3 has covered the process of gradual deconstruction of the confessional representation system in Syria in the 1950s and 1960s, and has shown that the rise of centralizing regimes inspired by Arab and national Syrian ideologies imposed restrictions that have sometimes severely damaged the Armenian system of communal cultural preservation. Armenian political parties, associations, schools, and media had often no better alternatives than discontinuing activities, retreating to less visible communal dimensions, or – at best – accepting a significant loss of autonomy and strict control. Chapter 4 has shown that a partial recovery of the conditions of the Armenians in Syria has been possible since the 1970s: the take-over of power by Hafiz Al-Asad marked the beginning of a phase of relaxation of the relations between the state and social groups that could be integrated in a corporatist system of support to the regime.

A second conclusion is that both in Lebanon and in Syria the evolution of the approach of the state toward ethno-cultural diversity has been dictated primarily by the needs of legitimacy and stability of the state itself, of the political system, or of the political leadership, rather than by a recognition of the value of cultural diversity *per se*. The two states represent two interesting case studies for scholars of ethno-politics of the Middle East. The perceived (potential or actual) problems for stability posed by the presence of diverse centres of ethnic and sub-ethnic allegiance have been addressed by resorting to different political-constitutional techniques: in Lebanon, essentially, by adopting a power-sharing, consociational political system; in Syria, at times by adopting policies aimed at suppressing, or gradually eliminating alternative allegiances, at times by exploiting the potential of ethno-cultural allegiances in a complex system of alliances between the regime and diverse communal groups, at times by resorting to a combination of the two. Neither in Lebanon nor in Syria, though, has the question of 'cultural rights', or of any 'right to diversity' played a central role in defining the approach of the state to ethno-cultural groups.

Thirdly, while recognising that the Lebanese consociational arrangement gave the Armenians remarkable chances to preserve their diverse identity, this book warns against fast-drawn, clear-cut conclusions presenting the Lebanese system as a successful, sustainable model for the preservation of ethno-cultural diversity. The two major breakdowns of the national pact, in 1958 and between 1975 and 1990, have fully exposed the precariousness of the Lebanese political system, and the tragic consequences that similar breakdowns may have for the Lebanese people and the Armenian-Lebanese community, regardless of its approach to national crises. Besides, the book has provided clear indications of the limitations of the Lebanese consociational formula in fairly representing the people of Lebanon even during those phases in which the inter-communal agreement appears to hold. The democratic gap in the current representation of the Armenian community, but also – conversely – the inability of the Lebanese state to guarantee democratic processes *within* the community, are clear examples of these limitations.

More generally, this book suggests that neither in Lebanon nor in Syria does a sustainable or consistent model for the accommodation of ethno-cultural diversity appear to be in place. Since independence, the Lebanese state has been chronically caught between the formal engagement to get past political confessionalism, and the pressures to maintain it and consolidate it. If the first option is made difficult by a complex interplay of vetoes, the consolidation of the consociational confessional system does not appear as a sustainable option either. The Lebanese state continues to suffer from a structural difficulty to accommodate social change within the system of confessional representation. Major adjustments of the confessional balance have often taken place at the cost of dangerous national crises. In Syria, the current approach of the state toward ethno-cultural diversity remains ambiguous: formally, the political recognition of ethno-cultural groups continues to be a taboo; *de facto*, in spite of the fact that the policy of construction of a Syrian national identity has been in part successful, the regime continues to value and to extract benefits from the persisting communal-confessional allegiances. The bases of this arrangement, however, appear both uncertain and volatile: as relations between the regime and a community like the Armenians are maintained at a merely informal level, they tend to offer no guarantees and they are potentially subject to sudden policy changes (and, obviously, to the consequences of a change of regime).

On the basis of these considerations, the comparatively successful preservation of Armenian ethno-cultural diversity in Lebanon and Syria may be described – rather paradoxically – as a 'by-product' of the two states' unresolved search for a solution to the political problems raised by the non-homogeneity of their society, or, in other words, as a temporary condition in their 'search for legitimacy': ethno-cultural diversity has continued to exist not because of its value *per se*, but because the stability of the state could not do without it until a more solid legitimacy, based on cross-cultural allegiances and cleavages could be found.

How long this 'temporary condition' can last, and how change could affect the future of the Armenian communities in the Levant is hard to tell. Of course, as the saying goes, *rien ne dure comme le provisoire*, and the Lebanese consociational republic and the Syrian regime inaugurated by Hafiz Al-Asad (and continued by his son Bashar) have long outlived many predictions of their transformation or collapse. When, and if change comes, the question of the approach of the state toward ethno-cultural diversity is bound to be raised again. Approaches which are sustainable, and that do not lead to the disappearance of diversity, would probably require that the question of ethno-cultural diversity is examined under the light of the concepts of 'cultural rights', or 'rights to diversity'; they would require, in other words, that state recognition of diversity as a value *per se* goes beyond mere declarations of principles. In the case of the Armenians, this could mean that Armenian culture is allowed, on the one hand, to maintain its connections with Armenia and the diaspora, and on the other to find recognition, and perhaps encouragement and protection as a component of Lebanese and Syrian national culture.

# Bibliography

## Books and Periodicals

Abrahamian, A.G. 1964–1967. *Hamarot Urvagits Hay Gaght'avayreri Patmut'ian* [Concise Outline of the History of the Armenian Expatriate Communities], 2 Vols., Yerevan: Hayastan.

Academy of Sciences of the Armenian Soviet Socialist Republic. 1967–1984. *Hay Joghovrdi Patmut'iun* [History of the Armenian People], 8 vols., Yerevan: Academy of Sciences of the Armenian Soviet Socialist Republic.

Alpoyachian, A. 1941–1961. *Patmut'iun Hay Gaghtakanut'ian: Hayeru Tsruume Ashkharhi Zanazan Masere* [History of Armenian Emigrations: the Dispersal of Armenians in Different Parts of the World], 3 Vols., Cairo: Nor Astgh.

Altounian, A.M. ca. 1997. *A la Recherche du Temps Retrouvé Avec Mon Père – l'Architecte Mardiros Altounian*, Beirut: Sipan.

H.H. Aram I. 1997. *The Challenge to Be a Church in a Changing World*, New York: The Armenian Prelacy.

Arpee, L. 1946. *A History of Armenian Christianity*, New York: The Armenian Missionary Association of America.

Arpee, L. 1946. *A Century of Armenian Protestantism 1846–1946*, New York: The Armenian Missionary Association of America.

Artinian, V. 1988. *The Armenian Constitutional System in the Ottoman Empire 1839–1863*, Istanbul: publisher unknown.

As'eed, M.S. 2002. *Al-Barlaman al-Suri fi Tatawouru al-Tarikhi 1919–2001*, Damascus: Al Mada.

Assaf, R. and Barakat, L. (ed.). 2003. *Atlas du Liban*, Beirut: Presses de l'Université Saint-Joseph.

Atamian, P.P. 1964. *Histoire de la Communauté Arménienne Catholique de Damas*, Beirut: Institut Patriarcal de Bzoummar.

Atamian Bournoutian, A. 1997. 'Cilician Armenia', in R.G. Hovannisian (ed.), *The Armenian People from Ancient to Modern Times*, Vol. 1, Basingstoke and London: Macmillan, 273–291.

Atiyeh, G.N. (ed.). 1995. 'The Book in the Modern Arab World: The Cases of Lebanon and Egypt', in G.N. Atiyeh (ed.), *The Book in the Islamic World. The Written Word and Communication in the Middle East*, New York: State University of New York Press.

Ayoubi, N. 1995. *Over-stating the Arab State*, London and New York: I.B. Tauris.
'Azazian, H. 1993. *Nubdha Tarikhiya Mujaza 'an al-Jaliyat al-Armaniya fi al-Bilad al-Arabiya*, Latakia: publisher unknown.
Babloyan, M.A. 1986. *Hay Barperagan Mamoul: Madenakidagan Hamahavak Tzoutzag 1794–1980* [The Armenian Printed Press: Bibliographical List 1794–1980], Yerevan: The Armenian Soviet Socialist Republic Academy of Sciences.
Bariguian, H. and Varjabedian, H. 1973. *Badmoutioun Surio Hay Debaranneru* [The History of Syrian Armenian Printing Houses], Aleppo: AGBU Bibliographical Committee.
Barsoumian, H. 1997. 'The Eastern Question and the Tanzimat Era', in R.G. Hovannisian, *The Armenian People from Ancient to Modern Times*, Vol. 2, Basingstoke and London: Macmillan, 175–201.
Barton, J.L. 1930. *Story of Near East Relief (1915–1930): An Interpretation*, New York: MacMillan Co.
Batatu, H. 1981. 'Some Observations on the Social Roots of Syria's Ruling Military Group and the Causes of its Dominance', *Middle East Journal*, 35(3), 331–344.
Bedrosian, R. 1997. 'Armenia during the Seljuk and Mongol Period', in R.G. Hovannisian (ed.), *The Armenian People from Ancient to Modern Times*, Vol. 1, Basingstoke and London: Macmillan, 241–271.
Bengio, O. and Ben-Dor, G. (eds). 1999. *Minorities and the State in the Arab World*, Boulder and London: Lynne Rienner.
Botiveau, B. 1996. 'Il Diritto dello Stato-Nazione lo Status dei Non Musulmani in Egitto e in Siria', in A. Pacini (ed.), *Comunità Cristiane nell'Islam Arabo*, Turin: Fondazione Giovanni Agnelli, 121–138.
Boukhaima, S. 2002. 'Le Mouvement Associatif en Syrie', in S. Ben Néfissa (ed.), *Pouvoirs et Associations dans le Monde Arabe*, Paris: CNRS, 2002, 77–94.
Boyajian, D.H. 1962. *The Pillars of the Armenian Church*, Watertown: publisher unknown.
Braude, B. and Lewis, B. (eds). 1982. *Christians and Jews in the Ottoman Empire*, 2 Vols., New York and London: Holmes & Meier.
Cardia, C. 1988. *Stato e Confessioni Religiose*, Bologna: Il Mulino.
Chabry, L. and Chabry, A. 1984. *Politique et Minorités au Proche-Orient: Les Raisons d'une Explosion*, Paris: Maisonneuve et Larose.
Chahinian, K. 1988. *Œuvres Vives de la Littérature Arménienne*, Antélias: Catholicosat Arménien de Cilicie.
Chakmakjian, H.A. 1985. *The Armenian Evangelical Movement*, Fresno: Rev. Dr. Chakmakjian.
Chaliand, G. and Ternon, Y. 1991. *1915, Le Génocide des Arméniens*, Bruxelles: Complexe.
Chami, J.G. 2002–2003. *Le Mémorial du Liban*, Tomes 1–4, Beirut: Joseph G. Chami.
Cholakian, H. 1982–1984. 'Halebi Azkayin Nersessian Oussoumnarana: Aghchegantz yev Mancheru Tebrozner 1876–1919' [The National Nercessian School of Aleppo: Schools for Girls and Boys, 1876–1919], *Haigazian Armenological Review*, 10, 243–266.

Cleveland, W.L. 1971. *The Making of an Arab Nationalist: Ottomanism and Arabism in the Life and Thought of Sati' Al-Husri*, Princeton: Princeton University Press.

Collings, D. (ed.). 1994. *Peace for Lebanon? From War to Reconstruction*, London: Lynne Rienner.

Courbage, Y. and Fargues, P. 1997. *Christians and Jews under Islam*, London: I.B. Tauris.

Dadoyan, S. 2003. *The Armenian Catholicosate from Cilicia to Antelias*, Antelias: Armenian Catholicosate.

Dadrian, V.N. 1995. *Autopsie du Génocide Arménien*, Bruxelles: Complexe.

Dagher, A. 1995. *L'Etat et l'Economie au Liban: Action Gouvernementale et Finances Publiques de l'Indépendance à 1975*, Beirut: CERMOC.

Dakessian, A. 1990. *Hay Antzialen Losanegarnerov* [Pictures from the Armenian Past], Aleppo.

Darbinian, R. 1953. 'In Retrospect: A Glance at the Last Thirty Years', *Armenian Review*, 6(3–23), 49–65.

Dasnabedian, H. 1988. *Histoire de la Fédération Révolutionnaire Arménienne Dachnaktsoutioun 1890/1924*, Milan: Oemme Edizioni.

Debié, F. and Pieter, D. 2003. *La Paix et la Crise: Le Liban Reconstruit?* Paris: Presses Universitaires de France.

Dekmejian, R.H. 1997. 'The Armenian Diaspora', in R.G. Hovannisian (ed.), *The Armenian People from Ancient to Modern Times*, Vol. 2, Basingstoke and London: Macmillan, 413–443.

Der Khatchadourian, A. 1971. 'Fifty Years of Armenian Press in Lebanon (1921–1971)', *Haigazian Armenological Review*, 2, 263–296.

Der Khatchadourian, A. 1972. 'A History of the Armenian Press in Syria', *Haigazian Armenological Review*, 3, 195–230.

Eckstein, H. 1966. *Division and Cohesion in Democracy: A Study of Norway*, Princeton: Princeton University Press.

Elphinston, W.G. 1946. 'The Kurdish Question', *International Affairs* (Royal Institute of International Affairs 1944–), 22(1), 91–103.

Esman, M.J. and Rabinovich, I. (eds). 1988. *Ethnicity, Pluralism, and the State in the Middle East*, Ithaca and London: Cornell University Press.

Furnivall, J.S. 1948. *Colonial Policy and Practice: A Comparative Study of Burma and Netherlands India*, Cambridge: Cambridge University Press.

Gannagé, P. 2001. *Le Pluralisme des Statuts Personnels dans les Etats Multicommunautaires: Droit Libanais et Droits Proche-Orientaux*, Beirut: Université Saint-Joseph.

Gates, C.L. 1998. *The Merchant Republic of Lebanon: Rise of an Open Economy*, Oxford: Centre for Lebanese Studies.

Gelvin, J.L. 1998. *Divided Loyalties: Nationalism and Mass Politics in Syria at the Close of the Empire*, Berkeley, Los Angeles and London: University of California Press.

Gerges, F. 1997. 'Lebanon', in Y. Sayigh and A. Shlaim (eds.), *The Cold War and the Middle East*, Oxford: Clarendon Press, 77–101.

Greenshields, T.H. 'The Settlement of Armenian Refugees in Syria and Lebanon 1915–39', in J.I. Clarke and H. Bowen-Jones (eds), *Change and Development in the Middle East: Essays in Honour of W.B. Fisher*, London and New York: Methuen, 1981, 233–241.

Guingamp, P. 1996. *Hafez El-Assad et le Parti Baath en Syrie*, Paris: l'Harmattan.

Gunter, M.M. 1990. *Transnational Armenian Activism*, London: Research Institute for the Study of Conflict and Terrorism.

Gürün, K. 1985. *The Armenian File: The Myth of Innocence Exposed*, Nicosia and Istanbul: K. Rustem and Brother.

Gutmann, A. (ed.). 1994. *Multiculturalism: Examining the Politics of Recognition*, Princeton: Princeton University Press.

Haddad, G. 1950. *Fifty Years of Modern Syria and Lebanon*, Beirut: Dar al-Hayat.

Hanf, T. 1980. 'Education and Consociational Conflict Regulation in Plural Societies', in F. Van Zyl Slabbert and J. Opland (eds), *South Africa: Dilemmas of Evolutionary Change*, Grahamstown: Institute of Social and Economic Research, Rhodes University, 224–248.

Harik, I.F. 1972. 'The Ethnic Revolution and Political Integration in the Middle East', *International Journal of Middle Eastern Studies*, 3(3), 303–323.

Hewsen, R.H. 'The Geography of Armenia' in R.G. Hovannisian (ed.), *The Armenian People from Ancient to Modern Times*, Vol. 1, Basingstoke and London: Macmillan, 1997, 1–17.

Hinnebusch, R. 2001. *Syria: Revolution from Above*, London and New York: Routledge.

Hinnebusch, R. 1995. 'State, Civil Society, and Political Change in Syria', in A.R. Norton (ed.), *Civil Society in the Middle East*, Leiden, New York and Köln: E.J. Brill, 214–242.

Hottinger, A. 1961. '*Zu'ama*' and Parties in the Lebanese Crisis of 1958', *Middle East Journal*, 15(2), 127–140.

Hottinger, A. 1966. '*Zu'ama*' in Historical Perspective', in L. Binder (ed.), *Politics in Lebanon*, New York, London and Sydney: John Wiley and Sons.

Hourani, A. 1946. *Syria and Lebanon: A Political Essay*, London, New York and Toronto: Oxford University Press.

Hourani, A. 1947. *Minorities in the Arab World*, London, New York and Toronto: Oxford University Press.

Hourani, A. 1976. 'Ideologies of the Mountain and the City', in R. Owen (ed.), *Essays on the Crisis in Lebanon*, London: Ithaca Press, 33–41.

Hovannisian, R.G. 1974. 'The Ebb and Flow of the Armenian Minority in the Arab Middle East', *Middle East Journal*, 28(1), 19–32.

Hovannisian, R.G. (ed.). 1997. *The Armenian People from Ancient to Modern Times*, 2 Vols., Basingstoke and London: MacMillan.

Hovannisian. R.G. 1997. 'The Armenian question in the Ottoman Empire, 1876–1914', in R.G. Hovannisian (ed.), *The Armenian People from Ancient to Modern Times*, Vol. 2, Basingstoke and London: Macmillan, 203–239.

Hovannisian, R.G. (ed.). 1999. *Remembrance and Denial: The Case of the Armenian Genocide*, Detroit: Wayne State University Press.

Hudson, M.C. 1977. *Arab Politics: The Search for Legitimacy*, New Haven and London: Yale University Press.

Hudson, M.C. 1968. *The Precarious Republic: Political Modernization in Lebanon* New York: Random House.

Hudson, M.C. 1999. 'Lebanon after Ta'if: Another Reform Opportunity Lost?', *Arab Studies Quarterly*, 21(1), 27–40.

Humphreys, R.S. 1991. *Islamic History: A Framework for Inquiry*, London and New York: I.B. Tauris.

Hutchinson, J. and Smith, A.D. (eds). 1996. *Ethnicity*, Oxford and New York: Oxford University Press.

Hyland, F.P. 1991. *The Armenian Terrorism: The Past, the Present, the Prospects*, Boulder, San Francisco and Oxford: Westview Press.

al-Imam, M.R. 1995. *Al-Arman fi Misr: al-Qarn al-Tasi' 'Ashar*, Cairo: Nubar Printing House.

al-Imam., M.R. 1999. *Tarikh al-Jaliya al-Armaniya fi Misr*, Cairo: al-Hay'ah al-Misriyah al-'Ammah lil-Kitab.

Inalcik, H. 1998. *Essays in Ottoman History*, Beyoglu, Istanbul: Eren.

Inalcik, H. and Quataert, D. (eds). 1994. *An Economic and Social History of the Ottoman Empire, 1300–1916*, Cambridge and New York: Cambridge University Press.

Inati, S.C. 1999. 'Transformation of Education: Will it Lead to Integration?', *Arab Studies Quarterly*, 21(1), 55–68.

Iskandar, A.J. 2000. *La Nouvelle Cilicie: Les Arméniens du Liban*, Antélias, Catholicosat Arménien de Cilicie.

Issawi, C. 1980. *The Economic History of Turkey 1800–1914*, London and Chicago: University of Chicago Press.

al-Jahmani, Y.I. 2001. *Turkiya wa al-Arman* [Turkey and the Armenians], Damascus: Dar al-Hawran.

Jebejian, R. 1994. *A Pictorial Record of Routes and Centres of Annihilation of Armenian Deportees in 1915 within the Boundaries of Syria*, Aleppo: Violette Jebejian Library.

Jebejian, R. 2000. *Malamih min Tarikh al-Haraka al-Riyadiya fi Suriya – Musahamat al-Riyadiyeen al-Arman fi al-Riyada al-Suriya* [Lineaments of History of the Sporting Movement in Syria – Participation of Armenian Sportsmen in Syrian Sport], Aleppo: R. Jebejian.

Karal, E.Z. 1982. 'Non-Muslim Representatives in the First Constitutional Assembly, 1876–1877', in B. Braude and B. Lewis (eds), *Christians and Jews in the Ottoman Empire*, Vol. 1, New York and London: Holmes & Meier, 387–400.

Karam, K. 2002. 'Les Associations au Liban: Entre Caritatif et Politique', in S. Ben Néfissa (ed.), *Pouvoirs et Associations dans le Monde Arabe*, Paris: CNRS, 57–75.

H.H. Karekin II, Catholicos of Cilicia. 1989. *The Cross Made of the Cedars of Lebanon*, Antelias: Catholicosate of Cilicia.

H.H. Karekin II, Catholicos of Cilicia. 1994. *The Council of Chalcedon and the Armenian Church*, Antelias: Catholicosate of Cilicia.

Karpat, K. 1982. '*Millets* and Nationality: The Roots of the Incongruity of Nation and State in the Post-Ottoman Era' in B. Braude and B. Lewis (eds), *Christians and Jews in the Ottoman Empire*, Vol. 1, New York and London: Holmes & Meier, 141–170.

Kassir, S. 1994. *La Guerre du Liban: De la Dissension Nationale au Conflit Régional*, second edition, Paris and Beirut: Karthala and CERMOC.

Kassir, S. 2000. 'Dix Ans après, Comment ne pas Réconcilier une Société Divisée?', *Monde Arabe Maghreb-Machrek*, Numero spécial, 169, 6–22.

Kassir, S. 2003. *Histoire de Beyrouth*, Paris: Fayard.

Kerr, S.E. 1973. *The Lions of Marash: Personal Experiences with American Near East Relief 1919–1922*, Albany: State University of New York Press.

Kévorkian, R.H.. 1998. 'L'Extermination des Déportés Arméniens Ottomans dans les Camps de Concentration de Syrie-Mésopotamie (1915–1916): La Deuxième Phase du Génocide', *Révue d'Histoire Arménienne Contemporaine*, Tome 2.

Khadduri, M. 1951. 'Constitutional Development in Syria, with Emphasis on the Constitution of 1950', *Middle East Journal*, 5(2), 137–160.

Khayat, T. 2001. 'La Route de la Discorde: Construction du Territoire Municipal et Aménagement Métropolitain a Borj Hammoud', in A. Favier (ed.), *Municipalités et Pouvoirs Locaux au Liban*, Beirut: CERMOC, 207–225.

al-Khazen, F. 2000. *The Breakdown of the State in Lebanon, 1967–1976*, Cambridge, MA: Harvard University Press.

Khoury, P.S. 1987. *Syria and the French Mandate: The Politics of Arab Nationalism 1920–1945*, London: I.B.Tauris.

Kolvenbach, P-H. April–June 1971. 'Note sur l'enseignement Arménien au Liban', *Travaux et Jours*, 39, 71–76.

Kouymjian, D. 1994. 'From Disintegration to Reintegration: Armenians at the Start of the Modern Era: XVIth–XVIIth Centuries', *Revue du Monde Arménien*, 1, 9–18.

Kouymjian, D. 1997. 'Armenia from 1375 to 1604', in R.G. Hovannisian (ed.), *The Armenian People from Ancient to Modern Times*, Vol. 2, Basingstoke and London: Macmillan, 1–50.

Kubursi, A.A. 1999. 'Reconstructing the Economy of Lebanon', *Arab Studies Quarterly*, 21(1), 69–95.

Kurtz, A. and Merari, A. 1985. *ASALA, Irrational Terror or Political Tool*, Jerusalem: The Jerusalem Post and Westview Press.

Kymlicka, W. and Norman, W. (eds.). 2000. *Citizenship in Diverse Societies*, Oxford and New York: Oxford Unversity Press.

Kymlicka, W. (ed.). 1995. *The Rights of Minority Cultures*, Oxford and New York: Oxford University Press.

Kymlicka, W. 1995. *Multicultural Citizenship*, Oxford: Oxford University Press.

Lang, D.M. 1970. *Armenia, Cradle of Civilisation*, London: Allen and Unwin.

Lang, D.M. and Walker, C.J. 1987. *The Armenians*, London: Minority Rights Group.

Lepsius, J. 1897. *Armenia and Europe: An Indictment*, London: Hodder and Stoughton.

Lijphart, A. 1977. *Democracy in Plural Societies*, New Haven and London: Yale University Press.

Longrigg, S.H. 1958. *Syria and Lebanon under French Mandate*, London, New York and Toronto: Oxford University Press.

Longuenesse, E. 1979. 'The Class Nature of the State in Syria: Contribution to an Analysis', *MERIP (The Middle East Research and Information Project) Reports* 77, 3–11.

Lust-Okar, E.M. 1996. 'Failure •of Collaboration: Armenian Refugees in Syria', *Middle Eastern Studies*, 32(1), 53–68.

Lybyer, A.H. 1913. *The Government of the Ottoman Empire in the Time of Suleiman the Magnificent*, Cambridge: Harvard University Press.

McCarthy, J. 1983. *Muslims and Minorities*, New York and London: New York University Press.

McCarthy, J. 2001. *The Ottoman Peoples and the End of Empire*, London: Arnold.

McCarthy, J. and McCarthy, C. 1989. *Turks and Armenians: A Manual on the Armenian Question*, Washington D.C.: Assembly of Turkish American Associations.

McLaurin, R.D. (ed.). 1979. *The Political Role of Minority Groups in the Middle East*, New York: Praeger.

Maktab al-Dirasat al-Suriya wa al-'Arabiya. 1951. *Min Houwe*, Damascus: Matba' al-'Awlum wa al-Adab Hashemi Ikhwan.

Mangassarian, A., Makhlouf, J., and Saade, S. 1991. 'Eglises Arméniennes du Liban: Relevé Archéologique', *Haigazian Armenological Review*, 11, 85–124.

Masters, B. 2001. *Christians and Jews in the Ottoman Arab World*, Cambridge: Cambridge University Press.

Matthews, R.D. and Akrawi, M. 1949. *Education in the Arab Countries of the Near East*, Washington: American Council on Education.

Mécérian, J. 1961. *Un Tableau de la Diaspora Arménienne*, Beirut: Imprimerie Catholique.

Mécérian, J. 1965. *Histoire et Institutions de l'Eglise Arménienne*, Beirut: Imprimerie Catholique.

Ménassa, B. 1995. *Constitution Libanaise: Textes et Commentaires et Accord de Taëf*, Beirut: Edition L'Orient.

Mermier, F. 2000. 'Beyrouth, Capitale du Livre Arabe?', *Monde Arabe Maghreb-Machrek*, 169, 100–108.

Messerlian, Z. 2002. 'Armenian Participation in the Lebanese Legislative Elections during the Presidency of Bishara Kouri 1943–1952', *Haigazian Armenological Review*, 22, 271–305.

Minassian, G. 2002. *Guerre et Terrorisme Arméniens*, Paris: Presses Universitaires de France.

Minassian, M. 1981. 'New Discoveries of Armenian Periodicals', *Haigazian Armenological Review*, 9, 295–304.

Morgenthau, H. 1918. *Ambassador Morghentau's Story*, New York: Doubleday, Page and Company.

al-Mudawwar, M. 1990. *Al-Arman abr al-Tarikh*, 2nd edition, Damascus.

Nahas, C. 2000. 'L'Economie Libanaise et ses Déséquilibres', *Monde Arabe Maghreb-Machrek*, 169, 55–69.

Nalbandian, L. 1963. *The Armenian Revolutionary Movement*, Berkeley, Los Angeles and London: University of California Press.

Nansen, F. 1928. *Armenia and the Near East*, London: Allen and Unwin.

Nasr, S. 1978. 'Backdrop to Civil War: The Crisis of Lebanese Capitalism', *MERIP (The Middle East Research and Information Project) Reports*, 73, 3–13.

Nasrallah, F. 1994. 'Syria after Ta'if: Lebanon and the Lebanese in Syrian Politics', in E. Kienle (ed.), *Contemporary Syria: Liberalization between Cold War and Cold Peace*, London: British Academic Press, 132–138.

Nasri Messarra, A. 1994. *Théorie Générale du Système Politique Libanais*, Paris: Cariscript.

Nassif, N. 2000. 'Les Elections Législatives de l'Eté 2000', *Monde Arabe Maghreb-Machrek*, 169, 116–127.

Nordiguian, L., and Salles, J.-F. 2000. *Aux Origines de l'Archéologie Aérienne: A. Poidebard (1878–1955)*, Beirut: Presses de l' Université Saint-Joseph.

Ofeish, S.A. 1999. 'Lebanon's Second Republic: Secular Talk, Sectarian Application', *Arab Studies Quarterly*, 21(1), 97–116.

Ormanian, M. 1955. *The Church of Armenia*, London: A.R. Mowbray and Co.

Owen, R. 1976. 'The Political Economy of the Grand Liban, 1920–1970', in R. Owen (ed.), *Essays on the Crisis in Lebanon*, London: Ithaca Press, 23–32.

Owen, R. 1988. 'The Economic History of Lebanon, 1943–1974', in H. Barakat (ed.), *Towards a Viable Lebanon*, London: Croom Helm, 1988, 27–41.

Pacini, A. (ed.). 1996. *Comunità Cristiane nell'Islam Arabo*, Turin: Fondazione Giovanni Agnelli.

Perthes, V. 1995. *The Political Economy of Syria under Asad*, London and New York: I.B. Tauris.

Petran, T. 1972. *Syria: A Modern History*, London and Tonbridge: Ernest Benn.

Picard, E. 1996. *Lebanon, a Shattered Country: Myths and Realities of the Wars in Lebanon*, New York and London: Holmes & Meier.

Quataert, D. 2000. *The Ottoman Empire 1700–1922*, Cambridge: Cambridge University Press.

Rabbath, E. 1973. *La Formation Historique du Liban Politique et Constitutionnel*, Beirut: Université Libanaise.

Raslan, A.F. 1997. *Arminiya: al-Ummah wa al-Dawlah*, Cairo.

Roberts, D. 1987. *The Ba'th and the Creation of Modern Syria*, London and Sydney: Croom Helm.

Rondot, P. 1947. *Les Institutions Politiques du Liban*, Paris: Institut d'Etudes de l'Orient Contemporain.

Rothschild, J. 1981. *Ethnopolitics*, New York: Columbia University Press.

Russell, J. 1997. 'The Formation of the Armenian Nation' in R.G. Hovannisian (ed.), *The Armenian People from Ancient to Modern Times*, Vol. 1, Basingstoke and London: MacMillan, 19–35.

Russo, M. 2001. 'The Formation of the Kurdish *Hamidiye* Regiments as Reflected in Italian Diplomatic Documents', *Armenian Review*, 47(1–2), 55–77.

Sahagian, J.-D. 1986. *Le Mouvement Evangelique Arménien dès Origines a Nos Jours*, Marseille: J.-D. Sahagian.

Saïdi, N. 1998. *Growth, Destruction, and the Challenges of Reconstruction: Macroeconomic Essays on Lebanon*, Beirut: Lebanese Center for Policy Studies.

Salt, J. 2003. 'The Narrative Gap in Ottoman Armenian History', *Middle Eastern Studies*, 39(1), 19–36.

Sanjian, A.K. 1965. *The Armenian Communities in Syria under Ottoman Dominion*, Cambridge, Massachusetts: Harvard University Press.

Sanjian, A. 2001. 'The Armenian Minority Experience in the Modern Arab World', *Bulletin of the Royal Institute for Inter-Faith Studies*, 3(1), 149–179.

Sayigh, Y. and Shlaim, A. (eds.). 1997. *The Cold War and the Middle East*, Oxford: Clarendon Press.

Schaebler, B. 2001. 'Identity, Power, and Piety: The Druzes in Syria', *ISIM (International Institute for the Study of Islam in the Modern World) Review*, 7/01, 25.

Schatkowski Schilcher, L. 1992. 'The Famine of 1915–1918 in Greater Syria', in J.P. Spagnolo (ed.), *Problems of the Modern Middle East in Historical Perspective: Essays in Honour of Albert Hourani*, Reading: Ithaca Press, 229–258.

Seale, P. 1965. *The Struggle for Syria: A Study of Post-War Arab Politics*, Oxford, New York and Toronto: Oxford University Press.

Seale, P. 1988. *Asad of Syria: The Struggle for the Middle East*, London: I.B. Tauris.

Seale, P. 1997. 'Syria', in Y. Sayigh and A. Shlaim (eds.), *The Cold War and the Middle East*, Oxford: Clarendon Press, 48–76.

Setian, N.M. 1992. *Gli Armeni Cattolici nell'Impero Ottomano: Cenni Storico-Giuridici (1680–1867)*, Rome.

Sonyel, S.R. 1987. *The Ottoman Armenians, Victims of Great Power Diplomacy*, London: K. Rustem & Brother.

Suleiman, M.W. 1967. *Political Parties in Lebanon: The Challenge of a Fragmented Political Culture*, New York: Cornell University Press.

Suleiman, Y. 2003. *The Arabic Language and National Identity*, Edinburgh: Edinburgh University Press.

Tabet, J., Ghorayeb, M., Huybrechts, E. and Verdeil, E. 2001. *Beyrouth*, Paris: Institut Français d'Architecture.

Tanielian, J. 1973. 'A Short Account of the Armenian Press in Lebanon', *Haigazian Armenological Review*, 4, 237–282.

Tanielian, J. 1977–1978. 'Issues Pertaining to the History of the Armenian Press', *Haigazian Armenological Review*, 6, 267–320.

Tanielian, J. 1980. 'New Armenian Periodicals of the Armenian Diaspora', *Haigazian Armenological Review*, 8, 301–324.

Tanielian, J. 1981. 'New Armenian Periodicals of the Armenian Diaspora – Part II', *Haigazian Armenological Review*, 9, 253–294.

Tanielian, J. 1986. *Lipananahay Debakroutioune Baderazmi Darineroun 1976–1984* [Armenian Lebanese Printing during the War Years 1976–1984], Beirut.

Tanielian, J. 2002. *Lipananahay Tebrotze: Tiver yev Mdoroumner* [The Armenian Schools in Lebanon: Numbers and Considerations], Beyrouth.

Tapper, R. (ed.). 1992. *Some Minorities in the Middle East*, London: Centre of Near and Middle Eastern Studies, School of Oriental and African Studies, University of London.

Tarrab, J. 1982. *Paul Guiragossian*, Beyrouth: Emmagoss.

Ter Minassian, T. 1997. *Colporteurs du Komintern: L'Union Soviétique et les Minorités au Moyen-Orient*, Paris: Presses de Sciences Po.

Ternon, Y. 1977. *Les Arméniens, Histoire d'un Génocide*, Paris: Seuil.

Thompson, E. 2000. *Colonial Citizens: Republican Rights, Paternal Privilege and Gender in French Syria and Lebanon*, New York: Columbia University Press.

Tibi, B. 1997. *Arab Nationalism between Islam and the Nation-State*, 3rd edition, Houndmill, Basingstoke and London: MacMillan.

Tibi, B. 1990. 'The Simultaneity of the Unsimultaneous: Old Tribes and Imposed Nation-States in the Modern Middle East', in P.S. Khoury and J. Kostiner (eds.), *Tribes and State Formation in the Middle East*, Berkeley, Los Angeles and Oxford: University of California Press, 127–152.

Tölölyan, K. 2002. *Redefining Diasporas: Old Approaches, New Identities*, London: Armenian Institute.

Tomiche, N. (ed.). 1969. *Le Théâtre Arabe*, Paris: UNESCO.

Topouzian, H.K. 1986. *Suriayi yev Lipanani Haigagan Kaghtojiakhneri Badmoutioun 1841–1946* [History of the Armenian Communities in Syria and Lebanon 1841–1946], Yerevan: Armenian Soviet Socialist Republic's Academy of Sciences, Orientology Institute.

Torrey, G.H. 1964. *Syrian Politics and the Military, 1945–1958*, Columbus: Ohio State University Press.

Tortarolo, E. 1998. *Il Laicismo*, Rome and Bari: Laterza.

Turkey (Republic of), Foreign Policy Institute. 1982. *The Armenian Issue in Nine Questions and Answers*, Ankara: Foreign Policy Institute.

Turkey (Republic of), Prime Ministry. 1995. *Armenian Atrocities in the Caucasus and Anatolia According to Archival Documents*, Ankara: Prime Ministry State Archives.

Uras, E. 1988. *The Armenian History and the Armenian Question*, Istanbul: Documentary Publications.

Valter, S. 2002. *La Construction Nationale Syrienne: Légitimation de la Nature Communautaire du Pouvoir par le Discours Historique*, Paris: CNRS.

Varjabedian, S.H. 1977. *The Armenians*, Chicago: S.H. Varjabedian.

Walker, C.J. 1990. *Armenia, the Survival of a Nation*, revised edition, London: Routledge.

Walker, C.J. 1997. 'World War I and the Armenian Genocide', in R.G. Hovannisian (ed.), *The Armenian People from Ancient to Modern Times*, Vol. 2, Basingstoke and London: Macmillan, 239–273.

Zaroukian, A. 1977. *Des Hommes sans Enfance*, translation from Armenian by S. Boghossian, Paris: Editeurs Français Réunis.

# Interviews

Mr. Armen Abdalian, Bourj Hammoud, 30 October 2003.
Mgr. Vartan Achkarian, Beirut, 5 June 2002.
H.H. Aram I, Catholicos of Cilicia, Antelias, 11 November 2002.
Mr. Vosguéperan Arzoumanian, Beirut, 9 May 2002.
Father Norayr Ashekian, Catholicosate of Cilicia, Antelias, 24 October 2003.
Mr. Vahe Ashkarian, 'Anjar, 24 October 2003.
Father George Assadourian, Beirut, 11 May 2002.
Mr. Paul Ayanian, Dora, 23 October 2003.
Dr. Christine Babikian-Assaf, Beirut, 8 November 2002.
Mr. Joe Baroutjian, Awkar, 20 October 2003.
Ms. Manoushag Boyadjian, Dbayeh, 6 and 27 November 2002.
Ms. Chahantoukhd, Bourj Hammoud, 30 October 2003.
Mr. Krikor Chahinian, Antelias, 16 October 2003.
Mr. Garbis Dantziguian, Mkelles, 29 October 2003.
Mr. Sarkis Demirdjian, Bourj Hammoud, 31 October 2003.
Mr. Hagop Doniguian, Antelias, 23 October 2003.
Mr. Krikor Dounkian, Aleppo, 26 November 2003.
Judge Krikor Eblighatian, Aleppo, 12 November 2003.
Mr. Matig Eblightian, Aleppo, 11 November 2003.
Mr. Berge Fazlian, Zalqa, 30 October 2003.
Mr. Robert Fisk, Beirut, 9 November 2002.
Father Antranik Granian, Zalqa, 30 October 2003.
Rev. Paul Haidostian, Beirut, 8 and 20 November 2002.
Mr. Movses Herguelian, Zalqa, 21 October 2003; 'Anjar, 24 and 25 October 2003.
Mr. Dickran Jimbashian, Mezher, 23 November 2002.
Mr. Sebouh Kalpakian, Beirut, 4 July 2002.
Mr. Shahan Kandaharian, Bourj Hammoud, 3 May 2002.
Father Vartan Kazanjian, Bzoummar, 11 May 2002.
Dr. Paolo Kazazian, Dora, 8 and 11 December 2003.
Mr. Manuel Keshishian, Aleppo, 13 November 2003.
Seta Khadeshian, Bourj Hammoud, 15 May 2002.
Mr. Varoujian Khandjian, Bourj Hammoud, 9 December 2003.
Ms. Hasmig Khanikian, Beirut, 9 November 2002; Damascus, 4 November 2003.
Mr. Haroutioun Khoshmatlian, Damascus, 4 November 2003.
Father Agostino Kousa, Aleppo, 28 November 2003.
Mr. Raffi Madoyan, Beirut, 13 December 2003.
Mgr. Boutros Marayati, Aleppo, 19 June 2002.
Rev. Serop G. Megerditchian, Aleppo, 27 November 2003.
Mr. Zaven Messerlian, Beirut, 4 July 2002.
Mr. Sarkis Najarian, Beirut, 17 October and 15 December 2003.
Mr. Jean Oghassabian, Dora, 17 October 2003.
Ms. Suzy Ohannessian, Antelias, 24 October 2003.

Mr. Hagop Pakradouni, Bourj Hammoud, 14 and 26 November 2002.
Mr. Karim Pakradouni, Beirut, 18 October 2005.
Ms. Maral Panossian, Beirut, 15 December 2003.
Ms. Seta Pamboukian, Bourj Hammoud, 7 June 2002.
Mr. Jirair Reisian, Aleppo, 19 June 2002.
Mr. Jean Salmanian, Bourj Hammoud, 17 May 2002.
Rev. Robert Sarkissian, Bourj Hammoud, 7 June 2002.
Mr. Sebouh Sekayan, 'Anjar, 25 October 2003.
Mr. Vicken Seropian, Beirut, 12 November 2002.
Mr. Aharon Shekerdemian, Beirut, 10 June 2002.
Mr. Sounboul Sounboulian, Aleppo, 14 November 2003.
Mr. Vartan Tachjian, Bourj Hammoud, 15 October 2003.
Mr. Jirair Tanielian, Beirut, 17 October 2003.
Mr. Vartan Tashjian, Bourj Hammoud, 15 October 2003.
Mr. Garbis Tomassian, Aleppo, 14 November 2003.
Mr. Toros Toranian, Aleppo, 26 November 2003.
Mr. Serge Toursarkissian, Zalqa, 22 October 2003.
Mr. Zohrab Yacoubian, Bourj Hammoud, 20 October 2003.
Mr. Benjamin Vousakjian, Beirut, 13 November 2002.

## Unpublished Dissertations

Babikian, C. 1983. 'L'Evolution du Rôle Politique des Arméniens au Liban de 1945 à 1975', BA dissertation. Beirut: Université Saint-Joseph.

Bedian, A.N. 1961. 'A Study of Elementary Schools in Syria, Related to their History, Background and Teacher's Beliefs', MA dissertation. Beirut: American University of Beirut.

Bedoyan, H. 1973. 'Armenian Political Parties in Lebanon', MA dissertation. Beirut: American University of Beirut.

Kaloustian, K.M. 1958. 'A Study of Armenian Schools in Lebanon', MA dissertation. Beirut: American University of Beirut.

Kalpakian, S. 1983. 'The Dimensions of the 1958 Inter-Communal Conflict in the Armenian Community in Lebanon', MA dissertation. Beirut: American University of Beirut.

Keuroghlian, A.A. 1970. 'Les Arméniens de l'Agglomération de Beyrouth, Étude Humaine et Économique', BA dissertation, Beirut: Université Saint-Joseph.

Kouyoumjian, K.D. 1961. 'The Recent Crisis in the Armenian Church?, MA dissertation. Beirut: American University of Beirut.

Loussararian, M.G. 1960. 'A Study of the Armenian Elementary School System in Beirut', BA dissertation. Beirut College for Women.

Messerlian, Z.M. 1963. 'Armenian Representation in the Lebanese Parliament', MA dissertation. Beirut: American University of Beirut.

Ragland, J.K. 1969. 'The Free Educational System of the Republic of Lebanon', Ph.D. dissertation. University of Oklahoma.

Schahgaldian, N.B. 1979. 'The Political Integration of an Immigrant Community into a Composite Society: The Armenians in Lebanon, 1920–1974', Ph.D. dissertation. New York: Columbia University.

Young, P.J. 2001. 'Knowledge, Nation and the Curriculum: Ottoman Armenian Education (1853–1915)', Ph.D. dissertation. University of Michigan.

## Daily Newspapers, Weeklies

*Ararat* (Beirut), various years.
*Ardziv* (Beirut), various years.
*Arevelk* (Aleppo), various years.
*Ayk* (Beirut), various years.
*Aztag* (Beirut), various years.
*Aztag Shapatoriak* (Beirut), various years.
*Joghovurti Tzain* (Beirut), various years.
*Kantsasar* (Damascus), various years.
*L'Hebdo Magazine* (Beirut), various years.
*L'Orient-Le Jour* (Beirut), various years.
*Tidag* (Beirut), various years.
*Zartonk* (Beirut), various years.

## Websites

http://groong.usc.edu
http://www.hamazkayin.com
http://www.homenmen.org
http://www.norserount.org

## Other

AGBU (Armenian General Benevolent Union). 2001. *A Brief Overview of AGBU in Lebanon*, pamphlet. Beirut: AGBU.

Anonimous, 'Hazkayine Khorhourt 1976–1977', brochure.

Armenian Relief Cross (Lebanon). Ca. 1998. *Together for a Healthier Future*, pamphlet. Beirut.

Authors unknown. Ca. 1929. Fragment of Armenian Apostolic yearbook (?) published in Syria.

Carnegie Endowment for International Peace. 1924. *The Treaties of Peace 1919–1923*, Vol. 2, New York: Carnegie Endowment.

Dantziguian, K. 1985. *Yev Hatchoghetsa* [...and I succeeded], collection of memoirs.
G. Doniguian & Sons Printing Press. 2004. Catalogue of the 80th anniversary.
Garabedian, G. 1965. *Garo*, motion picture. Beirut.
Haigazian University. 1995. *Celebrating the Fortieth Anniversary of Haigazian University College*, pamphlet. Beirut.
Homenetmen. 1993. Pamphlet issued for the 75th anniversary of the club. Beirut.
Howard Karagheusian Commemorative Corporation, *Director's Annual Report*, various years, Beirut: HKCC.
Jam'aiya Dar al-Tarbiya al-Thaqafiya. 1994. *Madrasa Dar al-Tarbiya*, pamphlet celebrating the 65th anniversary of the Dar at-Tarbiya-Grtasirats school of Aleppo. Aleppo.
Jinishian Memorial Programme. 2001. *Serving the Least of These: the 35th Anniversary of the Jinishian Memorial Programme*. Louisville, Kentucky: The Presbiterian Church.
*Keghart* (Aleppo), 1996.
"Manuel". Ca. second half of the 1970s. *Lipanan* [Lebanon], song from the album *Yerevan, Lipanan* [Yerevan, Lebanon]. Beirut.
Sanjian, A. 2000. 'Armenians and the 2000 parliamentary elections in Lebanon', in *Armenian News Network/Groong*, 2000, http://groong.usc.edu/ro/ro-20000907.html, site accessed on June 12, 2007.
Social Action Committee of the Armenian Evangelical Union. 1970. *A Survey of Social Problems and Needs Within the Armenian Community in Lebanon*. Beirut: Armenian Evangelical Union.
Tölölyan, K. 2001. 'Elites and Institutions in the Armenian Transnation', paper presented to the conference on *Transnational Migration: Comparative Perspectives*, Princeton University 30 June–1 July 2001.
*Travaux et Jours* (Beirut), No. 39, April–June 1971.
United Nations Development Programme, Regional Bureau for Arab States. 2002. *Arab Human Development Report 2002: Creating Opportunities for Future Generations*, New York: UNDP.
United Nations Human Rights Committee. 1996. General Comment 25 (57), *General Comments under Article 40, Paragraph 4, of the International Covenant on Civil and Political Rights, Adopted by the Committee at its 1510th Meeting*, U.N. Doc. CCPR/C/21/Rev.1/Add.7.
VV.AA. 1972. *The Middle East and North Africa*, 19 (1972–73), London: Europa Publications.

# Index